The Priest Is
Not His Own

&

Calvary and
the Mass

A spiritual guidebook to becoming the father God has called you to be.

Fulton J. Sheen

The Priest Is Not His Own

&

Calvary and the Mass

(A Spiritual Guidebook to Becoming the
Father God Has Called You to Be.)

Copyright © 2021 by Allan Smith

Bishop Sheen Today
280 John Street
Midland, Ontario, Canada
L4R 2J5
www.bishopsheentoday.com

Unless otherwise noted, Scripture quotations in the main text are taken from the Douay-Rheims edition of the Old and New Testaments, public domain.

Library of Congress Cataloging-in-Publication Data

Names: Sheen, Fulton J. (Fulton John), 1895-1979, author.

Smith, Allan J, editor.

Sheen, Fulton J. (Fulton John), 1895-1979, The Priest is Not His Own, by Fulton J. Sheen. Registered in the name of Fulton J. Sheen, under Library of Congress catalog card number: A 625917, following publication November 9, 1938.

Nihil Obstat: *Austin B. Vaughan, S.T.D., Censor Librorum*

Imprimatur: *Francis Cardinal Spellman, Archbishop of New York*, April 11, 1963

Sheen, Fulton J. (Fulton John), 1895-1979, Calvary and the Mass: A Missal Companion. Registered in the name of P.J. Kenedy & Sons under Library of Congress catalog card number: A 93597, following publication April 1, 1936.

Smith, Al (Allan J.) editor – Lord Teach us to Pray: A Fulton Sheen Anthology. Manchester, New Hampshire: Sophia Institute Press, 2019, ISBN 9781644130834.

Title: The Priest Is Not His Own & Calvary and the Mass: A Spiritual Guidebook to Becoming the Father God Has Called You to Be.

Identifiers:

ISBN: 978-1-998229-58-1 (paperback)

ISBN: 978-1-998229-59-8 (eBook)

ISBN: 978-1-998229-60-4 (hardcover)

Fulton J. Sheen; compiled by Allan J. Smith.

Includes bibliographical references.

Subjects: Jesus Christ — Priesthood – Fatherhood – Victimhood – Seven Last Words – Calvary – The Mass – The Eucharist

To Mary

Who Mothered Christ

Both Priest and Victim

And who Mothers all Priests

Both Offerers and Offered

With Her Divine Son

This Book is Dedicated

That She May, through these pages

Whisper to Us as at Cana

"Whatsoever He Shall say to You, Do Ye"

Contents

The Priest Is Not His Own

Calvary and the Mass

The Priest Is Not His Own

The Priest Is Not His Own is far more than a book for priests or for those considering the priesthood as a vocation. In these penetrating, deeply pondered discussions of the priesthood, Archbishop Fulton J. Sheen has produced a work of lasting value, a book that will perhaps change many hundreds of lives, and certainly a book that will also interest readers who have no direct concern with the priesthood as a calling.

Inspiration for this volume came while Archbishop Sheen was writing his famed *Life of Christ,* and it was out of those "dark days," as he describes them, that the thoughts of priesthood, illumined by the vision of Christ the Savior, were first formulated.

Just as the earlier work was based on the thesis that Christ offered no other sacrifice but Himself, so in this new book, Archbishop Sheen envisages the priest as a man sacrificing himself in the prolongation of Christ's Incarnation.

Archbishop Sheen writes of how all priests whether pagan or in the Old Testament offered victims distinct from themselves, such as lambs. But in Christ and the Christian conception, priest and victim are united inseparably.

Drawing on his profound knowledge of Scripture, Archbishop Sheen is able to describe the exact and true significance of the individual priest, and in vibrant detail, his constant, unending sacrifice — as victim.

He writes, "God still thunders to his priests: *I have set watchmen, Jerusalem, upon thy walls, that shall never cease crying aloud, day or night; you that keep the Lord in remembrance, take no rest, nor let Him rest either….* (Isaiah 62:6,7)

"Watchmen are we," adds Archbishop Sheen, "who have been put on the walls of the Church by the High Priest... What we are, the

Church is, and what the Church is, the world is... Night and day, giving God no rest, we will utter over and over again: *I dedicate myself for their sakes, that they too may be dedicated through the truth."* (John 17:19)

In considering the priest's many obligations and roles, and his ever more gratifying fulfilment of them, Archbishop Sheen has created a series of unsurpassed meditations and presents a very concrete guide to the many ways in which each priest can enrich his own spiritual life, as well as the lives of all those around him.

The Priest Is Not His Own is the work of a great and beloved inspirational leader — a world-famous priest himself writing eloquently and insistently to his colleagues and to those who would join him in a calling he understands and has most brilliantly realized.

✠ J.M.J. ✠

Introduction

Most books on the priesthood may be grouped under three categories: theological, pastoral and sociological.

The theological treatises emphasize the priest as the minister and ambassador of Christ; the pastoral is concerned with the priest in the pulpit, the priest in the confessional, the priest at prayer, etc. The sociological, which is the latest type, refrains almost entirely from the spiritual, and is concerned with the statistical reaction of the study of the faithful, the unbelievers, and the general public to the priest. Is there room for another?

Such a possibility presented itself in writing our *Life of Christ*. In that book, we tried to show that unlike anyone else, Our Lord came on earth, not to live, but to die. Death for our redemption was the goal of His sojourn here, the gold that He was seeking. Every parable, every incident in His life, even the call of the Apostles, the temptation, the Transfiguration, the long conversation with the woman at the well, were focused upon that salutary Death. He was, therefore, not primarily a teacher, but a Savior.

The dark days in which that Life was written were hours when ink and gall did mix to reveal the mystery of the Crucifix.

More and more that vision of Christ as Savior began to illumine the priesthood, and out of it came the thoughts in this book. To save anyone from reading it through, we here state briefly the thesis.

We who have received the Sacrament of Orders, call ourselves "priests." The author does not recall any priest ever having said that "I was ordained a 'victim,'" nor did he ever say, "I am studying to be a victim." That seemed almost alien to being a priest. The seminary always told us to be "good" priests; never were we told to be willing victims.

And yet, was not Christ the Priest, a Victim? Did He not come to die? He did not offer a lamb, a bullock, or doves; He never offered anything except Himself.

> "*He gave Himself up on our behalf, a sacrifice breathing out fragrance as He offered it to God.*"

(Ephesians 5:2)

Pagan priests, Old Testament priests, and medicine men, all offered a sacrifice apart from themselves. But not Our Lord. He was *Sacerdos-Victima.*

This being so, just as we miss much in the life of Christ, by not showing that the shadow of the Cross cast itself even over the crib and the carpenter shop, as well as His Public Life, so we have a mutilated concept of our priesthood if we envisage it apart from making ourselves victims in the prolongation of His Incarnation. There is nothing else in this book, but that idea. And if the reader would like to hear that chord struck a hundred times, he may now proceed.

✠ J.M.J. ✠

~ 1 ~

More Than a Priest

The priesthood of Christ was different from that of all pagan priests and from the Levitical priesthood of the family of Aaron. In the Old Testament and in pagan religions, *the priest and the victim were distinct and separate*. In *Our Lord, they were united inseparably.*

The Jewish priests offered bullocks, goats and sheep, victims that were less a part of themselves than the robes they wore. It is easy to shed someone else's blood, as it is easy to spend someone else's money. The animal lost its life, but the priest who offered it lost nothing. Often, he did not even have to slaughter the victims. Except in the case of national offerings, when they were killed by the priest, the one who offered a victim himself slew it (Leviticus 1:5). This provision foreshadowed the part Israel itself would later play as the executioner of the Divine Victim. But it applies to us too; in a deeper sense, every sinner must regard himself as putting the Savior to death.

Pagan people, without knowing it explicitly, sensed the truth that *"unless blood is shed, there can be no remission of sins"* (Hebrews 9:22). From the earliest times, through the kings and priests, they offered animals, and sometimes even humans, to turn away the anger of the gods. As in the Levitical priesthood, however, *the victim was always separate from the priest*. The sacrifice was a vicarious one, the animal representing and taking the place of the guilty humans, who thus sought to expiate their guilt in the shedding of blood.

But why, it may be asked, did the pagans, without the help of revelation, reach the conclusion expressed by St. Paul under Divine inspiration that "without the shedding of blood there was no remission of sins"? The answer is that it is not hard for anyone who ponders on sin and guilt to recognize: first, that sin is in the blood; and second, that life is in the blood, so that the shedding of blood expresses appropriately the truth that human life is unworthy to stand before the face of God.

Sin is in the blood. It can be read in the face of the libertine, the alcoholic, the criminal and the assassin. The shedding of blood, therefore, represented the emptying of sin. The Agony of the Garden and its bloody sweat were related to our sins which the Lord took upon Himself, for

Christ never knew sin, and God made him into sin for us.

(2 Corinthians 5:21)

That no creature is worthy to appear before the face of God was made known to man at a very early date. Adam and Eve found it out when they tried to cover their nakedness with fig leaves, after they had sinned.

Then the eyes of both were opened, and they became aware of their nakedness; so they sewed fig leaves together, and made themselves girdles.

(Genesis 3:7)

But fig leaves could not cover their nudity, either physical or spiritual, for the leaves soon dried up. What then was required? The sacrifice of an animal, the shedding of blood. Before they could be clothed with the skins of animals, there had to be a victim. And who made the skins which covered their shame? God did!

And now the Lord provided garments for Adam and his wife, made out of skins, to clothe them.

(Genesis 3:21)

This is the first hint in the Scriptures of the spiritual nakedness of man being covered up through the shedding of the blood of a victim. As soon as our First Parents lost the inner grace of soul, external glory was needed to make up for it. It is ever true that the more rich a soul is on the inside, the less need it has of luxuries on the outside. Excessive adornments and an inordinate love of comforts are a proof of our inner nakedness.

The Bible contains many incidents which suggest that a vicarious sacrifice of blood was necessary for our salvation. Typical are the accounts of the healing of the leper and of the expulsion of the scapegoat in Leviticus. In both cases there is a sacrificial victim, though (as in all pre-Incarnation sacrifices) the victim is separate from the priest.

The ritual connected with the healing of a leper clearly prefigures our purification from the leprosy of sin.

> *These are two living birds.... One of the birds must have its blood shed over spring water held in an earthenware pot; the one which is left alive must be dipped (together with the cedar wood, the scarlet stuff, and the hyssop) into the dead bird's blood, and with this the priest must sprinkle the defiled man seven times, to affect his due cleansing.*

(Leviticus 14:4-7)

The living bird was let loose in the open fields to symbolize the carrying away of the leprosy, but this freedom and release seems to have been purchased by the cleansing power of blood and water of the bird that was slain. The priest offered a sacrifice, but the oblation was distinct from himself.

Here we have a hint of vicarious redemption through blood. Our Lord, on the contrary, cured the leprosy of sin by no holocaust other than His own obedient will, through which we won the glorious liberty of the children of God.

The ceremony of the scapegoat, another example of priesthood and victimhood, is described in Chapter 16 of Leviticus. The priest had to wash himself completely — and not merely his feet — before the ceremony, foretelling that the great High Priest, Christ, would be "undefiled" (Hebrews 7:26); the priest also had to put on white linen and golden garments. As two birds were used in the former ceremony, two goats were now chosen, one to be slain and the other released. The ritual preceding release seems almost an anticipation of the *Hanc Igitur* at the Mass, for the priest lays his hands over the goat.

> *He must put both hands on its head, confessing all the sins and transgressions and faults Israel has committed, and laying the guilt of them on its head. And there will be a man standing ready to take it into the desert for him; so the goat will carry away all their sins into a land uninhabited, set at large in the desert.*

(Leviticus 16:21,22)

As the sins of the Israelites were carried off by the scapegoat, so our sins are cleansed by no effort of our own, but only by our incorporation into Christ.

The scapegoat was driven away into a land of separation, or a wilderness, to teach us how effectively our sins have been borne into oblivion by Christ.

> *I will pardon their wrongdoing; I will not remember their sins any more.*

(Hebrews 8:12)

The Incarnation

When the Son of God became man, He introduced something entirely new to the priesthood. Our Lord differed from the priests of the Old Testament, not simply because He came from a lineage other than that of Aaron, but also because, unlike all others, *He united in Himself both priesthood and victimhood.*

The consequences for all priests are tremendous, for if He did offer Himself for sins, then we must offer ourselves as victims. The conclusion is inescapable.

8

Scripture abounds in references to the complete identification of the offices of priest and victim in Christ.

A victim? Yet he himself bows to the stroke; no word comes from him.

(Isaiah 53:7)

The Epistle to the Hebrews quotes Psalm 39 [40, RSV], saying that the words of the Psalm were used by our High Priest as He entered the world.

As Christ comes into the world, he says, no sacrifice, no offering was thy demand; thou has endowed me, instead, with a body. Thou hast not found any pleasure in burnt sacrifices, in sacrifices for sin. See then, I said, I am coming to fulfill what is written of me, where the book lies unrolled; to do thy will, O my God.

(Hebrews 10:5-7)

The version of the Psalm quoted in the Epistle to the Hebrews is that of the Septuagint:

"Thou hast endowed me, instead, with a body," as if implying the Incarnation. Similarly, David foresaw the kind of sacrifice God would eventually ask for sins when he declared: "Thou hast no mind for sacrifice, burnt offerings."

(Psalm 50:18 [51:16, RSV])

The victimhood of our High Priest should not, however, be thought of as a tragedy in the sense that He had to submit to death, as the lambs had to submit to the knife of the Old Testament priests. Our Lord said:

Nobody can rob me of it [my life]; I lay it down of my own accord. I am free to lay it down, free to take it up again; that is the charge which my father has given me.

(John 10:18)

9

Our Lord came to die. The rest of us come to live. But His death was not final. He never spoke of being our sin oblation without speaking of His glory. His Resurrection and Ascension and His glorification at the right hand of the Father were the fruits of His voluntary offering as a Priest.

And now, His full achievement reached, He wins eternal salvation for all those who render obedience to Him. A high priest in the line of Melchizedek, so God has called Him.

(Hebrews 5:9,10)

The perfection of His humanity and His eternal glory as a priest resulted from His having once been in the state of a victim. His perfection came not so much from His moral stature as from His quality of a priest-Savior. It was by His interior devotion and obedience that He acquired glory, and not just by the sacrifice considered as a shameful death.

Describing the meekness of the Lamb led to the slaughter, Scripture says,

Christ, during his earthly life, offered prayer and entreaty to the God Who could save Him from death, not without a piercing cry, not without tears; yet with such piety as won Him a hearing.

(Hebrews 5:7)

There is a Jewish saying to the effect that three kinds of prayers can be distinguished, each loftier than the preceding one: prayer, crying and tears. Prayer is made in silence; crying with a raised voice, but there is no door through which tears do not pass. The prayer of the Victim in Gethsemane was such that it rose to a poignant cry and beyond that to the sweat of tears:

His sweat fell to the ground like thick drops of blood.

(Luke 22:44)

We find a symbolic representation of the union of the Priest and Victim in the very position of the cross suspended between earth and heaven, as if Jesus was rejected by man and abandoned by the Father. Yet He united God and man in Himself through obedience to the Father's Will and through a love for man so great that He would not abandon him in his sin. To His brethren He revealed the heart of a father; to His Father He revealed the heart of every son. Our Lord, therefore, is always priest and victim. No victim was worthy of priesthood save himself. Christ, moreover, was a victim not only in His body, but in His soul, which was sad unto death. No external nor internal sacrifice could be more united.

Two Scripture texts present paradoxical aspects of the priesthood and victimhood of Christ.

He was counted among the malefactors.

(Luke 22:37)

Such was the High Priest.... holy and guiltless and undefiled, not reckoned among us sinners.

(Hebrews 7:26)

Actually, the statements are not contradictory; they are complementary. He was reckoned with sinners, because He was the victim for their sins. But He was separated from sinners, because He was a priest without sin. He ate and mingled with sinners, shared their nature, and took on their sins. But He was separated from them by His innocence. One with sinners through sharing their nature, His sacrifice had infinite value, because He was not only man, but God.

Priests or Priest-Victims?

How often are we like the Galatians, bent on returning to the Old Law, in the sense that we see ourselves as priests but not victims? Do we offer Mass as if we presented a victim for sin who was totally unrelated to us, like the scapegoat or the bird? Do we ascend the altar as priests and not as victims? Do we offer the Christ-Savior to the Father, as if we were not dying with Him? Is our priesthood a two-story house to indicate our apartness, our reluctance to be a victim for others?

On the first floor is a family suffering physically, disturbed mentally, and lacking food and drink. On the second floor, we live. Through intermittent acts of charity, we descend to their misery from time to time to relieve it; but do we go back right away to the relative comfort of our own lodging?

Not so with Christ, the Priest. When He went into the depths of human suffering and sin, He never went back — not until all of its misery and guilt were relieved. Once He crossed that line, there was no thought of a return until Redemption was complete.

It is not as if our High Priest was incapable of feeling for us in our humiliations; He has been through every trial, fashioned as we are, only sinless.

(Hebrews 4:15)

...in God's gracious design He was to taste death and taste it on behalf of all.

(Hebrews 2:9)

If the priesthood and victimhood in Christ were one, how can they be dual in us? Rather,

You, too, must think of yourselves as dead to sin, and alive with a life that looks towards God, through Christ Jesus our Lord.

(Romans 6:11)

We cannot escape reproducing in our souls the mystery enacted on the altar. *Age quod agitis.* As Our Lord immolated Himself, so do we immolate ourselves. We offer our repose of body, in order that others may have peace of soul; we are pure, in order to recompense for the excesses of the flesh committed by sinners.

With Christ I hang upon the Cross.

(Galatians 2:20)

The Eucharist Reminds us that We are Victims

The Eucharist commits us to both life and death, priesthood and victimhood.

As regards life, it is clear beyond question that in the Eucharist we commune with it.

You can have no life in yourselves, unless you eat the flesh of the Son of Man, and drink His blood.

(John 6:54)

But this is only half the picture. Is there not a catabolic as well as an anabolic process in nature, a breaking down into elements as well as a building up into organisms? In nature, death is the condition of life. The vegetables which we eat at table have to be sacrificed. They must yield life and substance before they can become the sacrament, the holy thing nourishing the body. They must be torn up from their roots and subjected to fire, before they can give the more abundant life to the flesh. Before the animal in the field can be our meat, it must be subjected to the knife, to the shedding of blood, and to fire. Only then does it become the strong sustenance of the body. Before Christ can be our life, He had to die for us. The Consecration of the Mass precedes Communion.

The ultimate heresy of the Reformation was the divorce of sacrifice and sacrament, or the transformation of the sacrifice of the Mass into a "communion service," as if there could be giving of life without death. Is there not in the Eucharist not only a communion with life but also a communion with death? Paul did not overlook this aspect:

So it is the Lord's death that you are heralding, whenever you eat this bread and drink this cup, until He comes.

(1 Corinthians 11:26)

If we at Mass eat and drink the Divine Life and bring no death of our own to incorporate in the death of Christ through sacrifice, we deserve to be thought of as parasites on the Mystical Body of Christ. Shall we eat bread and give no wheat to be ground? Shall we drink wine, and give no grapes to be crushed? The condition for incorporation into the Resurrection and Ascension of Christ and into His glorification is incorporation into His death.

Those who belong to Christ have crucified nature, with all its passions, all its impulses.

(Galatians 5:24)

As priests we offer Christ in the Mass, but as victims do we offer ourselves with Christ in the Mass? Shall we tear asunder that which God hath joined, namely, priesthood and victimhood? Does not the intimate connection between sacrifice and sacrament also tell us that we are not priests alone but victims as well? If all we do in our priestly life is to drain chalices and eat the Bread of Life, then how shall the Church *fill up those sufferings that are wanting to the Passion of Christ.* (Colossians 1:24)

Do we lift up Christ on the cross at the moment of elevation, while present as mere spectators at a drama in which we are intended to play the first role? Is the Mass an empty repetition of Calvary? If so, what do we do with the cross we were bidden to take up daily? How can Christ renew His death in our own bodies. He dies again in us.

And the people of God? Do we teach them that they must not only "receive" Communion but "give" too? They may not accept life while giving no sacrifice. The communion rail is a place of exchange. They give time and receive eternity, they give self-denial and receive life, they give nothingness, and receive all. Holy Communion commits each to a closer union not only with Christ's life but also with His death — to greater detachment from the world, to surrender of luxuries for the sake of the poor, to death of the old Adam for rebirth in Christ, the new Adam.

First Application:
Three Kinds of Priest-Victims

The Canon of the Mass enumerates three kinds of victims who by prefiguring the sacrifice of Christ, became models for all priests. They were, in order, the offerings of the just son, Abel; the sacrifice of our patriarch, Abraham; and that which the High Priest Melchizedek offered. Abel offered a *blood* sacrifice, Abraham a *voluntary* sacrifice and Melchizedek a *sacramental* sacrifice. A priest may be victim in each of these ways.

Abel offered to God the choicest lamb of his flock, while his brother Cain offered only the fruits of the earth (Genesis 4:3,4). God looked with favor on Abel and on his blood sacrifice, but He rejected the sacrifice of Cain, as though it implied that sin could be forgiven without the shedding of blood. The blood sacrifice of Abel is thus a model for the missionaries who are martyred for their faith, for the priests who are victims of anti-God persecution, and for all the faithful who suffer unto death rather than deny the faith.

The sacrifice of Abraham serves as a model for the sacrifice of many in our days, those who endure all the stages of martyrdom under Communist tyranny yet are denied the formal crown of the shedding of their blood. It is for such especially that the figure of Abraham's sacrifice was intended. For them was it emphasized that the sacrifice received its full reward even though the blood of the victim was not poured out (Hebrews 11:19). This is the assurance for all who undergo a thousand martyrdoms by not being permitted to die by their persecutors, for those who are brain-washed and who spend their lives in prison or labor camps. They share in the promise and in the reward bestowed on Abraham because he was willing to sacrifice his own flesh and blood, his son, Isaac.

The third kind of priest-victimhood is that of Melchizedek. It is offered by all priests who live the mystery they enact sacramentally in the Mass. But how? By understanding the secondary meaning of the words of consecration. The primary meaning is clear and needs no elaboration. The mystery of transubstantiation takes place as we pronounce the words of consecration. There is, however, a secondary meaning because we are priest-victims. When I say "This is My Body," I must also mean: "This is my body"; when I say "This is My Blood," I must also mean: "This is my blood." "Thou, O Jesus, art not alone in the Mass," the consecrating priest must pray in his soul. "On the Cross Thou wert alone; in this Mass, I am with Thee. On the Cross, Thou didst offer Thyself to the Heavenly Father; in the Mass, Thou dost still offer Thyself but now I offer myself with Thee."

The consecration is then no bare, sterile repetition of the words of the Last Supper; it is an action, a re-enactment, another Passion in me. "Here, dear Jesus, is my body, take it; here is my blood, take it. I care not if the 'species' of my life remain — my particular duties in school, parish, or office; these are only the 'appearances.' But what I am, in my intellect, my will — take, possess, divinize, so that I may die with Thee on the altar. Then the Heavenly Father looking down will say to Thee and to me in Thee:

Thou art my beloved Son; in thee I am well pleased.

(Mark 1:11)

When I come down from the altar I will then, more than ever, be in Mary's hands as when she took Thee down from the Cross. She was not a priest, but she could say the words of consecration in a way no priest ever said them of that Body and Blood. As she held Thee she could say, as at Bethlehem: This is my Body; This is my Blood.' No one in all the world gave Him body and blood but me."

May she who was a victim with her Son teach us never to go to Calvary without having our hearts pierced with a sword. Woe indeed to us, if we come down from Calvary with hands unscarred and white! But glorious shall we be as priests and victims, when the Lord will see in our hands the marks of His Passion, for of such He said:

Why, I have cut thy image on the palms of my hands.

(Isaiah 49:16)

Second Application:
Be a Victim in the Breaking of the Bread

An unchanging ritual of the Mass is the Breaking of the Bread to remind us each time we celebrate, that the Lord was "broken" for our sins as a victim. The Old Testament already foreshadowed Christ's offering of Himself in the bread that was broken, for it was prescribed that the bread which the priest was to offer was to be "cut up into small pieces" (Leviticus 2:6). Even the Hebrew word for cakes of bread used in this passage is derived from a verb which meant "pierced" or "wounded." In this, the bread prefigured the condition of the victim which it symbolized:

Nay, here is one despised, left out of all human reckoning; bowed with misery, and no stranger to weakness; how should we recognize that face? How should we take any account of Him, a Man so despised?

(Isaiah 53:3)

As the bread was crushed, so too would Christ be crushed:

Ay, the Lord's will it was, overwhelmed He should be with trouble.

(Isaiah 53:10)

What was the sign by which the disciples on Easter Sunday afternoon knew the Risen Christ?

They recognized Him when He broke bread.

(Luke 24:35)

St. Paul's account of the Eucharist stressed this victim state of Our Lord:

... and gave thanks, and broke it.

(1 Corinthians 11:24)

Our priesthood must be like the pitchers which Gideon's army of three hundred carried into battle. Inside of each was a lighted candle (Judges 7:18-20). The light was there, but it did not shine forth to confound and defeat the enemy until the pitchers were broken. Only when we are "broken" do we shed the light of Christ to defeat the forces of Satan. It is not just the soul and mind of the priest that are involved in the exercise of his ministry: it is also his body, the body broken, mortified and made a victim.

Your bodies... are meant for the Lord, and the Lord claims your bodies.

(1 Corinthians 6:13)

Can we think that God will be any more satisfied with us, if we are only offerers and not also offered, than He was with the priests of the Old Testament? Did He not express disgust when they offered something apart and separate from themselves?

What do I care, the Lord says, how you multiply those victims of yours? I have had enough and to spare. Burnt offerings of rams, and the fat of stall-fed beasts, and the blood of calves and lambs and goats are nothing to me.

(Isaiah 1:11)

Will He not complain that our priesthood is incomplete, unless we "break the bread" which is our body? What is it then that He wants from us? It is the offering of ourselves.

I appeal to you by God's mercies to offer up your bodies as a living sacrifice, consecrated to God and worthy of his acceptance; this is the worship due from you as rational creatures.

(Romans 12:1)

The role of the body is so often forgotten. True, the body can be the occasion and the instrument of sin, but it is also an occasion and an instrument of merit. Can it be so vile as some old spiritual writers suggested, if it is "*meant for the Lord*" (1 Corinthians 6:13), if "*what is sown a natural body, rises a spiritual body*" (1 Corinthians 15:44), and if through the Eucharist it has been endowed with immortality? It is not our soul that prays; it is the person, the composite of body and soul. In sacrifice, in particular, the body is important. It is through its exhaustion in priestly ministrations, its constant use in preaching, teaching and converting, that it becomes a "living sacrifice."

Each time that priests "break bread" during the Mass, not only will they recognize the sacrifice of Christ for them, as did the disciples at Emmaus, but also He will recognize them. No unbroken bread, no unbroken bodies, will the High Priest accept from our hands. Was not the wheat already broken to become bread? Were not the grapes already crushed to become wine? Even nature suggests victimhood as inseparable from the priesthood of offering bread and wine at table.

St. Paul was merely stressing once again the inseparability of priest and victim when he wrote to the young priest, Timothy:

> *Then, like a good soldier of Christ Jesus, take thy share of hardship.... We are to share His Life, because we have shared His Death.*

(2 Timothy 2:3,11)

Third Application:
Vocations and Victimhood

Seminarians say: "I am studying for the priesthood." How often does a seminarian say or even think, "I am studying to be a priest-victim?" We insist on the dignity of our priesthood by quickly reprimanding those who show us disrespect. But do we ever insist on the indignity of our victimhood? We boast that our High Priest is Offerer and Offered. *We say that we offer Mass, but do we ever think that we are offered in the Mass?* Our Lord wants no more bullocks or goats; He wants those who "have crucified nature, with all its passions, all its impulses" (Galatians 5:24). St. Augustine said there is no need to look outside oneself for a sheep to offer to God. Each has within him that which he can crucify.

Could it be that one reason for the fewness of vocations is our failure to stress sacrifice? The young have a sense of victimhood which we underestimate. They want a mission, a challenge! When we follow the type of advertising appeal used by Madison Avenue to sell toothpaste, when we use commercial techniques in our vocation literature, do not the hearts of the young spurn our distance from the Cross? Do we not recruit fruits of propaganda rather than fruits worthy of penance?

Could it not also be that our failure to be victims discourages those who enter the seminary from persevering and becoming priests? We tell them that they cannot hope to be good priests unless they make a meditation each morning before Mass, but are there times when we ourselves jump direct from the bed to the altar? Does not this scandalize seminarians? On the other hand, how they are edified when they see their professors at early meditation with them and at their spiritual exercises! Lacking this example, they easily come to think of spirituality as something to be practiced only until the day of ordination.

A survey among 300 youths to determine what kind of priest inspired them most revealed that the first preference was for the foreign missionary; the second, for those who concerned themselves with the poor; the third, for an apostolate among the workers. The point is that the young prefer the heroic or sacrificial priest.

Vocations are more plentiful than many suspect. Of 3,500 boys under the age of fifteen questioned in a survey in one South American country, 1,800 said they felt that they had a vocation. And yet not more than forty young men are raised to the priesthood in that country each year. What happens to the others? Worldliness, the flesh? Yes. But it is proper to ask: Have we shown forth Christ Crucified to them? Those young people who feel called to a life of sacrifice, will they not draw back when they see that their ideal is not realized in us? But what encouragement is given them when they say: "That is the kind of priest I want to be." One reason why missionary societies attract the young is because their members give a living witness to their zeal for Christ. The hardships they endure, the souls they convert, the complete trust in God despite poverty and even persecution, these make the young love their priesthood through their victimhood. A survey among a group of seminarians revealed that 60 percent of them had been inspired to enter the seminary by contact with mortified and saintly priests.

It is so easy for us to be ready, like Peter at Caesarea Philippi, to confess the Divine Christ, but far from ready to accept the suffering Christ. It was the same Peter who said, "*Thou art the Christ, the Son of the Living God*" (Matthew 16:16), and who "*drawing Him to his side, began remonstrating with Him; Never, Lord, he said; no such thing shall befall Thee"* (Matthew 16:22).

Because of this, Our Lord called him Satan, for it was Satan who at the beginning of the public ministry tempted Him to reject the way of suffering by offering him three short cuts to His Kingdom without the Cross (Matthew 4:1-11). The denial of His victimhood appears to Christ as something satanic.

`When "*Satan sits enthroned*" (Revelation 2:13) at the end of time, Our Lord said that he would appear so much like Him "*that if it were possible, even the elect would be deceived*" (Matthew 24:24). But if Satan works miracles, if he lays his hands gently on children, if he appears benign and a lover of the poor, how will we know him from Christ? Satan will have no scars on hands or feet or side. He will appear as a priest but not as a victim.

We recognize fathers and sons, brothers and sisters, by family resemblances. In no other way will Our Lord know us and we Him. Our preparation for the day of His coming must accordingly consist of deepening our affinity with the Priest-Victim:

In this mortal frame of mine, I help to pay off the debt which the afflictions of Christ still leave to be paid, for the sake of His Body, the Church.

(Colossians 1:24)

Kenosis and Pleroma

Two words in Scriptures are often considered separately, when actually they are related as cause and effect. The two words, which represent another phase of the offerer-offered relationship, are *kenosis* and *pleroma*, that is to say, "emptying" and "filling." It is almost as if mountains were made by the emptying of valleys. St. Paul in a classic description of the humiliation and exaltation of Our Lord writes:

He dispossessed Himself, and took the nature of a slave, fashioned in the likeness of men, and presenting Himself to us in human form; and then He lowered His own dignity, accepted an obedience which brought Him to death, death on a cross. That is why God has raised Him to such a height, given Him that Name which is greater than any other Name; so that everything in heaven and on earth and under the earth must bend the knee before the name of Jesus, and every tongue must confess Jesus Christ as the Lord, dwelling in the glory of God the Father.

(Philippians 2:7-11)

Because He emptied Himself, He was exalted. Because there was Calvary, there was the sending of the Holy Spirit. Because His physical Body was broken, His Mystical Body grows in age and grace and wisdom before God and men.

Applying this principle to the priesthood, the emptying of self for the people of the parish produces the spiritual prosperity of the parish. The de-egotization of our lives prepares for the guidance of the Holy Spirit; the "vacancy" sign on our heart makes Christ come knocking at the entrance. He breaks down no locked doors. He will come in only if we open to Him. A box which is full of pepper cannot be filled with salt; a priest who is full of his own desires cannot be filled with the "power of the Holy Spirit" (Acts 1:2). St. Paul singled out Timothy from among his friends as the one who was always interested in others and least concerned with self. In him, "pleroma" was complete because of the "kenosis" of egotism.

I have no one else here who shares my thoughts as he does, no one who will concern himself so unaffectedly with your affairs; one and all have their own interests at heart, not Christ's.

(Philippians 2:20-21)

Shepherd – Lamb

To change the figure, we priests are not only shepherds but also lambs. Was not Our Lord Himself both the "Good Shepherd" and the "Lamb of God" (John 1:29)? As the Offerer, He is the Shepherd. As the Offered, He is the Lamb. It is this dual role of Christ which explains why He spoke at certain times during His trial and at other times was silent. He spoke as the Shepherd; He was silent as the Lamb.

The priest, too, is not only the Shepherd who cares for his sheep; he is also the Lamb who is offered in caring for them. This caring is what distinguishes Him from the hireling. One who cares for another assumes the weight of the other's condition on his own heart and bears it in love. The parishioners are not disturbers; they are our heart, our body, our blood.

The priest playing the role of a shepherd often goes to his death as a Lamb. The shepherd who would give more abundant life to the lost sheep is bound to have wolves howling about him and thus be led ultimately to his death. It was only the sight of the Shepherd crucified that made the sheep realize how much the Shepherd cared. It is interesting that St. Peter described Our Lord as "*your Shepherd, who keeps watch over your souls*" (1 Peter 2:25).

The shepherd's primary duty is to search out the lost sheep and stay with it once found. This is what distinguishes the true shepherd from the hireling, the intellectual from the intelligentsia. Both are degreed, learned and scholarly. The difference lies in their relation to the people. The intellectual never loses that compassion for the multitude which characterized the Word Incarnate. The intelligentsia, on the contrary, live apart from tears and hunger, cancer and bereavements, poverty and ignorance. They lack the common touch. Only the cream of bookish learning and not the milk of human kindness flows through their veins.

So with the priest. Contact with people for Christ's sake is the victimhood which makes the priesthood. Only by also being a lamb offered through forgetfulness of worldly superiority does the priest become the shepherd of souls.

✠ J.M.J. ✠

~ *2* ~

The Priest Is Like Jacob's Ladder

Every priest knows himself, by Divine election, to be a mediator between God and man, bringing God to man and man to God. As such the priest continues the Incarnation of Jesus Christ Who was both God and Man. Our Lord was not Priest because He was begotten eternally of the Father. He was a Priest because of the human nature He assumed and offered for our salvation. Thence derived the fullness of all priesthood, or to use the magnificent phrase of St. Thomas Aquinas, He became "fons totius sacerdotii."

St. Paul had already used an equally definitive expression to indicate our sacerdotal relationship to Christ on the one side, and to the people on the other:

That is how we ought to be regarded, as Christ's servants, and stewards of God's mysteries.

(1 Corinthians 4:1)

As Christ's servants, we are as dependent on Him for our powers as are the rays of light dependent on the sun. But Paul insists simultaneously that we are also the stewards of God's mysteries to indicate that we remain bound to our fellow men.

Every priest is like another Jacob's ladder. Exiled from home, fleeing from a resentful brother, the wandering son of Isaac made his evening couch on the ground, a stone slab his pillow. Man is most helpless when asleep, and it was while he was in that condition that God appeared to Jacob.

He dreamed that he saw a ladder standing on the earth, with its top reaching up into heaven; a stairway for the angels of God to go up and come down. Over this ladder the Lord himself leaned down, and spoke to Jacob, I am the Lord, He said, the God of thy father Abraham, the God of Isaac.

(Genesis 28:12,13)

Jacob forthwith changed the name of the place where he had this vision from Luza to Bethel. The name Luza originally signified "*separation,*" while Bethel meant the "*House of God*" (Genesis 28:19). We, likewise, called to mediate between God and man, become worthy priests of the House of God only by separating ourselves from the spirit of the world. God makes up for every abnegation by a greater blessing. The condition of serving "Bethel" is "Luza," detachment from the world.

The ladder is a simple and charming picture of the priesthood of Christ:

I am the way.

(John 14:6)

It is through His Death, Resurrection and Ascension to the right hand of God that Christ has become the Mediator and re-established relations between God and Man.

Certain details of the vision are particularly noteworthy:

1. The ladder was set upon the earth. Thus was the link between earth and heaven established through Christ becoming incarnate, taking human flesh, walking our earth and being lifted up on Calvary.

2. The ladder reached up to heaven, symbolizing that Christ risen and glorified is at the right hand of the Father.

3. Angels ascending and descending represent one of the functions of the priest whose task it is to carry sacrifices and prayers to heaven and bring back graces and blessings to earth.

The cross, the ladder of mediation, was set up on the earth. It was of earthly origin, in the sense that Pilate's soldiers fashioned it; but it was not of earthly origin as a means of atonement in so far as it came forth out of history and the Divine counsels. Its top reaches to Heaven, for the divine Mediator sits at the right hand of the Father. As Our Blessed Lord said: "*No one has ever gone up into heaven; but there is One who has come down from heaven*" (John 3:13). He is the ladder on which we ascend to God; no one goes to the Father except by Him.

Inasmuch as every priest is an alter Christus, each of us is another Jacob's ladder — having vertical relations to Christ in heaven and horizontal relations to men on earth.

The Top of the Ladder:
Vertical Relationship to Christ in Heaven

Of the many ways in which we are related to Christ, our High Priest in heaven, two call for mention here:

1. Our vocation derives from Him: "His vocation (that of the priest) comes from God, as Aaron's did; nobody can take on himself such a privilege as this" (Hebrews 5:4).

2. All the effectiveness of our priesthood comes from Him: the sacraments we administer, the truth we preach, the grace by which lost sheep are rescued, the youths whose vocations we foster, whatever supernatural work we perform.

What is the glorified Christ doing in heaven as we exercise our priesthood? "*He lives on still to make intercession on our behalf*" (Hebrews 7:25). Using human words to describe Divine things, we can say that each time we offer Mass, Our Lord shows His Heavenly Father the scars in His hands, His feet and His side; for this very reason He kept them. At the Consecration of the Mass, we can imagine Our Lord as saying: "In My Hand I have engraven their hearts. Not for their worthiness, but for My love unto death, grant them graces through the Holy Spirit. My wounds healed, but My scars I kept, that I might always hold them up before Thee, O Father, as pledges of My love. If Thou couldst not strike in justice the sinful people because the uplifted hands of Abraham stood in the way, then shall not My Hands win for them that mercy I won for them on Calvary? I am not just a *Sacerdos in aeternum; I am a Victima in aeternum."*

How did our High Priest enter into the heavenly sanctuary? Through the rending of the veil of His flesh. The Epistle to the Hebrews (9:11) compares the veil which hung before the Holy of Holies to the human flesh of Christ. Only once a year, and after the shedding of blood in sacrifice, could the High Priest pass through the veil which hid the Holy of Holies. Only after the shedding of His Blood on Calvary could Christ the High Priest enter the Holy of Holies of heaven.

The earthly life of Our Lord might be thought of as being led outside the veil, as many of the ceremonies of atonement in the Old Testament were enacted in the sanctuary outside the Holy of Holies. In yet another sense, Our Lord's preaching and miracles were restricted to a very small part of the world. His mission on earth was confined to Galilee and Judea. But after His Ascension and the coming of the Spirit, His priesthood was exercised even to the ends of the earth. His human nature was a veil, which kept Him for a time from manifesting His full glory. That veil of the flesh had to be rent on Calvary before He could enter into the full exercise of His priesthood.

Good Friday saw a double rending of the veil: One was the rending of the veil of the Temple which was torn from top to bottom. It signified that the Holy of Holies would now be open to all men:

And all at once, the veil of the temple was torn this way and that from the top to the bottom.

(Matthew 27:51)

But when Our Lord said "It is achieved" (John 19:30), the human flesh which had been a veil hiding the Unseen from man was rent asunder by the piercing of His flesh by the centurion's lance, and the Heart of Eternal Love was revealed,

28

bidding us cling to the hope we have in view, the anchorage of our souls. Sure and immovable, it reaches that inner sanctuary beyond the veil, which Jesus Christ, our escort, has entered already, a high priest, now, eternally with the priesthood of Melchizedek.

(Hebrews 6:18-20)

So long as that veil of the flesh was in place, it shut out man from the full vision of the Holy God, revealing Him only as "a confused reflection in a mirror" (1 Corinthians 13:12). But the mediation and intercession became heavenly after the shedding of blood.

The high priest in the Old Testament might stand amazed at the beauty of the veil, but he could not pass through it, except by blood. So with Christ:

It is His own blood, not the blood of goats and calves, that has enabled Him to enter, once for all, into the sanctuary; the ransom He has won lasts forever.

(Hebrews 9:12)

And again:

We can enter the sanctuary with confidence through the Blood of Christ.

(Hebrews 10:19)

The rending of the veil of the Temple from top to bottom was not the work of man but the act of God. So our Redemption is the work not of man but of God become Man.

Christ Our Only Mediator

The only intercession is that of our High Priest in heaven, for there is no other name given to men whereby they may be saved (Acts 4:12). The sand of the Moslem, the penances of the Hindu, the quietism of the Buddhist cannot avail for salvation. If proof of this affirmation were necessary, one need cite only the example of Moses.

The reason Moses was not permitted to enter the Promised Land was that he disobeyed the Divine Command and struck the rock when directed merely to speak to it. Two incidents involving a rock are recorded in the Bible story of Moses. One was at Rephidim in the second year after he had led them from Egyptian bondage. The other was at Cades in the 38th year of the wandering. In both instances the people were suffering from great thirst and the rock saved them, the rock which, as St. Paul says was Christ (1 Corinthians 10:4).

The first time the people needed water, God said to Moses, "Thou hast but to smite that rock" (Exodus 17:6); and immediately there flowed from it water. Some thirty-six years later, when there again was an acute drought, God told Moses to "lay thy command upon the rock here" (Numbers 20:8), that is, "speak." Instead, speaking in an egotistic way, Moses addressed the people:

Listen to me, he said, faithless rebels; are we to get you water out of this rock?

(Numbers 20:10)

Then Moses struck the rock instead of addressing it. Despite his pride, God gave Moses the water, but He told him that as punishment he would not enter the Promised Land.

Why did you not trust in Me, and vindicate My Holiness in the sight of Israel? It will not be yours to lead this multitude into the land I mean to give them.

(Numbers 20:12)

The Hebrew text uses a different word for "rock" in the two accounts. In the earlier incident, it is *Tsur*, so named to indicate its sharpness; in the later, *sela*, stressing its elevation. From St. Paul we know that the rock was Christ. We may, accordingly, surmise that the sharp rock directed by God to be struck was the symbol of Christ smitten in the sharpness of the Cross from Whom would come the waters of Redemption and the Spirit (John 7:39).

The second elevated rock which was not to be smitten but spoken to or interceded with, is it not a symbol of Christ risen and glorified in Heaven, to whom we need only speak in order to receive the living waters (John 7:37)? Redemption is already complete. No more Calvaries are needed.

> *The death He died was death, once for all, to sin; the life He now lives is a life that looks toward God.*
>
> (Romans 6:10)

Never again will there be a Rock which, when struck, will yield the waters of everlasting life. Redemption is only in Christ. Yet His role has not terminated. He continues to be our Advocate with the Father, and to apply the fruits of Redemption. In this, also, he differs from the priests of the Old Testament.

> *One who has no need to do as those other priests did. ..... What He has done He has done once for all; and the offering was Himself.*
>
> (Hebrews 7:27)

How else can our sins be forgiven except through His abiding forgiveness? There is no doubt that civil tribunals are of great use in adjudicating disputes. But what about the great sins against God, not only in the Church, but outside of it? For this we need Divine Redemption.

The two sons of Eli abused their office by oppression and debauchery. They, as priests, had a right to a certain part of the animal sacrifices that were offered; instead of being content with the parts God allotted them, they stole meat which God had ordered to be burned. To such disobedience the young priests added impurity and scandal which discouraged people from coming to the house of the Lord. Their father said to them:

If man does wrong to man, God's justice may yet be satisfied; if man sins against the Lord, who shall plead his cause for him?

(1 Kings 2:25 [1 Samuel 2:25, RSV])

To that question they could have no answer.

But God in His appointed time Himself answered it, and the answer is the Blood of the High Priest whose eternal act of love the priest has the power to renew in the Sacrifice of the Mass. If He is not invoked, or if He is rejected, then there is no forgiveness.

If we go on sinning willfully, when once the full knowledge of the truth has been granted to us, we have no further sacrifice for sin to look forward to.

(Hebrews 10:26)

Who can be our adversary if God is on our side? He did not even spare His own Son, but gave Him up for us all; and must not that gift be accompanied by the gift of all else? Who will come forward to accuse God's elect, when God acquits us? Who will pass sentence against us, when Jesus Christ, who died, nay, has risen again, and sits at the right hand of God, is pleading for us? Who will separate us from the love of Christ?

(Romans 8:31-35)

Our specific relation as priests is to the top of the ladder. It falls to us to contact the Eternal Lover in heaven Who "lives on still to make intercession on our behalf" (Hebrews 7:25).

The priesthood of Christ in heaven is an abiding and continuing one. Whatever man may need as man in each circumstance of effort, of conflict or of sin, he has an effective advocacy through Christ Who pleads our cause with the Father:

...if any of us does fall into sin, we have an Advocate to plead our cause before the Father in the Just One, Jesus Christ. He, in his own person, is the atonement made for our sins, and not only for ours, but for the sins of the whole world. (1 John 2:1,2)

This is the vertical side of our priesthood, whereby we contact the Holy of Holies, and whereby we are entitled to be called "*ministros Christi.*" At every moment of our priesthood, we are or should be in contact with the Divine Intercessor. Too often, when someone appeals for help in trouble and exposes to the priest his depressed soul, we tell him to pray. Certainly! But do we intercede? We have direct communication with the Divine Advocate; we have the privileges of an ambassador. To tell the one whom it is our office to help that he should pray while we intercede not, is to be unfaithful to our high office. To offer Mass from time to time for all who "*labour and are burdened*" (Matthew 11:28) is the mark of a holy priest who knows the way to the Holy of Holies.

The Bottom of the Ladder: Horizontal Relations with the People

In order to be our priest, Christ assumed a human nature. We likewise continue His Priesthood not alone by having contact with Him in Heaven, but also by remaining human and speaking to Him in the name of all humanity. Vertically we are related to Christ in Heaven; horizontally, we are related to men on earth. As Christ took upon Himself our infirmities, and bore our ills, so also we are representative of sinful humanity:

> *The purpose for which any high priest is chosen from among his fellow-men and made a representative of men in their dealings with God, is to offer gifts and sacrifices in expiation of their sins. He is qualified for this by being able to feel for them when they are ignorant and make mistakes, since he, too, is all beset with humiliations.*

> (Hebrews 5:1,2)

Why is it that Our Lord chose us who are so weak? Each of us knows many who would surely have been more responsive to the grace of ordination. It would be an insult to Divine Wisdom to imagine ourselves the best material available. Why did God not choose angels to mediate between sinners and God? Because sympathy, the compassion, the suffering together which only one who has suffered knows, would be lacking experimentally to the angel. Our Lord Himself assumed the "nature of a slave" (Philippians 2:7), in order the more specifically to share our woes and our wounds. No one can ever say that God does not know what it is like to suffer as he does. Even the one thing absent from His human nature, the quality of femininity, He compensated for to the greatest extent possible by calling "the Woman" to share (as much as Mary could) His Passion with Him.

Even outside His Passion, whatever He did for man in His compassion for his ills "cost" Him something. He never immunized Himself from our infirmities. He even seemed to lose something when He healed: "*a power has gone out from Me*" (Luke 8:46). He groaned when He raised Lazarus from the dead. "*And Jesus... sighed deeply, and distressed Himself over it*" (John 11:33).

We never offer Mass or say our Breviary as individuals. That is one reason why a server or other should assist at Mass. And though the Mass is offered to the Heavenly Father by the Church, its intercession is not for the Church alone but for those also who are not yet of the house of Israel, to whom also we are sent. Such is the meaning of those words which we recite at the Offertory when we offer in the four directions of the earth the chalice of Salvation *"pro nostra et totius mundi salute."*

The priest in the Old Testament was given detailed instructions which emphasized his bond to his people.

And whenever Aaron goes into the sanctuary, he will carry on his breast, on the burse that gives counsel, the names of Israel's sons, putting the Lord in mind of them eternally. And within the burse that gives counsel thou wilt put the touchstones of wisdom and of truth. These shall be on Aaron's breast, when he enters the Lord's presence; as long as he is there, he will be carrying on his breast the arbitrament of the sons of Israel.

(Exodus 28:29,30)

The names on the shoulder stones can be understood as the burden his people represented for him, as the cross would be our burden. But the breastplate, placed over the heart indicated that he still bore them affection and love. Because of our horizontal relations to the world, we must bear the name of Everyman in our hearts, and that not only in our private prayer, but whenever we offer the sacrifice of reparation and tearful intercession to the great High Priest in Heaven. The intentions of our Masses are wider than those who requested them. They embrace the faithful and the world.

> *Hark how the priests, that wait upon the Lord, make lament between porch and altar, crying aloud: Spare thy people, Lord, spare them; thy chosen people, do not put them to the shame of obeying heathen masters!*
>
> (Joel 2:17)

Always touched with sympathy for human infirmities, we bear the burden of nations in our hearts. Between the sanctuary and the tabernacle, clad in the vestments which identify us as the representatives of Christ, we speak for the dumb, atone for the sinful, plead for the Judases and intercede for those *"who do not know what they are doing"* (Luke 23:34).

The intercession of the priest before the throne of God must be a tearful one. In this our High Priest has given us an example of human sympathy, for He wept three times: once for human grief, misery, desolation and death, at the tomb of Lazarus; once for a city, a civilization, a decaying culture, a rotting government, corrupt priests, at Jerusalem; finally, for human sin, pride, greed, egotism, and all that catalogue of capital evils, at Gethsemane. If we start (as we must) at the bottom of the ladder, having compassion on all men, nothing that happens to others is foreign to us. Their grief is our grief, their poverty our poverty. No matter whose the souls that wax weary, no matter whose the hands that hard burdens bear, our reaction is always the same. "My woe," we cry in the deep of our own afflicted co-suffering spirit, "my grief, my cross!"

How Intercession affects Our Mass

Granted our identification with those who are ignorant and make mistakes (Hebrews 5:2), our thoughts will be their thoughts as we offer the Holy Sacrifice of the Mass.

At the Offertory, for example, we will see all humanity on the paten and in the chalice. As Our Lord obtained the first elements of His own human Body from a woman, so for the Eucharist He takes bread and wine from the earth. The bread and wine are thus representative of mankind. Two of the substances which have most widely nourished man are bread and wine. Bread has been called the marrow of the earth; wine, its very blood. In giving what has traditionally made our flesh and blood, we are equivalently offering all mankind on the paten.

The people no longer bring bread and wine as they did in the early church, but their contributions to the Offertory collection permit the purchase of the bread and wine. There would be less resistance to the collection basket if we made more effort to present it as a symbol of the incorporation of the entire congregation into the Sacrifice of the Mass. Similarly, we could simultaneously edify and win the Lord's blessing if we ourselves gave generously to every collection to which we ask the people to contribute. Why should we be exempt from a sacrifice for the Propagation of the Faith on Mission Sunday? "Be as generous as possible" is idle talk, if the generosity of the pastor has not preceded the generosity of his flock.

Before the bread could be placed on the paten and wine poured into the chalice, how many elements of the economic, financial and technical world had to be brought into play! The wheat needed farmers, fields, sacks, trucks, mills, commerce, finance, buying and selling. The grapes required. vineyards, bottles, winepresses, time, space, chemistry, a thousand years of accumulated skills.

At the Offertory, therefore, we gather up the whole world into the narrow compass of a plate and a cup. Every drop of sweat, every day of labor, the decisions of the economist, the financier, the draughtsman and the engineer, every exertion and invention that went into the preparation of the elements of the Offertory are symbolically redeemed, justified and sanctified by our act. We bring not only redeemed man, but unredeemed creation to the steps of Calvary and the threshold of Redemption.

As the wheat Mary ate and the wine she drank became a kind of natural Eucharist to prepare for the Lamb of God Who would sacrifice Himself for the world, so are all material things sanctified through the Offertory of the Mass.

In the Consecration, Christ renews His sacrifice in an un-bloody manner. The act of love that prompted that sacrifice is eternal, for He is the Lamb "*slain in sacrifice ever since the world was made*" (Revelation 13:8). What the priest does each time he speaks the words of Consecration, is to apply Calvary and its fruits to a particular place and a particular time. Localized at one point in space and one moment in time, Calvary is now universalized in space and time. The priest takes the Cross of Calvary with Christ still hanging on it, and he plants it in New York, Paris, Cairo and Tokyo, and in the poorest mission of the world. We are not alone at the altar; we are in horizontal relations with Africa, Asia, our own parish, our city — everyone.

Clinging to the chasuble of every priest, for example, are 600 million souls in China who as yet know not Christ. When the priest takes the host in his hand, he is looking at fingers gnarled from slavery in the salt mines of Siberia. As he stands before the altar, his feet are the bleeding feet of refugees tramping westward toward barbed wire beyond which lies freedom. The flame of the candles reflects the flow of blast furnaces tended by gaunt men who for their labors are denied economic justice. The eyes gazing on the host are wet with the tears of the widow, the suffering and the orphan. The stole is a sling in which the priest carries on his shoulder living stones, the burden of the churches, the missions of the entire world. He drags the whole of humanity to the altar, where he joins heaven and earth together. For his hands raised at the Consecration merge into the Hands of Christ in heaven, who "lives on still to make intercession on our behalf" (Hebrews 7:25).

In the Offertory, the priest is like a lamb led to the slaughter. In the Consecration, he is the lamb slaughtered as the sacrificial victim. In the Communion, he finds that he has not died at all, that he has on the contrary really come to the abundant life which is union with Christ. The one who surrenders himself to the material and allows himself to be possessed by it, is like a drowning man weighed down by the water that has entered and taken possession of his lungs. Such a one can never recover himself. But where the surrender is to God, we get ourselves back ennobled and enriched. We find that our death was after all no more permanent in the Consecration than was the death of Calvary, for Holy Communion is a kind of Easter. We give up our time, and get His eternity; we give up our sin, and receive His grace; we give up petty loves, and receive the Flame of Love.

In this union with Christ we are not alone, for Communion is not merely the union of the individual soul and Christ; it unites Christ to all the members of the Mystical Body and in an extended way through prayer to all humanity.

The one Bread makes us one Body, though we are many in number; the same Bread is shared by all.

(1 Corinthians 10:17)

Sharing the Body of Christ in Holy Communion wipes out all accidental distinctions of race, class or condition. Here we are one with the whole of redeemed humanity, and indirectly with the earth, of which Christ described His true followers as the salt.

But we who offer this Chalice and eat of this Bread must constantly remind ourselves that this priestly office imposes spiritual obligations. The Israelites in the desert were fed with manna on their journey and drank water from the rock, and yet

for all that, God was ill pleased with most of them; see how they were laid low in the wilderness.

(1 Corinthians 10:5)

Not everyone who receives Communion is saved. It avails us not to be priests unless we are victims, for only those who die with Him will live with Him.

Our nccd to die in Christ before we can live to Christ reflects one of the great differences between the High Priest and his human priests; He was without sin, but we are not. Hence, the priest must offer Mass, not only for the people but also — and this is often forgotten — for himself:

And, for that reason, must needs present sin offerings for himself, just as he does for the people.

(Hebrews 5:3)

On the cross Our Lord, as priest, begged forgiveness for sinners: "Father, forgive them" (Luke 23:34); sinless, He asked no pardon for Himself. With us, on the contrary, it is not so. We must offer the Holy Sacrifice for our own failings and sins.

The Old Testament priest was obligated to offer for himself a greater sacrifice, a more expensive animal. Since his blessings were greater, his sins also were greater.

He will offer the bullock to make intercession for himself.

(Leviticus 16:6)

The analysis of this text developed in the Epistle to the Hebrews so impressed the author as a seminarian that he resolved to let no week of his priestly life go by without offering a Mass in honor of Our Blessed Lady and to the Great High Priest in reparation for his failings and sins. This resolve he has kept for decades and hopes with God's grace to keep until the divine Mercy finally calls him to eternal union with the Tremendous Lover.

Conclusion

No priest should ever so act that Jacob's remark about himself could be applied to his meditations on the priesthood. When Jacob arose from his vision at Bethel, he said:

Why, this is the Lord's dwelling place, and I slept here unaware of it!

(Genesis 28:16)

As Jacob failed to recognize the nearness of God, the priest often fails to recognize the greatness of his calling. How often we sleep, unmindful of the Eucharist, His dwelling place! Only in rare moments do we come to the frightening realization of our vocation. We are more conscious of the bottom of the ladder than the top. Humanity is nearer to us; we can feel it. But the top is seen only by faith. It takes a kind of Luza, of separation from the world to make us see Bethel, the House of God. Our priesthood is best illumined in the fires of victimhood. We become significant to our fellow men not by being a "regular guy" but by being "another Christ." Our effectiveness at the bottom of the ladder depends on our communication with the top. Popularity is not necessarily influence. "Woe upon you," said Our Lord, "*when all men speak well of you*" (Luke 6:26). Greatest is our compassion for others and our ability to elevate them when we have come down from heaven (John 3:13). The bottom of the ladder is best discovered from the top.

First Application:
Separation from the World

Though as priests we are taken from among men and must therefore never be unsympathetic to their afflictions, though we are in the world, we are never of it, for our High Priest has called us out of this world. The Epistle to the Hebrews presents a profound reason why this must be so:

Let us, too, go out to Him away from the camp, bearing the ignominy He bore.

(Hebrews 13:13)

What did "away from the camp" mean? It meant to be the rejected one of the world. The "camp" in Scripture was the city of Jerusalem, the religious center of the world. The Temple had expelled Him, the priests had delivered Him over to the Gentiles; they denied Him a place to die in the city, as they denied Him an inn at His birth. Outside the camp was always the place of reproach. It was there the refuse and the trash were dumped.

And now, to make amends for his fault, ... the skin and all the flesh... he will carry away from the camp... and burn them over a wood fire.

(Leviticus 4:8,11,12)

Unless the world sees a difference in the places we frequent, in our activities and in the pleasures in which we indulge, in the language we use, in our dress, it will not respect our testimony. Separated from the world, separated unto God these are the negative and positive sides of our priesthood.

In fact, the more success and prestige we enjoy in the world, the more honors laid on us, the more we must refuse to avail ourselves of worldly rewards and consolations. The temptation to be "of the world" becomes great when a priest has popularity thrust on him because his work calls on him to utilize the mass media, the press, television or radio. Then more than ever must he impress on himself that it is one thing to be popular, another to be influential. Pope John XXIII once gave thanks to God because a well-known cleric, who had great success among all classes of people, had suffered. This is what keeps him humble, he said. In the proportion in which we seek what the world can give, we become unable to give what the world needs. Great inspirations come in the desert, or away from the world.

The word of God came upon John, the son of Zachary, in the desert.

(Luke 3:2)

Silence constitutes an integral part of this isolation. It is not always proper to speak all that we know.

Do not cast your pearls before swine.

(Matthew 7:6)

Some like to talk about religion endlessly, as Herod did until John the Baptist introduced Herod's own moral problem. Religion is less a subject for discussion than for decision.

Be sure thou dost not tell any man of it.

(Matthew 8:4)

Be sure nobody hears of this.

(Matthew 9:30)

Our High Priest stands between us and displays of popular applause, of surface approbation. Like Jacob's ladder, though we are rooted in the earth, we must be supported by heaven, else is there no ascending or descending of the angels. At each moment of our apostolate, the world must say of us what the Sanhedrin said of Peter and John after the Resurrection, that they "recognized them now as having been in Jesus' company" (Acts 4:13). If the fires which enkindle our activity are other than the flame of the Holy Spirit, we are but "echoing bronze, or the clash of cymbals" (1 Corinthians 13:1).

Every priest should meditate frequently on the two newly ordained priests, the sons of Aaron. Aaron and Moses had offered their sacrifices and God had shown approval by consuming them with miraculous fire. The new priests, Nadab and Abiu, without waiting for instructions, prepared to make a return to God for His gift by the offering of incense, which was symbolic of prayer. But they ignited their thuribles, not with the sacred fire of the altar (Leviticus 16:12) but with a strange fire which God had forbidden.

> *There were two of Aaron's sons, Nadab and Abiu, who took up their censers and put coals and incense into them, to burn unhallowed fire in the Lord's presence, not in accordance with His command; whereupon the Lord sent down fire which devoured them, and they died there in the Lord's presence.*

(Leviticus 10:1,2)

What this strange fire which they offered was, we do not know. All we do know is that as they reached the door of the tabernacle where Moses and Aaron were standing, they were met by a consuming blast of fire. They had used some fire of the world, not the fire of God symbolic of the Holy Spirit.

The scene recalls a similar one described in the Acts of the Apostles (5:1-10), the destruction of Ananias and Saphira, who used not the spirit of Pentecost in their giving, as Nadab and Abiu did not use the fire of God in their priesthood. Fire that is of our own kindling does not make a pleasing sacrifice to God. Only the Spirit of God can provide an acceptable fire.

> *Those who follow the leading of God's Spirit are all God's sons.*

(Romans 8:14)

The nearer men are to God, the more exposed they are to the touch of His chastening hands. What might pass unnoted in others will be punished in them.

The priest who does not depend upon the Holy Spirit but seeks to furnish a fire or a spirit of himself, provokes the Lord by presumption. God accepts only what His Spirit inspires. We must bring back to God what He has given. He rejects all counterfeits. He will have Divine fire or none. Otherwise, the fire of Divine approval becomes the fire of Divine wrath. Strange fire was punished with hallowed fire. God's fire quenched their censers together with the light of their life.

Twice we are reminded that Nadab and Abiu had no children (Numbers 3:4 and 1 Paralipomena 24:2 [1 Chronicles 24:2, RSV]). Priests whose ministry is not inspired by the Holy Spirit have a sterile priesthood. It is not continued through vocations. If they lack the Spirit of Christ, so will they lack spiritual progeny. The priestly life enkindled by the *ignis alienus* of the world cannot grow old with the comfort of young priests whose vocations it fostered. But the priest on fire with the Holy Spirit will never be barren. His parish, and his school will flower with vocations. Thus has every priest a measure of the fire which blazes in his soul. The Nadabs and the Abius cannot enkindle love of Christ, but was there ever a Paul without a Timothy?

Second Application: Loss of Our Ego

Christ our High Priest, the Ladder of Jacob, was not a human Person, though He had a human nature. His manhood was not the center of personality; the human nature had no conceivable existence apart from the Eternal Word who called it into being and made it His own.

The human nature was a garment with which He clothed His Divine Person, or rather an *instrumentum conjunctum Divinitatis* by which He acted on humanity. It was not a separable instrument, in the way in which a pencil is separable from the hand of the writer, but one eternally united to the Word, even now in heaven, as the pledge, pattern and model of our resurrection and glory.

Through the instrumentality of this human nature, Our Blessed Lord exercised three offices. He was Teacher, King and Priest; these three offices which He communicated to His Church to be exercised by the human instruments He chose to be His ministers. Consequently, in His Mystical Body, He still continues to teach, to govern and to sanctify. What He did through the Body He took from

Mary, He does now through the Body He took from humanity and filled with His Spirit at Pentecost.

Now if our Mediator brought together God and man, heaven and earth, eternity and time, in the unity of His Divine Person, what does that mean for us priests? How does it affect the ideal of the priesthood in the Church? What it specifically does is to submerge the human personality of the priest so that he can say: "I am no longer my own." Human personality answers the question, "Who is it?" Our human nature answers the question, "What is it?" The priest who continues the Life of Christ seeks to be one with Him so completely that the personality which governs his every thought, word and deed is the Personality of Christ Himself. As the human nature of Christ had no human person, so the priest seeks to have no source of responsibility other than Christ Himself. We strive to eliminate the "Ego" and substitute the *"Christus-Sacerdos-Victima."*

Though the Hypostatic Union can never be repeated, every priest must try in a distant and imperfect way to reproduce it in his priesthood. We too seek to have "two natures in one person." One nature we have inherited from Adam; the other "nature" is grace, by which we are made "partakers of the Divine Nature." While, in no strict sense, are these like the two natures in Christ, they help to point up the problem of our "ego." The ideal is so to submerge our personality in the Person of Christ as to think with Him, will what He wills, make Him the source of our responsibility and our power.

If a painter felt the urge to create a beautiful picture but had available only a canvas that did not belong to him, he might decide that it would not be worth the effort. The analogy is one that can be applied to the great High Priest; if He does not own us, if He is not the directing Personality of all our actions, He will not work through us as He works through those who belong to Him. We operate too much through our power, not His.

I, as a person, use a pencil as an instrument. If the pencil were endowed with its own personality, it might say: "I will not write," or "I will go up when you want me to go down," or "I will blunt my point." There would be little I could do with that instrument. So it is with us, if our personality is in conflict with His; or if it has a little secret garden of some petty love or secret sin, which He cannot enter. In such a case, the fault of our priesthood is not in Him, but in us. Our ego "frustrates" Divinity. He wills one thing; we will another. We become but broken rungs on the ladder to heaven.

Maybe the Nestorian heresy is alive today — and in us? Nestorius taught that there were two persons in Christ. Do not we sometimes live as if there were two persons in us; the person who wishes to be rich and the Person of Christ Who had nowhere to lay His Head? The person who seeks to escape work, and the Person of Christ Whose greatest conversions were made when He was tired? The person who never makes a convert, and the Person of Christ Who is always in search of the lost sheep.

He called us as persons to the priesthood bidding us to crucify ourselves, to de-egotize and to make ourselves empty vessels for the heavenly treasure. That is why we are bidden to live a life "hidden with Christ in God." Only in self-forgetfulness does Christ reign in us.

To Christ Crucified

I am not moved to love Thee, O my Lord,
By any longing for Thy Promised Land;
Nor by the fear of hell am I unmanned
To cease from my transgressing deed or word.

'Tis Thou Thyself dost move me — Thy blood poured
Upon the cross from nailed foot and hand;
And all the wounds that did Thy body brand;
And all Thy shame and bitter death's award.

Yea, to Thy heart am I so deeply stirred
That I would love Thee were no heaven on high —
That I would fear, were hell a tale absurd!
Such my desire, all questioning grows vain;

Though hope deny me hope I still would sigh,
And as my love is now, it should remain.

Translated by Thomas Walsh*
From the book *An Introduction to Spanish Literature*,
by George Tyler Northup, University of Chicago.

As the scientist learns the secrets of nature by being passive before it, so we learn the mysteries of our High Priest by being passive before Him. Nature would never unfold the pages of its laws, if the scientist imposed his mind upon it; so neither will the High Priest confer that fullness of power upon us, unless we are like empty vessels before Him. St. Paul says that he kept down his self-will and was made weak in everything that involved his personality, in order that he might increase within himself in the power of God.

But He told me, My grace is enough for thee; My strength finds its full scope in thy weakness. More than ever, then, I delight to boast of the weaknesses that humiliate me, so that the strength of Christ may enshrine itself in me. (2 Corinthians 12:9)

There is nothing that God could not do without me. But there are many things that He has elected to do through me, provided I am a supple instrument in His Hand. The true continuation of the Priesthood is, therefore, the giving of ourselves so completely to the great High Priest that we have no other feelings, or emotions, or desires than Christ Himself:

Yours is to be the same mind which Christ Jesus shewed.

(Philippians 2:5)

Why when land was about to be divided among the twelve tribes did the tribe of Levi receive none? Because it was the tribe of the priesthood. What did they need since they possessed the Lord? What a lesson!

That is why the Levites have no lands assigned to them like their brethren, the Lord thy God has promised them that He himself will be their portion.

(Deuteronomy 10:9)

Third Application:
The Importance of Ex Opere Operantis

When we act in the Church's name in dispensing the sacraments, we are instruments of God by which grace is conferred by the simple performance of the action, or as the Scholastics said, ex *opere operato*. Sunlight is not polluted by passing through a dirty window. God can write straight with crooked lines. A person could be as validly baptized by a Judas as by a Peter.

This is true of the sacraments. But the priest is bound to perform many other duties, to console the sick, to preach the Gospel, to convert sinners, to stir souls to penance, to foster vocations, and all these duties require our own sacrifice, our detachment and the laborious fashioning of ourselves to the image of Christ. The effectiveness of such actions *ex opera operantis* requires the surrender of our personality to Christ.

Speaking of the actions of Christ, the theologians say that everything He did was a Divine act because He was a Divine Person, a principle they express by the statement that *actiones sunt suppositorum*. This principle can by analogy be applied to the priest. All of the actions of his nature are to be attributed to the Person Christ:

Whatever you are about, in word and action alike, invoke always the name of the Lord Jesus Christ, offering your thanks to God the Father through Him.

(Colossians 3:17)

We act, live, think, preach not in our name or personality, but in His. We are only branches. He is the Vine (John 15:1-10). The vine and the branches have the same life, are nourished by the same sap, and work together in the production of the same fruit. They form but one being, they have one and the same action. Our oneness in Him is so total, that we cry out with Paul:

I hang upon the Cross, and yet I am alive; or rather, not I; it is Christ that lives in me.

(Galatians 2:20)

Our sublime dignity does not consist exclusively in the priestly character given in Holy Orders, but in what this character also demands as its complement, namely, Christ taking the place of our personality. Then we grow in Christ as Mary did. Certainly, Our Blessed Mother was richer spiritually on Christmas Day than on the day of the Annunciation; richer at Cana than at Bethlehem, richer at Calvary than at Cana, and richer in the Upper Room at Pentecost than on Golgotha.

The ideal is accordingly to have the Person of Christ as the single source of our responsibility both in acts which produce their effect *ex opere operato* and in those which are fruitful *ex opere operantis*. Our sinful life does not destroy the essential value of the former kind. When in the confessional the priest says, "I absolve," it is Christ Who absolves; when at Mass he says, "This is My Body," it is Christ Who offers His Body to the Father. And so on for all the sacraments. But in the priest's other acts, it should be Christ Who is again visiting the sick and instructing those who seek truth. This kind of union with Christ, however, does not come simply from ordination. It demands mortification.

The faithful see Christ in us at the altar and in the confessional and at the font. Do they see Christ in us at the table, in the school, on the golf course, or in the hospital? Are these places for our ego to assert itself, or are they occasions for others to see Christ in the dining room of a Simon or a Lazarus? Christ does not come off with the chasuble, nor is our ordination folded in a pocket as easily as a stole. Unbelievers do not see us investments; they see us in shops, in theatres, at meetings. Whether they see Christ in us depends on whether we act like Christ.

An electric wire attached to the generator will give no light if the bulb is burned out. One of the reasons why Christianity does not influence the world more is that few Christians shine more brightly than those who lack the faith. Is this not true also of many priests, in spite of the fact that the priest should be a different person from all others, because he is the Person of Christ?

St. Francis de Sales saw a young priest on his ordination day about to enter the church for his first Mass. The young priest stopped as if he was talking to someone invisible; the problem seemed to be who should pass first. The priest explained to St. Francis de Sales: "I just had the happiness of seeing my Guardian Angel. Previously, he always walked before me; now that I am a priest, he insists on walking behind me."

By the surrender of our ego to the Person of the High Priest we exercise an influence like that of the eighteenth-century French court preacher, Bishop Jean Baptiste Massillon on Louis XIV. "Father," the king complimented him one day, "I have heard many orators in this chapel, and I was always very satisfied; but every time I hear you, I am dissatisfied with myself."

Holy priests always make sinners say what the Samaritan woman said to the menfolk of her city:

Come and have sight of a man who has told me all the story of my life; can this be the Christ?

(John 4:29)

✠ J.M.J. ✠

~ 3 ~

Spiritual Generation

"Increase and multiply" is a law of sacerdotal no less than of biological life. The production of new life is generation, a function that does not pertain exclusively or even primarily to the flesh. God is the source of all generation.

Begetting is not an impulse from below but a gift from above; rather than an evolution from animals, it is a descent from Deity.

What, says the Lord thy God, shall I, that bring children to the birth, want power to bring them forth?

(Isaiah 66:9)

Every mother who begets a child, every hen which hatches its young, every mind which conceives a new idea, every bishop who ordains a priest, every priest who fosters a vocation, all reflect that eternal act of generation in which the Father says to his Son:

Thou art my son; I have begotten thee this day.

(Psalm 2:7)

The understanding of the eternal generation of the Second Person of the Trinity provided by such carnal generation is, however, very remote and obscure. Somewhat more precise — though still of course analogical — is the operation of the human intellect when it "conceives" ideas. Where do we get the idea of "fortitude," "relationship" or "spirituality?" We have never seen these concepts in the pedestrian world of oranges, sidewalks and coins. Whence came they? The mind generated them; once begotten, they remain distinct from the mind, but not separate from it. The fruits of thinking, namely, ideas, do not drop from the mind like apples from a tree, or the newborn from parents. They exist in the mind and yet with characters of their own.

In like manner, does God as the Eternal Thinker have a Thought, a Word. Because this Wisdom was "generated," we call God Who Thinks the Father, and the Word or Idea Who is "generated" the Son. The Father was not first and then the Son. An unbelieving father said to his son who asserted that the Father and Son were equal: "I existed before you did, and therefore the Father existed before the Son." The boy answered: "Oh no! You did not begin to be a father until I began to be a son."

The Blessed Virgin Mary and Generation

Was not the Blessed Mother herself generated in the Mind of God? Before she was immaculately conceived in the womb of her mother, St. Anne, she was "immaculately conceived" in the Mind of God. That is why the words of Proverbs (8:22-30) are applied to her:

The Lord made me His when first He went about His work, at the birth of time, before His creation began. Long, long ago, before earth was fashioned, I held my course. Already I lay in the womb, when the depths were not yet in being, when no springs of water had yet broken; when I was born, the mountains had not yet sunk on their firm foundations, and there were no hills; not yet had He made the earth, or the rivers, or the solid framework of the world. I was there when He built the heavens, when He fenced in the waters with a vault inviolable, when He fixed the sky overhead, and leveled the fountain springs of the deep. I was there when He enclosed the sea within its confines, forbidding the waters to transgress their assigned limits, when He poised the foundations of the world. I was at His side, a master-workman, my delight increasing with each day, as I made play before Him all the while.

The Apostles and Generation

Just as God the Father has a Divine Son and countless millions of adopted sons by grace, so Mary had not only Jesus as her Son, but all those other children who were, in the person of John, commended to her on Calvary.

Fecundity, generation and fruitfulness mark the teachings of the faith, beginning with the command to "*increase and multiply*" (Genesis 1:22). So it is to the end, for the final book of the Bible declares that the Tree of Life itself is fecund, "*the tree that gives life, bearing its fruit twelvefold*" (Revelation 22:2). In the same vein, the Apostle Paul describes his converts as the fruits of his generation: "*It was I that begot you in Jesus Christ, when I preached the gospel to you*" (1 Corinthians 4:15). Timothy he addressed as "my own son in the faith" (1 Timothy 1:2), and again as "*his well beloved son*" (2 Timothy 1:2).

So too does James assure us that God has begotten us in Truth:

It was His will to give us birth, through His true word, meaning us to be the first-fruits, as it were, of all His creation.

(James 1:18)

And John stresses the theme of our Redemption by reminding us that carnal generation is as nothing compared to the spiritual generation by grace:

Their birth came, not from human stock, not from nature's will or man's, but from God.

(John 1:13)

God hates sterility. He punishes disobedience with barrenness. When He promises His people a blessing, it is expressed in terms of fecundity:

There shall be no unfruitfulness in thy land.

(Exodus 23:26)

But the one who has no spiritual children is under a curse. Only those who walk with the Lord and yield to the Spirit are gifted with fruitfulness:

Thou shalt be blessed as no other people is blessed; man and woman, sire and dam shall breed.

(Deuteronomy 7:14)

The Spiritual Generation of Priests

The priest is pledged to celibacy, not because human generation is wrong, but because it must yield so that he can devote himself wholly to a higher form of generation: the begetting of children in Christ by bringing to Him those who never knew Him, by restoring to Him those lost in sin, and by arousing in those who already love Christ the inspiration to serve Him more fully as religious or priests. The energy which otherwise would be used for the service of the flesh is not buried in a napkin. It is transformed so that it serves chaste generation in the Spirit.

Too often the vow of chastity is presented negatively as the avoiding of carnal and sinful pleasures. But is pure water only the absence of dirt, a white diamond merely the negation of carbon? Chastity is sometimes mistakenly called cold, but not by Francis Thompson, who proclaims it a "passionless passion, a wild tranquility." Chastity is fire. No life is produced without fire. Even the virginal conception of Our Lady had its fire — not human indeed, but the Fire of the Holy Spirit. At that moment, she undoubtedly had an ecstasy of soul surpassing the flesh ecstasy of all humans combined. Such is the joy of begetting through the Pure Love of the Spirit.

"Father"

No form of address is so widely used for a priest, and none so appropriate as "Father." It stresses precisely the priest's close relationship to God,

The Father of Our Lord Jesus Christ, that Father from whom all fatherhood in heaven and on earth takes its title.

(Ephesians 3:14,15)

But if the priest is thus a father, then God may properly inquire of him where are his offspring. The bishop alone, of course, has the power to beget a priest in ordination, but every priest has the power and duty to foster the vocation. When we go before the judgment seat of God, each of us will be asked: "Whom have you begotten in Christ?" Woe to those who are barren! When Our Lord comes to us looking for the fruit of our Fatherhood, we must not be as the barren fig tree which merits only a curse.

Physical maternity is not without its labor, and to a mother in labor, Our Lord likened His Passion: "... *because now her time has come*" (John 16:21). But spiritual parenthood, our mission, is not without its labor too, as Paul said of Onesimus:

And I am appealing to thee on behalf of Onesimus, the child of my imprisonment.

(Philemon 1:10)

The mother of Samuel the Prophet was, after many years of sterility, blessed with a son who was to prove mighty in Israel because her heart was right with God. Those who desire the glory of God, she proclaimed in thanksgiving, will find that the life which has been barren can become unusually fruitful:

See how at last the barren womb bears many.

(1 Kings 2:5[1 Samuel 2:5, RSV])

And what above all things will assure us of begetting children in Christ, if it be not our oneness with the Christ Victim? Having enumerated seven miracles or signs which Our Lord worked to prove His divinity; St. John observed that few who had witnessed the signs had been convinced by them (John 12:37). But Christ had yet another way to win souls:

Yes, if only I am lifted up from the earth, I will attract all men to Myself.

(John 12:32)

Miracles are not a cure for unbelief. On being informed that Lazarus had been raised from the dead, some of the Pharisees sought to kill him and thus destroy the evidence. But the spiritual harvest which Our Lord assured us would come from His Cross cannot be denied. The means He proclaimed to draw souls to Himself constitute an infallible source of spiritual fecundity for those who live in its shadow.

Convert Making

Has administration taken precedence in the life of many pastors over evangelization? Has organization swallowed up shepherding? Are souls to be reckoned only on index cards? Are the sheep in the fold to be used only for shearing, or is each member of the laity to be encouraged and helped to develop his own specific apostolic vocation? The question is one that each pastor can answer for himself only by searching the depths of his own conscience. What he has to remember is that he is the father not only of the sheep who are in the fold:

I have other sheep too, which do not belong to this fold; I must bring them in too.

(John 10:16)

Does not Canon Law make the pastor responsible for all souls in his parish? Yet how many pastors devote themselves seriously to trying to incorporate those not of the fold into the Mystical Body of Christ? Every priest should ask himself how many adults he baptized in the past year as the fruit of his zeal; how many fallen-away Catholics he brought back to the Father's House. Why do some priests never make a convert while others make hundreds? Can it be because one takes his title of "Father" seriously while the other does not?

When I preach the gospel, I take no credit for that; I act under constraint; it would go hard with me indeed if I did not preach the Gospel.

(1 Corinthians 9:16)

Administration is absolutely essential; to ignore it would be to overlook the fact that each member has a specific function in the Mystical Body. But the Holy Spirit has not called us to be mere bankers, real estate men or blueprint experts. Such activities are at best incidental to a primary function which the Apostles understood. The Spirit was not given them to sit at counting tables:

It is too much that we should have to forego preaching God's word and bestow our care upon tables.

(Acts 6:2)

On the other hand, it is not enough to be "sacristy" priests devoutly beseeching the Lord to send souls to us, while ignoring His command:

You must go out to the street corners and invite all whom you find there.

(Matthew 22:9)

All around us potential converts abound. The tragedy is not only that they lack faith, but that we seldom ask them to embrace it. A non-Catholic lawyer was asked on his deathbed by his Catholic partner of twenty years, "Now, that you are nearing your end, how about coming into the Church?" The dying man raised his eyebrows. "If your faith meant so little to you during the twenty years you have known me," he replied, "it cannot make that much difference now."

Conversions are not more difficult in our times than before; but the approach must be different. Today, people are looking for God, not because of the order they find in the universe, but because of the disorder they find in themselves. They are coming to God through an inner disgust, a despair that may be called creative.

Out of the depths I cry to Thee, O Lord.

(Psalm 129:1[130:1, RSV])

Religion is sometimes said to be losing its influence in the world. To the extent that such is the case, part of the reason undoubtedly is that we do not appear to the unbeliever as different from anyone else. The missionary, the priest who lives in the slums, the saintly priest who spends himself with souls — these always inspire, and they inspire because they reveal Christ and Him Crucified.

Doubting Thomas must not be judged too harshly for the conditions he laid down before he would believe. All he asked for was fair evidence.

Until I have seen the mark of the nails on His hands, until I have put my finger into the mark of the nails, and put my hand into His side, you will never make me believe.

(John 20:25)

No deep conviction is aroused in the incredulous until they see the scarred hands and the broken heart of the priest who is a victim with Christ. The mortified priest, the priest who is detached from the world — these inspire, edify and Christify souls.

Being a father of many children requires work. Our Lord made His two greatest converts when He was tired. The eight-hour day, five-day week is not prescribed in the Scriptures. God gave Moses hundreds of details about the tabernacle, but one piece of furniture was not mentioned. The tabernacle lacked a chair. Altar, laver, table, lamp, censers and drapes are all listed, *but there was no place for the priest to sit down.* When are we meant to sit down in the sense of resting from our priest-victimhood? Our Lord "sat" after He had spent Himself for our Redemption:

whereas He sits forever at the right hand of God, offering for our sins a sacrifice.

(Hebrews 10:12)

We also read of Him "standing" in heaven. When Stephen was stoned, he saw "*Jesus standing at God's right hand*" (Acts 7:55), suggesting that when His Church is persecuted, Our Lord stands in heaven. If such is the symbolic meaning, the High Priest surely stands today to strengthen the third of the people of the earth who groan interiorly under the beating of the hammer and the cutting of the sickle of Communism!

Certainly, for the priest, work is his lot while on earth: "*Finish your journey while you have the light*" (John 12:35). It was no oversight on God's part to omit a chair when furnishing the tabernacle. The priest was not ordained to be a sitter. Christ's promise is that those who overcome will "sit" with Him at the Heavenly Banquet.

The earthly father must work for and be with his family; the spiritual father in like manner, must work for and be with souls. Our Lord gave us the example:

There they crucified Him, and with Him two others, one on each side with Jesus in the midst.

(John 19:18)

In the great moment of redemptive love, He is found in the midst of saved and sinners, among good thieves and bad thieves. His mediators and ambassadors can no more isolate themselves from sinners than He did. We are separated from them as holy priests, but one with them as victims for sins. Nor do we go there amongst them to convince them of their error so much as to break bread for their starving souls.

The spirit of the true father is less canonical than evangelical. Canon Law concerns the relations of the Church and its members. The Gospel concerns the mission of the Church to the world. The parish or the diocese is not the limit of our fatherliness. As Our Lord got closer to the cross, He had more and more dealings with those who were not Jews. After the cross, His message was to the world. Two things always seem to go together in a bishop or a priest: love of conversions and love of the foreign missions. The Catholics close to us we must indeed sanctify, but souls in distant lands who have never heard the good tidings, must also be redeemed.

Conversion is Victimhood

Can it be that the Communists excel us in their zeal to spread their beliefs? Zeal unfortunately is not always in direct proportion to truth. Fire has two qualities: light and heat. Light is truth. Heat is love. We have the truth, but sometimes not the zeal or love; we have the light, but not always the heat. But the Communists have the heat and not the light, the zeal and not the truth.

There is a dangerous tendency among many in modern times who call themselves Christians to divorce Christ and the cross.

And what would Christ be without the cross? Another teacher like Buddha or Lao-tse; a sociologist spreading whipped cream on socially disapproved behavior; a psychoanalyst reducing guilt to a complex and banishing sin as a "hangover" from savagery; a preacher too polite to mention hell or divorce; a reformer for whom all discipline is masochistic and who proclaims self-restraint and moderation as unnatural and in conflict with the biological urge to self-expression.

And who picks up the cross without Christ? The Communists! Into a disordered and falsely liberal world, they introduce order, law, obedience, discipline, study, conformity to the all-holy will of the Party, detachment from Western excesses, and above all, a crushing of the ego for the sake of the kingdom of earth. But as the Christ without the cross would be a weak, effeminate Christ unable to save us from sin, so the cross without Christ is tyranny, dictatorship, concentration camps, slavery and Sovietism.

Are we living in a world distinguished by an abundant outpouring of the anti-Pentecostal spirit? Has part of the earth caught fire with the flames of hell, while the fires of Pentecost sputter in our hands like little candles incapable of setting the world ablaze?

To suggest that the fires of Pentecost are dying would be not only blasphemy but a denial of proud facts; for the hope and glory of our age are to be found in the endurance of the Church of Silence and the unveiling of new fires by our missionaries. Yet is there not many an individual priest who should sadly contrast his own smugness with the zeal of the Communists and ask himself why some who want to be good and who profess the truth, still lack a passionate conviction for Christ. The Lord said to Moses:

The fire on the altar must burn continually. Never must the altar be empty of this perpetual fire.

(Leviticus 6:12,13)

Under the Law of Moses the priest had each morning to feed the fire with fresh logs and carry the ashes away from the camp (Leviticus 6:10,12). The morning fires of meditation, the self-denial which carries from the heart the dead things of the world —these are the conditions of the perpetual fire which burned in St. Paul for the conversion of the entire human race:

Thus, nobody has any claim on me, and yet I have made myself everybody's slave, to win more souls.... I have been everything by turns to everybody, to bring everybody salvation.

(1 Corinthians 9:19,22)

Fostering Vocations

Another aspect of the role of the father in begetting spiritual children in Christ is the fostering of vocations. It is accordingly appropriate for the priest to ask himself what contribution he is making. It is often said that there is a decline in vocations, but it is necessary here to distinguish between vocation and response. God calls. That is the Divine side. We respond. That is the human side. Pius XII in the Encyclical *Menti Nostrae* said:

The Church will never lack priests sufficient for its mission.

Every study of vocations reveals that many youths under fifteen feel the call. One survey indicated that 40 per cent of students in secular schools and 50 per cent of students in Catholic schools thought of a vocation after they were twelve. In another survey, 60 per cent of boys in normal school, 23 per cent in professional schools, 37 per cent in technical schools and 66 per cent in classics affirmed that at some time in their life they hoped to become priests or religious.

Many who have felt the call just wander away. Rather than a deliberate turning aside, there is compromise or straying. Youths with vocations, like sheep in a field, look around the world instead of up to heaven; and before they know it, they have lost sight of the Good Shepherd. The reasons are many, but often one of them is the failure of the priest to talk to an altar boy about the priesthood, to neglect to thank him when he gets up to serve the early Mass. A cutting reprimand for a trivial misdemeanor may alter a young man's plans — for such a cause Tito left the Church.

Now, son of man, prophesy doom to... the shepherds of my flock. This be thy message from the Lord God: Out upon Israel's shepherds, that had a flock to feed, and fed none but themselves.

(Ezekiel 34:2)

We must surely hope that we do not fall under this Divine Judgment. Nevertheless, as God's word, it must urge us to greater care of the young:

The milk drank, the wool wore, the fat lambs slaughtered, but pastured these sheep of mine never at all! The wasted frame went unnourished, the sick unhealed; nor bound they the broken limb, nor brought strayed sheep home, nor lost sheep found; force and constraint were all the governance they knew. So my sheep fell a-wandering, that shepherd had none; every wild beast fell a-preying on them, and they scattered far and wide.

(Ezekiel 34:3-5)

When we appear before the Lord to be judged by the use to which we put the chrism with which our hands were anointed, He will ask us if we have continued our priesthood?

I will hold them answerable for the flock entrusted to them, and they shall have charge of it no more, feed themselves out of its revenues no more. From their greedy power I will rescue it; no longer shall it be their prey.

(Ezekiel 34:10)

What young priest and religious will then proclaim our fruitfulness? What aid that we gave the Society for the Propagation of the Faith, or the *Opus Sancti Petri* for educating native seminarians will be recorded in the Book of Life? In how many Catholic homes will we have encouraged the vocations of worthy youths by our visits? What spiritual exercises will be noted as conducted by us for young men and women who felt drawn to the priesthood or the religious life?

How fruitful a vineyard of vocations is the sacristy! To see a priest making his meditation before Mass does more for an altar boy's vocation than a thousand pieces of inspirational literature.

Being a spiritual father to future priests requires dedication. Aaron and the priests of the Old Testament were anointed in three places: the right ear, the right thumb and the big toe of the right foot (Leviticus 14:14-28). The threefold anointing suggests a three-fold dedication: to be attentive to the hearing of the Word of God, for the ear signifies obedience (Exodus 21:6), as Our Lord was obedient unto the death of the Cross (Philippians 2:8); to use his hands constantly in performing good deeds, as Christ finished the work given to Him by the Father (John 4:34; 9:4; 18:4; Hebrews 10:5,7); and to walk always in the ways of God, for sweet are the feet of those who spread the news of the Gospel.

See where they bring good news on the mountain heights, proclaiming that all is well.

(Nahum 1:15)

The secret of fostering vocations may be summed up in this Old Testament ceremony, namely, the encouraging of spiritual sensitivity, of good works and of flight from evil.

1. The young must first hear the call of God. It is then the priest's role to keep his soul sensitive to God's voice. As in Baptism, we touch both ears saying, *"Ephphetha"* ("Be opened"), so in preparation for Orders, we keep the soul alert to God's whisper, for He does not shout a vocation.

2. The ear needs the hands to translate into good works the pious inspiration of God. Aspirants to the priesthood therefore serve the altar, instruct children in the faith, act as counselors to the young, thus fitting their hands to be anointed one day by the bishop.

3. Vocations prosper through discipline, too, for the priest must walk the narrow path to salvation, not the broad way to destruction (Luke 13:24). The world and the flesh have strong solicitation for youth. They must be protected from sin as God protected the Jews in going out of Egypt:

> *Thus the people had Pharao's leave to go on their way; but God did not lead them by the nearest road, the road through Philistia. Here they would have found themselves met by armed resistance, and perhaps, in despair of their enterprise, returned to Egypt.*

> (Exodus 13:17)

Canon Law places an obligation on every priest, especially pastors, to foster the signs of vocation observed in youths with whom they come in contact.

Dent operam sacerdotes, praesertim parochi, ut pueros, qui indicia praebeant ecclesiasticae vocationis, peculiaribus curis a saeculi contagiis arceant, ad pietatem informent, primis litterarum studiis imbuant divinaeque in eis vocationis germen foveant (Canon 1353 from the Code of Canon Law, 1917).

One parish in the United States had no vocations in forty years. A new pastor in a single year developed ten vocations. The difference was due to his spirituality. His ear heard the call of the Lord of the Harvest for vocations, his hands were busy in promoting devotions to the Sacred Heart, and his feet visited every family in his parish.

Some years ago I was eating in a hotel restaurant when a boy about twelve, who shined shoes for a living, began to swing on a velvet curtain at the entrance. The headwaiter yelled at him and ordered him out of the hotel.

I followed the boy into the street. He told me he had been expelled from a Catholic school by a pastor and a nun who assured him that he could never again attend a Catholic school. I took him to the pastor and the nun involved and reminded them of three other "bad" boys expelled from religious schools: one for drawing pictures during geography class, another for fighting too much, the third for keeping bad books under his mattress. They were respectively Hitler, Mussolini, and Stalin. How different, under God, might world history have been if their leaders had taken more pains to reform them!

The pastor and the nun agreed to re-admit the boy. In due course he was ordained a priest and today he is a missionary in the Arctic.

What a blessed life is ours! What a beautiful role celibacy plays when it facilitates a higher kind of generation, when it inspires the priest to imitate the Father in begetting the Word, to imitate the Christ Who begot us in the Spirit as an *alter Christus!*

Our days are blessed by a deepening of liturgical devotion and an upsurge of participation in the Eucharistic mysteries on the part of the laity. Such developments are a tribute but also a warning to the clergy, for as the laity become more spiritual, so must they. The Church is in danger when the laity are more spiritual than the clergy:

You are the salt of the earth; if salt loses its taste, what is there left to give taste to it?

(Matthew 5:13)

Much earlier the prophet Hosea had issued the same warning:

Priest, now, shall fare no better than people.

(Hosea 4:9)

It is not possible to create esteem for the priesthood except through an admiration for the priest's victimhood. No mother brings a child into the world without labor. No priest begets a vocation or makes a convert or sanctifies a soul except under the shadow of the cross. And as an *alter Christus*, every priest must realize his ability to beget in the spirit. We are usually conscious of our sacramental power at Mass and in the confessional, but do we have confidence in our power to excite vocations? When we place our hand on a boy who gives spiritual promise and say, "Some day you will be a priest," do we believe Our Lord will support our judgment and our blessing? Many a priest can look back on the blessing he gave a youth who is now an ordained priest. He did not confer the vocation on the young man. God did that. But there is such a thing as a priestly strengthening of the vocation in the soul. As Our Lord prayed to His Father, so must we pray confidently to the Lord:

And He will bring honour to Me, because it is from Me that He will derive what He makes plain to you.

(John 16:14)

How happy the death of the priest who knows that he has passed on the torch of life which Christ ignited in his soul. And until that hour, without the benefit of sitting down in the tabernacle of the Lord, each of us will say with Paul to those whose vocation we have fostered:

My little children, I am in travail over you afresh, until I can see Christ's image formed in you!

(Galatians 4:19)

~ 4 ~

The Holiness of the Priest

The moral and spiritual life of the priest is related in two ways to the Mystical Body of Christ. His holiness helps to make the faithful holy. The sanctity of the Christian community, in turn, helps to make him holy.

At the Last Supper, Our Lord gave His priests a compelling reason why they had to be holy, holding Himself up as the example:

I dedicate Myself for their sakes, that they too may be dedicated through the truth. It is not only for them that I pray; I pray for those who are to find faith in Me through their words.

(John 17:19,20)

He sanctified Himself not for Himself alone, but for them too. They in turn were to sanctify themselves for the Church and all future believers. Spirituality begins at the top, not at the bottom. The mirror reflects the light of the sun, but does not create it. Sanctity is a pyramid:

Gracious as balm poured on the head till it flows down on to the beard; balm that flowed down Aaron's beard, and reached the very skirts of his robe.

(Psalm 132:2 [133:2, RSV])

God is holy; that holiness comes to earth in Christ. He bestows it on His priests with their cooperation; they, in the measure in which they accept, contribute to making the people holy. The people do not give the priest the special powers to sanctify which he possesses. It is Our Lord who gave these powers, and He gave them to enable the priest to make the people holy. From the mountain, where one communes with God, sanctity descends:

> *So Moses went down again to the people, and rid them of defilement.*
>
> (Exodus 19:14)

For the sake of the Church, Our Lord came into the world and (as He said) He sanctified Himself. But what precisely does this expression mean? How can one consecrate himself? Could Aaron consecrate himself? Could I consecrate myself? But He could consecrate Himself, because He is a "high priest, now, eternally with the priesthood of Melchizedek" (Hebrews 6:20). He could sanctify Himself, because He was both priest and victim:

> *Order your lives in charity, upon the model of that charity which Christ shewed to us, when He gave himself up on our behalf, a sacrifice breathing out fragrance as He offered it to God.*
>
> (Ephesians 5:2)

In Biblical usage, to dedicate or sanctify meant to set apart as an offering to God, a sacrifice.

> *Thou shalt set apart for the Lord thy God all the firstborn of thy cattle and sheep.*
>
> (Deuteronomy 15:19)

> *There is no ransoming the first-born of ox or sheep or goat; they are set apart for the Lord.*
>
> (Numbers 18:17)

All Old Testament sacrifices were holy to the Lord as types of the "first-born" (Luke 2:7) who, in a special way became sanctified, that is, was set apart as a sacrifice for our salvation, on Good Friday. His own official sanctification, as He affirmed the previous night, was the meritorious cause of His priests and people being sanctified. St. Paul understood this clearly:

Christ shewed love to the Church when He gave Himself up on its behalf. He would hallow it.

(Ephesians 5:25,26)

The High Priest's "Our Father"

From the foregoing it is clear that Our Lord made Himself "holy" or "priestly" or "saintly" for our sakes. To reproduce this holiness in us priests, the help of heaven is needed. The night of the Last Supper He spoke to the Heavenly Father in our behalf, saying His own "Pater Noster." Previously, He had said to the apostles, when they asked how they were to pray:

And He told them, when you pray, you are to say, Father.

(Luke 11:2)

Our Lord never said "Our Father" of Himself and us together, but "My Father" and "Your Father," because He is the Natural Son; we, the adopted sons. His sacerdotal prayer of Holy Thursday night, like the prayer He had given the apostles on the earlier occasion, contained seven petitions. The first "Our Father" was for everyone, but this "Our Father" is for priests alone. It sums up the virtues that distinguish the priest.

1. *Perseverance: "Holy Father, keep them true to Thy name"*.

(John 17:11)

2. *Joy: "That My joy may be theirs and reach its full measure in them"*.

(John 17:13)

3. *Deliverance from evil: "That Thou shouldst keep them clear of what is evil"*.

(John 17:15)

4. *Holiness through sacrifices: "Keep them holy, then, through the truth".*

(John 17:17)

5. *Unity: "That they may all be one; that they too may be one in Us, as Thou Father, art in Me, and I in Thee".*

(John 17:21)

6. *His Constant Companions: "This, Father, is my desire, that all those whom thou hast entrusted to Me may be with Me where I am.*

(John 17:24)

7. *Enjoy His glory in heaven: "So as to see My glory".*

(John 17:24)

How often the note of joy and glory and happiness is struck! And everything is conditioned on being "with Him"; this was His purpose in choosing them as His priests. But before He offered that prayer, He told us that we would never be immune from trial. The "joy" set before us is similar to that with which He embraced the Cross. But the victory is certain. We have already won! Only the news has not yet leaked out!

In the world, you will only find tribulation; but take courage, I have overcome the world.

(John 16:33)

What Holiness Involves

Our Lord sanctified Himself for our sakes, and that — as has been indicated — involved sacrifice. He immolated Himself, just as whatever was dedicated to the Lord under the Old Testament was immolated.

As the shepherd, so the sheep; as the priest, so the people. Priest-victim leadership begets a holy Church. What the priests are in the parish, the diocese, and the nation, that likewise will the faithful be. As multitudes got the bread at Capharnaum through the disciples, so the faithful get the sanctification of Christ through our sanctification. Seeing this goal reached, the last outburst of Our Lord's sacerdotal soul was: *"It is achieved"* (John 19:30). The tens of thousands of lambs who shed their blood as types were no longer needed. The Lamb of God had immolated Himself. Every priest must perform a like act of self-oblation, and then pass on its fruits to the whole people: *"Do this for a commemoration of me"* (Luke 22:19).

The specific thing Christ directed every priest to repeat and renew was the sacramental symbol of His death. The living out of this death is sanctification.

But why must the Cross be taken up daily? Because there is a ransom price on every soul. Some of them cost much. They require a great sacrifice. It is not that Christ withholds His Mercy, but that He has willed to dispense it through our hands. And unless the hands of the priest are scarred hands, Christ's mercies do not so readily pass through them. Blessings, power, healing, influence get clogged by worldliness.

The Church makes no impression in the world so long as those outside see it only as a "sect" or an "organization' or "*one of the great religions*." Our Lord made His impact through His Cross (John 12:32). The wounded Christ redeemed; and only a wounded Church can effectively apply that Redemption. When the Church is making progress, where conversions are numerous, there Christ is poor again, tired again from missionary journeys, a victim once again in His saintly priests.

Every worldly priest hinders the growth of the Church; every saintly priest promotes it. If only all priests realized how their holiness makes the Church holy, and how the Church begins to decline when the level of holiness among priests falls below that of the people! God still thunders to His priests:

I have set watchmen, Jerusalem, upon thy walls, that shall never cease crying aloud, day or night; you that keep the Lord in remembrance, take no rest, nor let Him rest neither, till He has restored Jerusalem, spread her fame over all the earth.

(Isaiah 62:6,7)

Watchmen are we, who have been put on the walls of the Church by the High Priest. Day and night we must pray and preach without ceasing so as to merit the description given by St. Augustine: *"aut precantes aut praedicantes."*

Our dedication to the people is not only on Sundays, or at Mass once a day, or hearing confessions on Saturdays. We are told to do two things: (1) "Take no rest" — strange as it may seem. No chairs! Remember? (2) "Give God no rest." Did we ever tell a beggar who wanted money, "Ask me for it when I cross the street; if I do not give it to you, follow me and seize my coat; if that does not get you what you want, throw a stone at my window at midnight." But God does say: "Wrestle with me, as Jacob did. Give me no rest." Like the importunate widow who aroused the judge, so we are to cry to the Priest-Victim in the face of the enemies of the Church:

Give me redress against one who wrongs me.

(Luke 18:3)

I tell you, even if he will not bestir himself to grant it out of friendship, shameless asking will make him rise and give his friend all that he needs.

(Luke 11:8)

What we are, the Church is; what the Church is, the world is. The world and all it contains is finally a highway on which the Bride, the Church, goes to meet the Bridegroom for the heavenly nuptials. Politics does not ultimately determine war and peace. What is decisive is the spiritual state of the Church living in and leavening the world. To read the Old Testament is to recognize that history is the hand of the Lord who blesses and punishes nations according to their deserts. What we do to sanctify ourselves sanctifies the world. When the shepherd is lazy, the sheep are hungry; when he sleeps, they are lost; when he is corrupt, they grow sick; when he is unfaithful, they lose their judgment. If the shepherd is not willing to be a victim for his sheep, the wolves come and devour them.

Each morning we priests hold in our hands the Christ Who shed blood from His veins, tears from His eyes, sweat from His Body to sanctify us. How we should be on fire with that love, that we may enkindle it in others!

Do we suffer for the wandering sheep? Do we warm ourselves by a fire talking to maidservants as Peter did, while the Lord is crucified again in the souls of sinners? Do we adopt an intransigent position with the enemies of the Church, forgetting that a Saul was made a Paul? We dress in black; but it is not to mourn Christ, for He has conquered. We are in mourning for those who bar their doors against our knock, for those still unwilling to believe though one should rise daily from the dead, for those who reach us vinegar as we cry "Sitio!" (John 19:28). Night and day, giving God no rest, we will utter over and over again:

> *I dedicate Myself for their sakes, that they too may be dedicated through the truth.*
>
> (John 17:19)

Holy Christians Guarantee Holy Priests

Holiness descends in the Church from the all Holy God through Christ, His bishops and His priests, to the entire community which is the Mystical Body. But there is simultaneously an ascending movement of holiness from the Christian community to the all Holy God. Particularly is this true of vocations to the priesthood and the religious life.

There is no priest who does not go through the motions of urging the faithful to pray for vocations. But too often, the phrases are formal. They are what is expected of one. In the priest's mind, they are a part of the announcements, on a level with the card party for the Ladies Auxiliary or the CYO skating meet.

These other activities are, of course, not to be sneered at. They, too, foster a Christian life and therefore stimulate vocations. But can we put them in the same category as prayer? Out of hundreds of possible ways of fostering vocations, prayer was the single one Our Lord specified:

The harvest, He told them, is plentiful enough, but the laborers are few; you must ask the Lord to Whom the harvest belongs to send laborers out for the harvesting.

(Luke 10:2)

What prompted these words? Luke says that Christ spoke them on the occasion of choosing seventy-two disciples (Luke 10:1). Matthew sketches the background in more detail. It was after a long journey, he noted, and the Lord's heart was touched by compassion for the masses who hungered for knowledge of heaven but did not know where to search for what they lacked:

Yet still, when He looked at the multitudes, He was moved with pity for them, seeing them harried and abject, like sheep that have no shepherd. Thereupon He said to His disciples, The harvest is plentiful enough, but the laborers are few; you must ask the Lord to Whom the harvest belongs to send laborers out for the harvesting.

(Matthew 9:36,37,38)

Not only those already in the Church but equally those outside it make Him yearn for laborers, lest the plentiful wheat rot in the fields.

His compassion for the multitude was twofold. Because they were hungry, He miraculously fed the five thousand. Because their souls suffered, sheep without a shepherd, He was moved with pity.

Every true priest has the same heart-tearing pity as he flies over a great city, Paris, New York or London. Down below he sees with Christ's eyes millions of souls unfed by the Eucharist, unhealed by penance, living in houses built on sand because they know not the Rock. He sees in them what Our Lord saw when He looked at the multitudes danger of eternal loss! Here are countless acres ripe for harvesting, but how few the laborers to gather!

Our Lord indicates that this harvest of souls is convertible. He is enthusiastic about the prospects of winning souls, and His words are intended to project that enthusiasm to His priests. He made a similar expression of confident anticipation when the crowds streamed out of Samaria to hear His words:

> *Why, lift up your eyes, I tell you, and look at the fields, they are white with the promise of harvest already.*

(John 4:35)

As wheat does not oppose the sickle, so the masses will not oppose us. One wonders if we do not underestimate the possibility of conversions. The failure may simply be in our defective preparation and approach. The unbelievers will not go to hear philosophers, but they will go to hear saints. Priests who work in the slums amid the outcasts report that they rarely meet with an insult. Like the wheat, the masses will bend only before a certain kind of harvester. Not finding us as we should be, they turn their backs on us. But when they encounter a priest whose life expresses the message he brings, they are ready to be harvested.

What Our Lord asked us to pray for was laborers. He did not say: "My Father is Almighty; He can make the few accomplish much." He knew the extent of His Father's power, but He was also one with His Father in the divine plan to sanctify man with the aid of human means. In the Incarnation, His human nature was *instrumentum conjunctum divinitatis*. In the prolongation of His Incarnation, He uses us as instruments. Though He could reap the harvest without men, He will not.

But only laborers and not idlers are acceptable instruments. The priest must study to perfect his mind, not wearying the people with stale repetitions. It is true that "*words will be given you when the time comes*" (Matthew 10:19); but what Our Lord here promised was not inspiration for those who do not prepare their message, but the help of the Spirit for those persecuted beyond human resource. In the designs of Providence, the gift of final perseverance may depend for a priest not only on the amount of evil he has done, but on the good he has left undone.

The laborers must go into the harvest fields, to the masses, to the unbelievers, to the abandoned, the rudderless. Is it not possible that the Lord withholds many vocations from dioceses and mission societies because of the growing use of priests in strictly secular activities? Why specifically does God call a man to the priesthood? It is not easy to justify the placing of a priest in insurance, building, accountancy, banking, publicity, and promotion, when the need is so grave for convert-makers, for missioners to search out the lost sheep and lead them gently to the fold of Christ. Do we lack dedicated and reliable laymen able to do such tasks as well or better? If the Lord was so particular about the fragments of bread, which He ordered gathered up, then will He not insist jealously that His priests do precisely that for which He called them?

Why did Our Lord, when He spoke of vocations, single out precisely the word, "Pray!"? Because prayer is the expression of the Christian community and the yearning of the Church. As the Church gets the kind of Pope she deserves, so she gets the kind and number of priests she deserves. Why do Ireland and Holland have so many vocations? Because the Catholic people of these small but intense countries, rich in their faith, want priests, and they pray to be given the priests they want. Why do some countries have so few? Because few people, even few parents, pray for priests. "Ask, and the gift will come" (Luke 11:9). Can we hope to receive if we do not ask? There are probably hundreds of thousands of vocations hanging from heaven on silken cords; prayer is the sword that cuts them. The laborers are available potentially in the Heart of Christ; it is our petitions that actualize them. *"... And I was never consulted?"* (Isaiah 30:2).

Are there prayers in Church for vocations? Do mothers pray for vocations for their children? Do the faithful pray the Lord "*to send laborers out for the harvesting*" (Matthew 9:38)? Do school children pray for the call of God?

What the Christian community wants ardently, the Lord of the Harvest will grant. That is why Our Lord told us to pray. The command was intended for all, but it was given directly and specifically to the apostles and the disciples, as His ambassadors and co-workers among the people. Prayer in the Church is alone primary; publicity and its methods are secondary. The search for vocations begins on our knees. One bishop had no candidates for the priesthood in two years. He began a campaign of prayer in the schools of his diocese, and without any other publicity he had activated forty vocations at the end of one year.

The original Greek word (èkßálλw) for "sending" laborers into the fields is stronger than the Latin (Matthew 9:38). It means that the Lord of the harvest would thrust them out or propel them forward. The same Greek word is used by Matthew (8:31) for the expulsion of a devil out of a man (though different words are used in describing the incident in Mark 5:8 and Luke 8:29); it takes a great power to drive the priesthood into a man. This power Our Lord said He would exercise, if we prayed. It even suggests that from totally unexpected and impossible places, He would inspire vocations.

Effect on Community on Saintliness or Sinfulness

Every slightest failing on our part brings the community under the judgment of God. Every least increase of priestly virtue brings it blessing.

When the Israelites took Jericho (Joshua 6:1-21), God ordered that the city be destroyed, and its wealth given to Him as the fruit of victory. But one Israelite disobeyed. Yielding to temptation, Achan appropriated to himself a garment and some precious ornaments, violating the Divine command (Joshua 7:1). Later, when Joshua was routed in battle, the Lord revealed that the reason for his defeat was the secret sin of Achan. The evil of one brought destruction and death on his entire community.

Personal sins, even the most secret, have repercussions on all the Church. A cut finger pains the whole man. The ripple caused by a stone thrown into a pond touches every point on the shore. A hidden violation of Christ's law by any of His members reverberates through and disturbs the equilibrium of the entire Mystical Body.

Joshua, under the inspiration of God ordered the destruction of Achan and the stolen goods:

And there Joshua said, Thou hast brought trouble on us, and now it is the Lord's turn to bring trouble on thee.

(Joshua 7:25)

Now, if the sin of one layman so affected the ecclesia of Israel, how much more must the failings of one priest affect the ecclesia Dei! But the influence of one good soul, one saint, works to the good of the whole community. God was willing to spare Sodom and Gomorrah for the sake of a few just men. Abraham stopped at ten and the cities were destroyed (Genesis 18:16-19;28). But God does not necessarily stop at ten. Blessings, vocations and conversions abound, and judgments are averted, because of the few who are good. For Jacob's sake, God multiplied the flocks of Laban (Genesis 30:27). Out of respect for Joseph, God prospered the house of Potiphar (Genesis 39:5). The wicked city of Segor was saved because of the prayer of Lot:

Once again, said he, I yield to Thy entreaty; I will not overthrow the city Thou pleadest for.

(Genesis 19:21)

Because of Paul, 276 souls were saved in a violent storm at sea (Acts 27:24,34).

Before God sent Jerusalem into captivity as a punishment, He told Jeremiah that one good man would save it:

Go the rounds of Jerusalem, search the streets of it with hue and cry; and if you find one man there that faithfully does his duty, and keeps troth, then the city shall be pardoned.

(Jeremiah 5:1)

After He had inflicted judgment on Jerusalem, He gave the reason:

Who would close the breach, intercede with Me to spare the land from ruin? Never a man was found! What wonder if I have poured out My vengeance, burnt them up in My anger? It was but their deserts I gave them, says the Lord God.

(Ezekiel 22:30,31)

Finally, when the Last Judgment comes, the days of vengeance,

there would have been no human creature, if the number of those days had not been cut short; but those days will be cut short, for the sake of the elect.

(Matthew 24:22)

It could well be that God's wrath — and let us not forget that Revelation (6:16) speaks of *ira Agni* — is withheld from cities because of saintly souls among the clergy and the religious and the laity. God could not strike as long as Moses stood between Him and the people.

So the Lord relented, and spared His people the punishment He had threatened.

(Exodus 32:14)

What converts could prayer win in Mission lands! The materialism of Japan would fragment, like the shell of an egg, to reveal the life within, did we but pray for Japan. How slight would be the sacrifice, yet how much would it mean to the Vicar of Christ, if every priest who lives in comfort sent even a few of his Mass stipends to the Holy Father through his Society for the Propagation of the Faith!

O blessed intercessors are we! The salt of the earth! The lights of the world! Without good men, the world would be corrupted and in darkness. We sanctify ourselves not for us as individuals but for all as God's people. We do not save our soul alone; either we save it in the context of our neighbors and of the Mystical Body, or we lose it. No cell of my body can live normally outside my body, but my body can live without any given individual cell. *In toto Christo* we live and work.

To neglect intercession is to sin against God.

Never may I offend the Lord by ceasing to pray for you, and pointing you to the good paths, the right paths.

(1 Kings 12:23 [1 Samuel 12;23, RSV])

If we priests lack a heart to sigh and cry for the abominations and miseries of others, great is our reason to fear for ourselves. We cannot speak of unbroken fellowship with Our Lord without unbroken fellowship with the Church and the world.

God has proved His love to us by laying down His life for our sakes; we too must be ready to lay down our lives for the sake of our brethren.

(1 John 3:16)

Choosing Candidates for the Priesthood

Since the holiness of the priest in God's designs makes the Church holy, those who seek the priesthood but are wanting in holiness must be purged.

Have you never been told that a little leaven is enough to leaven the whole batch? Rid yourselves of the leaven which remains over, so that you may be a new mixture, still uncontaminated as you are.

(1 Corinthians 5:6,7)

When public relations techniques are used to promote vocations, with advertising in religious publications and direct mailings designed to encourage young people to join a given society or community, the danger is always present that stress will be placed on numbers to the neglect of quality. St. Thomas insists that the weeding out of the unfit is an obligation of those charged with the selection of candidates.

Deus numquam ita deserit Ecclesiam suam quin inveniantur idonei ministri sufficienter ad necessitatem plebis, si digni promoverentur et indigni repellerentur. Et sic non posset tot ministros inveniri, quot modo sunt, melius est habere paucos ministros bonos quam multos malos (Supp. q. 36, art. 4, ad I).

One cannot fail to be struck by the symbolic significance of the instructions God gave Gideon to identify the shock troops of his army:

Separate those who lap the water like dogs, and those who go down on their knees to drink.

(Judges 7:5)

And who were marked for elimination? Those who made themselves comfortable by lying flat on the ground and drinking leisurely. And who were taken?

But the Lord said to Gideon, These three hundred men who lapped the water shall win you deliverance.

(Judges 7:7)

Great truths are revealed to and placed in the custody of the few who are dedicated to the battle of faith. The imposing appearance of great numbers may blind us to the need for God's help, may make us overlook the necessity of training seminarians to be priest-victims. Hence the advice of St. Paul to Timothy:

As for the imposition of hands, do not bestow it inconsiderately, and so share the blame for the sins of others.

(1 Timothy 5:22)

To present candidates for ordination without due judgment, is to risk being held responsible for the subsequent defaults of those who fail the great High Priest. The priest must, therefore, avoid the methods of the world in promoting vocations. It is possible to win customers in business by publicity techniques, but vocations require a different approach. We may never be many, we may never be wise in the eyes of the world, but whatever we do must be done through the foolishness of the Cross.

> *Consider, brethren, the circumstances of your own calling; not many of you are wise, in the world's fashion, not many powerful, not many well born.... no human creature was to have any ground for boasting, in the presence of God.*

(1 Corinthians 1:26,29)

Value of Prayers for Vocations in the Family

Every family is a church within a church. "Greet the brethren at Laodicea, and Nymphas, with the church that is in his household" (Colossians 4:15).

The classic example of the prayers of a mother for a vocation is Hannah. Hannah was barren. "Why had the Lord denied her motherhood?" (1 Kings 1:5 [1 Samuel 1:5, RSV]). She promised God that if He would send her a son, she would consecrate him to God as a priest. In prayer, three times she humbly called herself the handmaid of the Lord, addressing Him as the "Lord of hosts" (1 Kings 1:11 [1 Samuel 1:11, RSV]). The *Magnificat* hearkens back to the prayer of Hannah. So fervently did she pray, that Eli the high priest thought she was drunk saying: "Wilt thou always be at thy cups? Give thy stomach a rest from the wine that so bemuses thee" (1 Kings 1:14 [1 Samuel 1:14, RSV]).

Hannah, however, was not drunk. She was only pouring out her soul to the Lord (1 Kings 1:15 [1 Samuel 1:15, RSV]). In due time, her prayer was answered, and she called the son Samuel, "in token that he was a gift she had won from the Lord" (1 Kings 1:20 [1 Samuel 1:20, RSV]).

Hannah had not just asked for a son, but a son whom she might dedicate to God. She puts him at the service of the temple where "as he grew he advanced in favour both with God and with men" (1 Kings 2:26 [1 Samuel 2:26, RSV]). Later, there was a formal unfolding of Samuel's vocation, when three times "the Lord's call came to Samuel" (1 Kings 3:4 [1 Samuel 3:4, RSV]). Each time Samuel thought it was Eli who called, running to him each time saying:

I am coming, he answered; then ran to find Eli, and said, I am here at thy summons.... Till then, Samuel was a stranger to the Divine voice; the Lord had not made any revelation to him.

(1 Kings 3:5,7 [1 Samuel 3:5,7, RSV])

Samuel mistook God's voice for Eli's, but Eli told him the next time he heard the voice to say: "Speak on, Lord; thy servant is listening" (1 Kings 3:9 [1 Samuel 3:9, RSV]).

God calls His servants to tasks which are manifested only by degrees. Too often we say: "Tell me first what you want me to do, and I will see whether I want to." But the advice of the old priest to Samuel was "Put yourself in God's hands. He will show you your work." St. Paul was told to go to Damascus and his vocation would be revealed. When we open our ears, God opens His lips. We know God's truth when we do His will. Later on Samuel was called to re-create Israel as Moses had created it.

The point of the story is that a vocation comes through prayer, often that of a mother, even when all seems hopeless. In a survey of a group of seminarians, three out of four indicated that their mothers were a major inspiration in the development of their vocation. St. Paul had already noted the influence of a mother and a grandmother in fostering the vocation of Timothy.

That faith dwelt in thy grandmother Lois, and in thy mother Eunice, before thee; I am fully persuaded that it dwells in thee too.

(2 Timothy 1:5)

St. Paul praises the faith of this young priest and finds the instrumental cause in a pious family background. It was the third generation of this faithful family which bore the fruit of a vocation. Origen conjectured that they were relatives of St. Paul. Like the celebrated mothers of Augustine, Chrysostom and Basil, and like the mother of many a priest today, their sincerity and unfeigned faith produced a heritage for the Church. Lord Shaftesbury once said: "Give me a generation of Christian mothers and I will change the face of the earth in twelve months."

The decay of the home is often blamed for the fewness of vocations in our times. While this is true, forget not Christian homes! We can too easily become like Elias bemoaning the corruption of Israel.

See how the sons of Israel have forgotten Thy covenant, thrown down Thy altars, and put Thy prophets to the sword! Of these, I only am left, and now my life, too, is forfeit.

(3 Kings 19:14 [1 Kings 19:14, RSV])

The Lord told him, nevertheless, that he had been more faithful than he suspected:

Yet I mean to leave Myself seven thousand men out of all Israel; knees that have never bowed to Baal.

(3 Kings 19:18 [1 Kings 19:18, RSV])

There is much good, did we but seek it out. What Pascal said applies equally to vocations and to converts: "There are only two classes of men who can be called rational — those who serve God

84

with all their hearts because they know Him, and those who seek Him wholeheartedly because they know Him not." *

(*Pascal's Pensées, "Apology,"* No. 2106, translated by H. F. Stewart, D.D., Pantheon Books, Inc., 1950.)

We can easily be too severe on others. When James and John suggested to Christ that He punish the Samaritans who would not receive Him, they drew this rebuke:

You do not understand, He said, what spirit it is you share. The Son of Man has come to save men's lives, not to destroy them.

(Luke 9:55)

Few are the priests whose level of service to their flocks is such as to merit the tribute paid by the Galatians to St. Paul, when they described him "as God's angel, as Christ Jesus" (Galatians 4:14); but the opportunity is at every moment present for every priest to feel his greatness and his littleness, his power and his nothingness.

O sacerdos! Tu quis es?
Non es a te, quia de nihilo.
Non es ad te, quia es mediator ad Deum.
Non es tibi, quia soli Deo vivere debes.
Non es tui, quia es omnium servus.
Non es tu, quia alter Christus es.
Quid ergo es? Nihil et omnia,
o sacerdos!

✠ J.M.J. ✠

~ 5 ~

The Holy Spirit and the Priest

Since the priest is an *alter Christus*, he must know the role the Spirit played in Christ's life.

At every moment of His life on earth, the Savior was completely under the guidance of the Spirit. Even as the breath of God stirred over the waters in the first dawn of creation and the Lord said, *"Let there be light"* (Genesis 1:3), so did the Spirit inspire Mary in the very moment of the Incarnation.

> *The Holy Spirit will come upon thee, and the power of the most High will overshadow thee. Thus this holy offspring of thine shall be known for the Son of God.*

(Luke 1:35)

At His Baptism, there was seen:

> *The Spirit like a dove, coming down and resting upon Him.*

(Mark 1:10)

He returned from the Jordan

> *full of the Holy Spirit and by the Spirit He was led on into the wilderness, where He remained forty days, tempted by the devil.*

(Luke 4:1,2)

While the chords of His Heart are still vibrating in response to a voice from heaven, He is summoned by the Spirit into the wilderness. Was not Saul, in the morning of his life in Christ, sent for three years to Arabia? Is not character compacted through struggle direct and personal, with the forces of both good and evil? "No one shall be crowned unless he has struggled..." He was led, by the Spirit's direction, into a wilderness for a trial. As Moses in Midian, as David around Bethlehem, as Elias around Horeb, so the Spirit draws the Savior into retreat. David must meet Goliath alone before he can meet the hosts of the Philistines. Each priest must first win the spiritual victory alone and within himself, before he can repeat that victory in the lives of others.

Next, the endowments for His mission on earth were communicated to Him from the same source. As Isaiah foretold:

One shall be born, on whom the Spirit of the Lord will rest; a Spirit wise and discerning, a Spirit prudent and strong, a Spirit of knowledge and of piety, and ever fear of the Lord shall fill His heart.

(Isaiah 11:2,3)

After He had put the tempter to flight, He returned to His home town of Nazareth and in the synagogue He read the appointed lesson of the day, paraphrasing Isaiah (61:1,2), and showing by His first words that His every action, especially His preaching, was the work of the Spirit. He had emerged from the conflict, not weakened but strengthened.

The Spirit of the Lord is upon Me; He has anointed Me, and sent Me out to preach the gospel to the poor, to restore the broken-hearted; to bid the prisoners go free, and the blind have sight; to set the oppressed at liberty, to proclaim a year when men may find acceptance with the Lord, a day of retribution.

(Luke 4:18,19)

Later on, it is by the Spirit that He vanquishes the mightiest of foes:

When I cast out devils, I do it through the Spirit of God.

(Matthew 12:28)

Evil is conquered by the Spirit, not by complaining and ranting. And to attribute such victory to any other power is blasphemy against the Spirit. Then comes the role of the Spirit in the Crucifixion — a sublime truth often forgotten.

> *...the blood of Christ, who offered Himself, through the Holy Spirit, as a victim.*
>
> (Hebrews 9:14)

He is both Priest and Sacrifice, through the Spirit, Who alone makes that unity, either in Him or in us. It is also the Spirit which gives the sacrifice an eternal efficacy. The Spirit helps us over the difficulty created by the fact that Our Lord's sacrifice took place on a hill, and yet belongs to a heavenly sanctuary. It is the Spirit, independent of time and place, which makes our daily renewal of Calvary possible.

The Spirit too played a role in His Resurrection and descent into Limbo.

> *In His mortal nature He was done to death, but endowed with fresh life in His Spirit, and it was in His Spirit that He went and preached to the spirits who lay in prison.*
>
> (1 Peter 3:18,19)

The same Holy Spirit is operative in communicating the merits of Redemption to mankind, and particularly through the priesthood. Even the pre-announcement of our salvation was effected through the Spirit. St. Peter looking back on all of the prophecies says that they looked forward to Christ through the Spirit:

> *Salvation was the aim and quest of the prophets, and the grace of which they prophesied has been reserved for you. The Spirit of Christ was in them, making known to them the sufferings which Christ's cause brings with it, and the glory that crowns them; when was it to be, and how was the time of it to be recognized?*
>
> (1 Peter 1:10,11)

Thanks to the Spirit, the prophets pre-announced Christ; thanks to the Spirit, the Apostles reported Him. Those who have the Spirit know Christ to be the center of the universe; that all history up to the moment of the Incarnation looked to Him, and that all history since the moment of the Ascension is a preparation for His second coming. Some modern scholars find only a "myth" in the Scriptures; Peter bids us recognize in them the Spirit. As the Spirit functioned in announcing Christ, so the Spirit functions in continuing Christ. The night of the Last Supper, Our Lord told His priests that the Father would send the Spirit in His name (John 14:26). After the Resurrection, He breathed on them saying:

Receive the Holy Spirit.

(John 20:22)

It almost seems that in the mystery of Redemption, each Person of the Blessed Trinity hides behind the other. The Son hides behind the Father, for it is the Son Who reveals the Father. Similarly, we would never know the Love of the Father, if He had not sent His Spirit. The Son in turn, hides behind the Holy Spirit, for it is through the Holy Spirit that we understand that Jesus is the Lord. Jesus Himself insisted on this aspect. He stressed that it was the Holy Spirit who would reveal Him.

At the Last Supper, Our Lord explained the role of the Holy Spirit in the lives of His priests. He had just been telling His disciples that they would be persecuted as He was persecuted. Now He tells them that though the Spirit would not manifest Himself visibly in a human form, as He had done, the Spirit would make them understand what He, Jesus, had said to them:

Well, when the truth-giving Spirit, who proceeds from the Father, has come to befriend you, He whom I will send to you from the Father's side, He will bear witness of what I was.

(John 15:26)

It is the Spirit who tells the priest the whole scope of his work as days roll on, as new problems arise, and as new enemies hate. New dimensions of meaning in Christ's life, of which we never dreamed before, will become clear. This inner witness of Christ's depth and worth will be our support in a hostile world. Our grasp of the Life of Christ will not be confined within the narrow limits of Bethlehem and Jerusalem.

And He will bring honor to Me, because it is from Me that He will derive what He makes plain to you.

(John 16:14)

To glorify or honor Christ means to manifest His hidden excellence when His human nature was admitted into the full participation of the power and glory of the Father. This the human mind cannot conceive or apprehend; to enter into this mystery is the work of the Spirit of the Glorified Christ.

Those who say they want only the "Jesus of the Gospels" forget that the Gospels speak of the full revelation of Our Lord through His Spirit. He proclaimed the very incompleteness of His words, insisting that fuller knowledge would come later.

Had Our Lord remained on earth, He would have been just an example to be copied. By abandoning the earth for heaven, He becomes a life to be lived. That is why it was better that He should go.

The Spirit Reveals Christ

A priest often meets a man, a good man, but one to whom God has not given the priceless gift of faith. That man will evaluate Jesus Christ. He will be fair to Him within the limitations of his own human judgment. Christ was a great thinker and a holy man, he will say, equating Him with Buddha, Confucius, Socrates and Plato. St. Paul, however, tells us:

It is only through the Holy Spirit that anyone can say, Jesus is the Lord.

(1 Corinthians 12:3)

They who have not the Spirit call him "a great man," a teacher," "a master"; but to see Him as the Lord of heaven and earth, as the Son of the Living God, comes only through the Holy Spirit.

This being so, may it not be that our failure to read the Scriptures, to preach redemption, to inspire converts, to give better spiritual direction, to convert sinners, is because we have not sufficiently pondered and absorbed the counsels given us by the Lord at the Last Supper?

Why do some feel uncomfortable in the Presence of God? Is it because of an excessive love of comfort, a spirit of envy and jealousy, a pleasure in their status as clerics, a kind of sword-activism in place of prayer and watching? May this want of the Spirit of Christ not explain a reluctance to appear more often and more joyously in His Eucharistic Presence? Would not a person who hated mathematics be unhappy at a convention of mathematicians? The soul that hated truth (to speak in inadequate human terms) would suffer more in heaven than in hell; analogically speaking, the want of the Spirit of Christ makes us shrink from His companionship.

Tryst there must be, if friends will meet and journey together.

(Amos 3:3)

The priest must not postpone this union with the Holy Spirit to a more convenient season (Acts 24:25). If he neglects growth, decay sets in. There comes a time when it is too late to repent, even to ask for a drop of water to "cool my tongue" (Luke 16:24).

Baptism makes every Christian a new creature and an ambassador of Heaven. Ordination intensifies these spiritual attributes in the priest. But though we dispense holiness, we are not automatically holy. It is the Spirit who makes us more priestly day by day because He takes the things of Christ and reveals them to us, bringing to remembrance all the words of Christ (John 16:14; 14:26). Becoming a holy priest is not completed the day of ordination, nor do the blessings of the Spirit flow to us without great effort on our part. We are "workers together with God." We stand in need of knowledge if we are to communicate it to others, if we are to bring our bodily appetites into subjection (1 Corinthians 7:29-31), and if we are to be patient under the pressure of work, loving every human being with that charity which flows from the consciousness that Our Lord died for them too. All these qualities are progressive, and it was one who himself had made that uphill fight who best expressed what it means:

> *And you too have to contribute every effort on your own part, crowning your faith with virtue, and virtue with enlightenment, and enlightenment with continence, and continence with endurance, and endurance with holiness, and holiness with brotherly love, and brotherly love with charity. Such gifts, when they are yours in full measure, will make you quick and successful pupils, reaching ever closer knowledge of our Lord Jesus Christ; he who lacks them is no better than a blind man feeling his way about; his old sins have been purged away, and he has forgotten it. Bestir yourselves then, brethren, ever more eagerly, to ratify God's calling and choice of you by a life well lived.*

(2 Peter 1:5-10)

The Role of the Holy Spirit in Intensifying Conflict

Every priest, though ordained to be a Peter, retains within him the frailty of the Simon-nature. St. Paul describes the resulting civil war between Peter and Simon.

> *Inwardly, I applaud God's disposition, but I observe another disposition in my lower self, which raises war against the disposition of my conscience, and so I am handed over as a captive to that disposition towards sin which my lower self*

93

contains. Pitiable creature that I am, who is to set me free from a nature thus doomed to death? Nothing else than the grace of God, through Jesus Christ our Lord. If I am left to myself, my conscience is at God's disposition, but my natural powers are at the disposition of sin.

(Romans 7:22-25)

Even before Paul, Plato had observed that there is a war in each of us against himself. Anyone who does not take up the sword against that lower nature is destroyed by it. Sin first takes possession of the flesh; and once entrenched there, it attacks the mind and finally displaces it from its position of authority.

A man may have priestly powers and yet be governed by nature, for the grace of ordination does not destroy the flesh:

To live the life of nature is to think the thoughts of nature; to live the life of the Spirit is to think the thoughts of the Spirit; and natural wisdom brings only death, whereas the wisdom of the Spirit brings life and peace.

(Romans 8:5,6)

The priest is like a mountain climber. The Holy Spirit bids him go higher, but below him are the abysses. What the Holy Spirit does in the soul of a priest is not only to make him more aware of the conflict within himself, but also to make him more conscious of sin. Divine grace does not so act as to prevent a man absolutely from sinning, but the Spirit takes the fun out of it. It is not possible for a priest to love a human being with the full powers of his soul, precisely because he has already fallen in love with the Perfect, namely, Christ through His Spirit. All other love is dissatisfying and bitter.

A sin committed by a priest, consequently, pains him more intensely than does the same sin to one not a priest. This is because of the greater gift of the Spirit. Imagine two men marrying two shrews who were identical in their disgruntled nature. One had enjoyed the love of a beautiful and devoted wife who died; the other was married for the first time.

Which of the two suffers the more? Obviously the one who knew before the better love. So with the priest. Having enjoyed the ecstasy of the Spirit of Love, he can never be satisfied with human substitutes.

At the Last Supper Our Lord told those He had chosen as His first priests how the Spirit would intensify the conflict.

He will come, and it will be for Him to prove the world wrong, about sin...

(John 16:8)

No man really understands sin who thinks of it merely as the breaking of the law. This is a defect which results from basing moral theology exclusively upon the Commandments. To do so is to develop in the young an attitude which makes them ask, "Is this a mortal or a venial sin? How far can I go without committing grievous sin?" The full understanding of sin comes only through the Holy Spirit, and until He enlightens the soul, it is blind to our sinfulness. No matter how great our powers of reasoning, we can produce real conviction of sin only through the Spirit.

But what does the Spirit do in the soul? Our Lord said the Holy Spirit would convict men of sin because "they have not found belief in Me" (John 16:9). By not believing in Him, men crucified Him. Hence, it is the crucifix that brings to the soul the profound consciousness of guilt. It becomes for each his autobiography. The skin of Christ is the parchment, His Blood the ink, the nails the pen. There we see written the story of our life. This close relationship between the sense of sin and the crucifix enabled St. Peter to win three thousand souls for the Lord on the day of Pentecost. He reminded his hearers that they had crucified Christ (Acts 2:36). To sin against faith thus means to refuse to believe in Christ to the point of rejecting and crucifying Him.

Unless the Spirit has mastery in this war of Simon and Peter, the priest remains but a child in the nursery, not an ambassador in the sanctuary. The Lord gives him milk, as St. Paul gave the Corinthians *not meat; you were not strong enough for it.... Nature still lives in you.* (1 Corinthians 3:2)

As some acorns sprout, yet never become great oaks, so some ordinations make only spiritual saplings, not trees planted by the waters of life. The spiritually undeveloped priest has two characteristics:

1.   A protracted infancy. There is a full assent to the Creed, but there is wanting the beauty of priestly holiness through the indwelling of God's Spirit. Because of this long infancy, there is a continual oscillation of sin and amendment, of failure and re-establishment in grace, of pettiness and the domination of the priest-state. There is a confession of individual sins, but no facing up to the fact that he is presuming on God's mercy and that he is living in a worldly state. The flesh is the rule of life and not the Spirit.

2.   The second mark of this carnal life is that it renders the priest unfit for receiving more spiritual truths; never being won away completely from the flesh, he never has that emptiness which is essential for receiving the Spirit. A man can be empty in soul like the Grand Canyon, but such emptiness is unprofitable. The fruitful kind of emptiness is that of a nest, which the dove of the Holy Spirit can fill, or the emptiness of a flute, through which the breath of the Holy Spirit can pipe the joyful tunes of being one with Christ.

The Spirit and Reparation for Sins

Because the Holy Spirit deepens our sense of sin in relation to the Crucifixion, the practical result should be to engage the priest in constant reparation for his sins. The Epistle to the Hebrews (5:3) bids the priest do precisely this; in our language, it tells him to offer Mass sometimes for himself. Our sins are more serious than the same sins in the laity, which is why God ordered greater sacrifices for priests. The ordinary people could offer a kid for their sins (Leviticus 4:28).

Even a ruler of a nation could do the same. But the priest had to offer a bullock.

Such a transgression, if it be committed by the high priest then in office, brings guilt upon the whole people, and he must make amends for it by offering to the Lord a young bullock without blemish.

(Leviticus 4:3)

Responsibility is in proportion to privilege. The priest represents the people, and therefore his sin affects the whole Church. He is the embodiment of the people's sanctity as a community of worshippers.

It would be quite wrong to imagine that those who do not live by the Spirit do not experience remorse, or that conflict is absent from their lives. Sin which does not come out properly in confession to be washed away by contrition and absolution, often comes out abnormally in complexes, such as imputing evil motives to others, hypercriticism, or a love of distracting pleasures. Such a condition can easily lead to despair. The devil then pounces gleefully on his prey. Revelation (12:10) calls the devil, "the accuser of our brethren." Before the sin, Satan assures us that it is of no consequence; after the sin, he persuades us that it is unforgivable. Before the sin, he represents himself as the friend of man urging him on to revolt; after the sin, he smothers the soul in a false belief that deliverance is impossible.

To doubt forgiveness is the beginning of hell. Scripture tells us that Cain found no place for repentance, though with tears he sought it (Genesis 4:13). Remorse, not contrition, brings unavailing tears, as it did to Saul over the loss of his kingship, Judas over the loss of his apostleship, and Cain over the loss of God's favor. But the Holy Spirit sees guilt in relation to Calvary to give us urgent hope and then pardon, for on that hill we hear the cry:

Father, forgive them; they do not know what it is they are doing.

(Luke 23:34)

This awakening of a sense of sin through the Spirit applies not only to the priest but to the faithful whom he shepherds. Sermons on hell fire awaken fear, but unless the Spirit is with the preacher, the fear is servile, not filial. Souls are led to repentance only through "the Sword of the Spirit, God's Word" (Ephesians 6:17). Now what does this Sword of the Spirit do in souls? It heightens the conflict between the body and soul, between the spirit of the world and the spirit of Christ.

> *God's Word to us is something alive, full of energy; it can penetrate deeper than any two-edged sword, reaching the very division between soul and spirit, between joints and marrow, quick to distinguish every thought and design in our hearts.*
>
> (Hebrews 4:12)

Sinners are melted into contrition through the Spirit; they see the civil war in their own souls through the Spirit; the Spirit reveals the hidden sins which they hoped no one could detect; the Spirit shows that man is a fallen creature and needs power from on high. The Spirit will convince atheists of their unbelief. No evil can be crucified until it is recognized and diagnosed and brought into the light. Self clothes itself in so many disguises that nothing but the Spirit can compel it to reveal its true sinful character. A priest with the Spirit of Christ will get a sinner to confession in circumstances in which the priest without the Spirit will fail. Scolding a sinner in the confessional may drive him away but lifting him up in the Spirit of Christ will make of him a true penitent. Even a priest who is naturally a poor speaker can through the Spirit of Christ make his words effective beyond his orative talents:

> *Human indeed we are, but it is in no human strength that we fight our battles. The weapons we fight with are not human weapons; they are divinely powerful, ready to pull down strongholds. Yes, we can pull down the conceits of men, every barrier of pride which sets itself up against the true knowledge of God; we make every mind surrender to Christ's service....*
>
> (2 Corinthians 10:3-6)

The Spirit and Love of Souls

Every priest, when he goes before the Lord for judgment, will be asked: "Where are your children?" The vocation of the priest is primarily to beget souls in Christ. Shall we mount the pulpit and denounce unnatural birth control in the flesh, while we practice it in the spirit? Shall mothers be blamed for not having more children when our baptismal records show no souls begotten in Christ in years? The limits of our parish and the boundary of our duty are not the faithful alone, but "other sheep too, which do not belong to this fold" (John 10:16). Every soul is our responsibility, and many would enter the Church, did we but ask them. The error of many priests is that they are concerned more with the administrative than with the evangelical.

Do we organize for soul-saving with the same zeal as we organize for "drives"? When money is needed, a priest thinks nothing of organizing a door-to-door canvas; but how often does he make a door-to-door canvas for converts? Are we having our parish continually replenished by souls that come to tell what God has done for them? Where the Holy Spirit is, there are conversions:

And each day the Lord added to their fellowship others that were to be saved.

(Acts 2:47)

Our conversions per priest per year in the United States are fewer than three. But who among us does not know many who have left the One Fold and One Shepherd, because of broken vows, lust for a second or third marriage, sophomoric pride, or any one of the seven pallbearers of a soul, commonly called the seven capital sins? Do we have catechetical centers and use them to train the laity to be apostles and to live out the full responsibilities of the Sacrament of Confirmation? Every parish should be a nursery of souls that are not of the fold; every priest, a shepherd in search of lost sheep; every Mass, a proclamation that redemption must be spread to the world:

What, cry they of Jacob, is the Lord so easily offended?

(Micah 2:7)

Is the Holy Spirit less bountiful to save souls now than at Pentecost? Is the tenor of our priestly life holding in check those fires and mighty winds of conversion? Why do the Pentecostal fires burn so brightly in the mission lands and so feebly in our parish? Has the tide of the Spirit run out of our harbors? The fault is not in the Spirit, for *"God does not repent of the gifts He makes"* (Romans 11:29). The rushing of the mighty winds has not calmed and stilled itself into stagnancy or sterility. The Holy Spirit is still ready to overshadow our priesthood, so that we may bring forth those who are holy.

The priest acts from without, the Holy Spirit from within. We wish one another blessings; He gives blessings. He alone can plant in a heart, by His divine husbandry, the seed that will blossom into a "new creature in Christ" (2 Corinthians 5:17). The selfishness and sloth which make us shrink from searching for souls can be consumed by His Spirit. All round about us, in our parishes, in our daily contacts with men, are countless masses of souls that are like gold ingots covered with dross. And we, if we but had the fire of the Spirit, would burnish them into jewels of the Kingdom of God!

✠ J.M.J. ✠

~ 6 ~

The Spirit and Conversion

As the Spirit does not fail, but is given to those who ask, souls are no more difficult to convert now than at any other time. The approach must be different, as the approach to the Roman was different from that to the Jew. In psychological terms, every conversion starts with a crisis, moral or spiritual. The moral crisis begins with a moment or a situation involving some kind of suffering, physical, emotional or spiritual, with a dialectic, a tension, a pull, a duality, or a conflict. The crisis is accompanied, on the one hand, by a profound sense of one's own helplessness, and on the other hand, by an equally certain conviction that God alone can supply what the individual lacks.

If there were only a sense of helplessness, there would be despair, pessimism, eventual suicide. This is, indeed, the condition of the post-Christian pagan: he feels the total inadequacy of his own inner resources against the overwhelming odds of a cruel universe and falls into despair. He has one half of the necessary condition for conversion — namely, a sense of crisis — but he fails to link up his powerlessness with the Divine Power which sustains and nourishes the soul. In such a situation, paganism gives place to what might be called creative despair: "despair," because the man recognizes his spiritual disease; "creative," because he knows that only a Divine Physician can bring healing.

The crisis of conversion is sometimes spiritual rather than moral. This is frequent among those who have been seeking perfection but are not yet possessed of the fullness of the faith and sacraments. Some such souls have led a good life on the natural plane; they have been generous to the poor and kind to their neighbors and have furthered at least a vague fellowship with all peoples. Others have had a smattering of the supernatural life; they have led as Christ-like a life as they knew how, living up to faith in Him as they saw His light. The crisis in their souls begins at the moment when they either recognize that they have tremendous potentialities not yet exercised or begin to yearn for a religious life which will make greater demands on them.

Up to that moment of crisis, they have lived on the surface of their souls. The tension deepens as they realize that, like a plant, they have roots which need greater spiritual depths and branches meant for communion with the heavens above. The growing sense of dissatisfaction with their own ordinariness is accompanied by a passionate craving for surrender, sacrifice, and abandonment to God's will. The shift from mediocrity to love may be occasioned through the example of a saint, the inspiration of a spiritual book, the desire to escape from mere symbols to divine reality. However, it comes, there is a duality present from the moment the soul hears Christ saying:

But you are to be perfect, as your heavenly Father is perfect.

(Matthew 5:48)

Conversion is the introduction of a new Spirit. The unconverted man has an incompatible spiritual Rh factor in his human nature, which is corruptive; it is overcome by making him "share the Divine Nature" (2 Peter 1:4) through a blood infusion of Calvary and Pentecost. Conversion, therefore, is totally different from proselytism, which is only a change in group membership, or the putting on of a new label. But conversion is a *metanoia*, a change of character, the becoming a new man.

The Spirit Makes Converts, Not Us

The work of conversion is accomplished by the Holy Spirit, through the use of human means. The Spirit may place a rod in the hands of a shepherd. His action may induce an awareness of the absence of God in the soul, or it may create a sense of God's presence and of His actual grace working in the soul. In all instances, the Holy Spirit illumines the mind to see a truth not visible before and strengthens the will to do things never before attempted. Job speaks of one way in which the Spirit touches the soul in suffering:

Sometimes in visions of the night, when deep sleep falls upon men as they lie abed, He speaks words of revelation, to teach them the lesson they need. This is one means by which He will turn a man away from his designs, purge him of his pride; and the grave is disappointed, the sword misses its prey. Or else He will use the pains of the sick-bed for a man's correction, and leave his whole frame wasted with disease.

(Job 33:15-19)

The priest must never think that his preaching and zeal won the convert. Lydia listened to Paul, but the Scripture says,

and the Lord opened her heart so that she was attentive to Paul's preaching.

(Acts 16:15)

Here was a woman already religious, described as a woman of prayer; yet her mind needed the tuition of the Holy Spirit in order to understand what she had heard. Incidentally, Lydia was the first convert in Europe, and it was from her house that the evangelization of Europe began.

Sometimes the revelation of the Spirit is gradual, as with the woman at the well. She first called Our Lord a "Jew" (John 4:9), then a "man" (John 4:12), then a gentleman when she addressed Him as "Sir" (John 4:15), then "a prophet" (John 4:19), then the "Messiah" (John 4:25), and finally "Saviour of the world" (John 4:42).

The jailer at Philippi was the second convert in Europe (Acts 16:27-34), and he was moved by the Spirit through fear and through the word of Paul. The Ethiopian treasurer illustrates how the Holy Spirit directs a priest to one whose conversion is divinely willed:

The Spirit said to Philip, Go up to that chariot and keep close by it.

(Acts 8:29)

The Ethiopian already had some concept of religion, for he was reading the fifty-third chapter of Isaiah. The Holy Spirit moves even souls dedicated to sorcery and magic. Such souls in their darkness may be searching for the truth. A sorcerer named Elymas had tried to turn the Proconsul, Sergius Paulus, from the faith, the rudiments of which he had received through the preaching of Paul. "Then Saul, whose other name is Paul, filled with the Holy Spirit,....." (Acts 13:8) blasted the sorcerer. Incidentally, this is the first time that the Scriptures give Saul the Roman name of Paul. Denouncing Elymas as a son of the devil, Paul struck him blind — his first miracle. One wonders if Paul recalled that he himself was struck blind at the time of his conversion. Was it in order that the temporary blindness might give light, as did his own? Venerable Bede says, "The Apostle remembering his own case, knew that by the darkening of the eye, the mind's darkness might be restored to light." Sergius Paulus then became strengthened in his faith. It was the first appearance of Christianity before a Roman aristocrat and official.

No soul is beyond conversion. The Lord assures us through the prophet Joel that He will make good the bad years.

Profitless years, when the locust ravaged you, Gnaw-all and Ruin-all and Spoiler, that great army of mine I let loose among you, they shall be made good.

(Joel 2:25)

Converting souls in keeping with our vocation to be "fishers of men" is not easy, because each catch takes its toll of effort. But losing is the condition of gaining in the realm of the Spirit. We never profit another without being "inwardly aware of the power" that has proceeded from us, as Our Lord was when He healed the woman with the issue of blood (Mark 5:30). But who are the energetic priests? Are they not the zealous priests? Nothing is as fatiguing as boredom. Filled with the Spirit of Christ, a priest working with souls is like the burning bush which was aflame, but did not burn out (Exodus 3:2). Every exhaustion of spiritual energy by a priest creates a vacuum for a richer endowment of the Spirit, until souls become his passion:

> *It is He Who gives the weary fresh Spirit, Who fosters strength and vigour where strength and vigour is none.*
>
> (Isaiah 40:29)

Every pastor should from time to time go through the baptismal record and see how many sheep have been brought to the Shepherd in the course of his ministry. How often does he find a name inscribed in the Book of Life with his own name listed in the column which reads: "Baptized by ___"? A parish can wither without converts for years, as for fifteen years the House of God lay unfinished, until God spoke to the people saying:

> *The Lord of hosts bids you put heart into the work; is not He, the Lord of hosts, at your side?*
>
> (Haggai 2:5)

So in a parish without spiritual stone being added to spiritual stone, the Lord bids us work. There can be no work apart from strength. We supply the work, God the power. It is comfort that makes us shirk the work of conversion. We are clothed, but are we warmed by the fire of Pentecost? The wages we earn — are they put into a bag with holes, or are we laying up the richer treasury of souls and covering up the mountain of our own failings? Saving souls is the assurance of our salvation.

> *My brethren, if one of you strays from the truth, and a man succeeds in bringing him back, let him be sure of this; to bring back erring feet into the right path means saving a soul from death, means throwing a veil over a multitude of sins.*
>
> (James 5:19,20)

We priests are only spiritual farmers; we till the soil, God drops the seed. We make no converts. We must never count up our converts or we will one day begin to think that we, not the Lord, made them. The same divine energy that wrought Creation and Redemption saves souls.

The Spirit and Instruction

Instructing is not arguing. One can win an argument and lose a soul. The priest must be patient with bigots. If we believed the lies they believe about the Church, we would hate it a thousand times more than they.

The priest must try to discover if the objections against the faith expressed by an enquirer are in fact intellectual, or if instead they are basically moral, that is, if they are rooted in some improper behavior. So-called "reasons" are sometimes rationalizations to justify the way people live. It is important to find out not only what people say about Christ and His Church but why they say it. This was the technique used by Our Lord with the woman at the well. She introduced a theological problem when her real problem was a moral one, namely, her five husbands. He, nevertheless, did not cast her aside even though He saw through her pretence. Instead, He showed her what her real problem was, and she was converted.

The priest's best approach to enquirers is neither to prove they are wrong, nor to prove that he is right, but simply to offer bread to the hungry and drink to the thirsty. Our Faith is the satisfaction of the soul's desire, not the didactic presentation of a syllogism. The priest must prepare himself carefully for every discussion with an enquirer. Before starting to instruct, he should spend an hour in thinking up analogies, examples, and answers to possible objections.

To save souls we must be holy. The Lord does not use dirty tools. How can we go to sinners if they say: "Physician, heal thyself" (Luke 4:23)? Nor can we bid fallen-aways to return to the obedience they owe the Church if they are able to question our own way of living and acting:

An errand these prophets ran, but none of Mine; a message they gave, but not of My sending. Privy to My design had they been, ah, then they should have uttered My own warnings, and so I might have turned My people aside from false paths, and erring thoughts!

(Jeremiah 23:21,22)

Instruction to the enquirer should be so formulated as to prove that we love what we believe. If we show little enthusiasm for the sublime truth we communicate, how shall the convert learn to love that truth?

The Spirit and Lost Sheep

Our love of souls must be persistent. We get used to reading the Parable of the Good Shepherd, but do we understand that for us priests it is a spelling out of our obligation to seek the lost sheep. Leaving a dinner, breaking an evening's entertainment, interrupting a siesta, all such efforts are summed up in leaving *those ninety-nine others on the mountain-side and go out to look for the one that is straying.* (Matthew 18:12)

Nothing unspiritual is sacred in the face of a spiritual need. Even the "banished" ones, those outside the Church through bad marriages, those who spurned the Sacred Heart though He spurned them not — are not these part of our ministry?

Never a soul will God suffer to be lost in the reckoning; still He busies Himself with remedies to save the life of him who is banished.

(2 Kings 14:14 [2 Samuel 14;14, RSV])

The banished son of the Church remains a son and the true priest grieves as long as he is away from his home. How many are the couples in invalid marriages who are ready to live as brother and sister, if only this possibility were properly presented to them? God's love is active on behalf of even the worst and the unworthiest of souls. Grace is given to many who were written off by priests of little faith, for God has said, "the sinner's death is none of My contriving!" (Ezekiel 33:11). Is not God a Father and is not the priest a "father"? We must never imitate the elder brother who would not receive back the prodigal. Here were two sons who lost the Father's love: one because he was "too good" and the other because he was "too bad"; but the latter it was who found that love again (Luke 15:11-32).

As His servants, we have confidence in His power:

There is a stronger power at work in you, than in the world.

(1 John 4:4)

Our zeal for conversions will go through three stages: a heavenly prayer, exhausting identification with others, and finally, the healing of the soul. St. Mark tells us (7:34) that Our Lord, when confronted with a deaf and dumb man, likewise performed the miracle of curing him in three steps. "... He looked up to heaven, and sighed; He said, Ephphatha, (that is, be opened)."

The condition of all apostolate is a realization that Heaven grants it. To look in the first instance anywhere else, for example, to publicity or organization, is to miss the source of power. If we make this mistake, we can next anticipate that costly pity and compassion in which we are one with the ignorant, the dull and the deaf. Only then is the eye opened to faith, the ear to the sound of the word of God. No one can give sight to the spiritually blind unless he gazes into heaven. What we give depends on what we receive.

How often Our Lord's sighs are mentioned in Scripture, for example, at the sight of the hardness of hearts and unbelief, at the sight of a leper, a hungry multitude, in the face of hostility and over the dead body of Lazarus! All the ills and evil of man's fate and conduct weighed on His priestly Heart. So, the worth of our efforts is in proportion to the expanse of sympathy and feeling we have for unconverted souls. The depth of a priest's compassion is the measure of his apostolic success.

Here, too, it is pertinent to meditate on the relation between the love of the Holy Spirit and the Eucharistic Presence on the one hand, and our sympathy for souls on the other. The gaze and the sigh went together in Our Lord. Likewise, the look at the tabernacle and the sympathy for the sick are twins. He who prays, sympathizes; he who has the Spirit has a body that takes up a cross daily for his people; he whose eyes sweep the heavens for the Spirit, has the keener gaze for the lost sheep of earth. The habitual communion with God is the root of the priest's compassion. Pity is second; Our Lord is first.

When the Spirit seeks to work in us for souls, our nature shrinks from the task. But it is something like swimming: it becomes a joy after the shock of the first plunge. We grow weary, of course, but God is unwearied in giving us new strength. Age is not the determining factor. The young who lack the Spirit tire more quickly than the old who have it.

> *Youth itself may weaken, the warrior faint and flag, but those who trust in the Lord will renew their strength, like eagles new-fledged; hasten, and never grow weary of hastening, march on, and never weaken on the march.*
>
> (Isaiah 40:30,31)

The natural man steadily tends to exhaustion. All life lived on the creature level digs its own grave. But the man who trusts in the Unwearied God does not follow the earthly law of fatigue. Unzealous priests are tired in mind before they are tired in body. Their exhaustion is ennui due to the loss of the Spirit. But the true apostle, though he may sit like his Master, "tired after His journey, by the well" (John 4:6), can nevertheless account a converted soul as "*food to eat of which you know nothing*" (John 4:32). Grace abhors a vacuum, as nature does. The empty house of the Gospel that was not filled by the Spirit was occupied by seven devils.

Thanks to the Spirit, though the priest grows older in years, he becomes younger through ascent to the altar of God where youth is renewed. Exertion without the Spirit is impatience; impatience, touched by the Spirit, is zeal for souls.

As the diamond cutter works diamonds and the sculptor stone, so the priest works souls.

Like a shepherd He tends them, gathers up the lambs and carries them in His bosom.

(Isaiah 40:11)

In the parish, in the school, the priest will watch that not one such soul is plucked out of his hands (John 10:11-28). Authority over the Church and its souls was not given to Peter until he had made a triple promise to love. Any authority the priest exercises has the same foundation. The priest will be as tender in love to his people as Jacob was to his flock:

I may lose a whole herd if I overdrive them.

(Genesis 33:13)

The Spirit and The Scripture

It has been said that a characteristic gesture of many priests, when they take the Bible from a shelf (after looking for it for several minutes), is to tap it with the hand to knock the dust off. This may explain why pulpit orators are so fond of a few routine texts, such as: "Come you that have received a blessing from My Father" (Matthew 25:34), or "Come to me, all you that labored and are burdened" (Matthew 11:28); and on Mission Sunday: "Go out, making disciples of all nations" (Matthew 28:19). Why is it that the less prepared the preacher is, the more he is inclined to find fault with his parishioners? And the less he examines his own conscience in meditation, the more he resorts to moralistic nagging.

The saintly priest, on the contrary, tells his flock: "We are Christ's ambassadors, then, and God appeals to you through us" (2 Corinthians 5:20). But if God appeals, He does so through His Word: "I preached God's Gospel to you" (2 Corinthians 11:7).

The preacher will do well to ponder on the technique used by St. Paul at Thessalonica:

Over a space of three sabbaths he reasoned with them out of the scriptures, expounding these and bringing proofs from them that the sufferings of Christ and His rising from the dead were fore-ordained; the Christ, he said, is none other than the Jesus whom I am preaching to you.

(Acts 17:2,3)

When he spoke to King Agrippa, Paul used exactly the same method of preaching:

Yet there is nothing in my message which goes beyond what the prophets spoke of, and Moses spoke of, as things to come; a suffering Christ, and One Who should shew light to His people and to the Gentiles by being the first to rise from the dead.

(Acts 26:22)

St. Peter uses the Scriptures in exactly the same way to develop the truths of the faith:

Salvation was the aim and quest of the prophets, and the grace of which they prophesied has been reserved for you. The Spirit of Christ was in them, making known to them the sufferings which Christ's cause brings with it, and the glory that crowns them; when was it to be, and how was the time of it to be recognized?

(1 Peter 1:10,11)

Can the preacher today do better than Peter and Paul? Regardless of how many times people hear the Scriptures, they can always find something new in them. St. Paul has set out the reason why this is so:

Everything in the scripture has been divinely inspired, and has its uses; to instruct us, to expose our errors, to correct our faults, to educate us in holy living; so God's servant will become a master of his craft, and each noble task that comes will find him ready for it.

(2 Timothy 3:16,17)

The scriptures are not merely a record of historical events that have passed. They constitute for every age a revelation of God's mind and will to each individual. Many of the incidents recorded in the Old Testament provide a perspective to give us a fuller understanding of events that occurred later and are described in the New Testament. Genesis 21:10-12, for example, recounts a quarrel in Abraham's family. Ishmael, his child by Hagar, mocked and insulted his younger child Isaac, the son of promise, whose mother was Sarah. Sarah sided with Isaac and decided that Hagar and Ishmael should be driven out of Abraham's house. Such family quarrels and maternal revenge may not seem to have much pertinence until we read Galatians 4:30, where St. Paul explains that the casting out of the bondwoman and her son was to show that they were yet in bondage to the Law and were consequently not entitled to share in the inheritance of the Gospel.

Not only does Scripture derive its inspiration from the Spirit, but the Spirit alone makes its meaning clear. Before his conversion Paul was versed in the Scriptures, yet could not see in them that the Lord was the Christ. Our Blessed Lord told the Pharisees that they poured over the Scriptures but did not realize that they referred to Him (John 5:39). Whatever beneficial effect was produced on the listener always came through the Holy Spirit.

Our preaching to you did not depend upon mere argument; power was there, and the influence of the Holy Spirit, and an effect of full conviction.

(1 Thessalonians 1:5)

When St. Paul recalled the effect of his preaching on the Corinthians, he probably had in mind his lack of success in Athens. St. Paul had given a very learned talk at Athens, quoting several of the Greek poets, but the effect was limited to one or two conversions. St. Paul thereupon left Athens for Corinth. During the forty-mile trip, he must have meditated on his want of success and tried to determine why he had failed. Later on, when he wrote to the Corinthians, he contrasted preaching by philosophy and eloquence, and preaching by the power of the Spirit.

So it was, brethren, that when I came to you and preached Christ's message to you, I did so without any high pretensions to eloquence, or to philosophy. I had no thought of bringing you any other knowledge than that of Jesus Christ, and of Him as Crucified.

(1 Corinthians 2:1-3)

There are two kinds of knowledge about Christ: the speculative and the practical. The former is obtained by study, the latter only through the Holy Spirit Who leads us to accept Jesus as Lord and Savior.

✠ J.M.J. ✠

~ 7 ~

The Spirit of Poverty

Poverty is not an economic but a spiritual condition. The vow of poverty not only allows for what is necessary to provide for one's material needs, but permits a man to live according to his state of life. Poverty, in relation to the priesthood, is a spirit. That is why Christ said:

Blessed are the poor in spirit.

(Matthew 5:3)

All men are poor in the sense that they have no natural claim to what is essential for the Kingdom of Heaven. Of themselves, they do not even know what they lack. Only when the Spirit takes possession of them, so that they become poor in spirit, do they recognize that they are destitute and blind and naked. That is why the beatitude referring to poverty in spirit is followed closely by one designed to console those who mourn. As poverty implies helplessness, so mourning implies a sense of guilt and corruption. The two are related like humility and patience, as Isaiah points out:

Nothing you see about you but I fashioned it, the Lord says; My Hand gave it being. From whom, then, shall I accept an offering? Patient he must be and humbled, one who stands in dread of My warnings.

(Isaiah 66:2)

The priest who is poor in spirit is a mendicus rather than a pauper. His most conscious moments testify to his emptiness, his dependence on God and his unworthiness. Only they will enter the Kingdom of Heaven who have cast off self-will, self-reliance, economic security as a substitute for Divine trust. The two attitudes are set out in sharp contrast in the message to the angel of the church of Laodicea recorded in Revelation (3:17), a message which we, in the richest nation in the world, can well take to heart. To those in the church of Laodicea who glory in their own success, saying

"I have come into my own; nothing, now, is wanting to me," the angel is directed to say: "And all the while, if thou didst but know it, it is thou who art wretched, thou who art to be pitied. Thou art a beggar, blind and naked; and my counsel to thee is, to come and buy from me what thou needest; gold, proved in the fire, to make thee rich, and white garments, to clothe thee, and cover up the nakedness which dishonors thee; rub salve, too, upon thy eyes, to restore them sight. It is those I love that I correct and chasten; kindle thy generosity and repent."

Poverty of spirit is based on the example of Our Blessed Lord.

You do not need to be reminded how gracious our Lord Jesus Christ was; how He impoverished Himself for your sakes, when He was so rich, so that you might become rich through His poverty.

(2 Corinthians 8:9)

He was a child of a poor mother born on a journey, first cradled among animals. His poverty was voluntary. He who had made the waters, asked for a drink; He who had made the beasts, borrowed one for a procession; He who had made the trees, borrowed a Cross. Satan offered Him all the riches of the world — the short cut to popularity — and He refused them, even though worn out by a forty-day fast. Joseph found Him a cave in which to be born; and another Joseph, a cave in which to lay His broken Body — for birth and death were equally alien to Him as God.

If such was the poverty of spirit of Christ, it is obvious that the priest, the *alter Christus*, has no choice but to cultivate a like spirit. The priest is already rich — rich with the grace of vocation, the grace of ambassadorship, the grace of Orders. Being rich in Christ, he has no need of being rich in Mammon. The Bible records that the tribe of Levi received no land, because the Lord was the riches of those chosen to be His priests:

> *This, too, the Lord said to Aaron: You are to hold no lands, no portion is to be assigned to you, among your fellow-Israelites. I am all thy portion; these others have their several possessions, thou hast Me.*

(Numbers 18:20)

The Riches of The Priest

Far greater is the wealth of the priests of the New Testament who enjoy the familiarity of the Incarnate Lord and the riches of the Spirit: "... how rich is the glory He bestows" (Romans 9:23); *"So rich is God's grace, that has overflowed upon us in a full stream"* (Ephesians 1:8).

The Catholic priest ought to be remarkable for his detachment from worldly things just as much as for his love of chastity.... avarice which the Holy Spirit calls the root of all evils, can lead a man to any crime. The priest who allows this vice to get hold of him, even though he may stop short of crime, is making common cause, whether he knows it or not, with the enemies of the Church, aiding them in their evil designs. (Pius XI, Encyclical on the Catholic Priesthood, December 20, 1935)

What abundance the priest possesses! He dispenses the pardon of Christ to those who repent of their sins. He has at his disposal the richness of the wisdom of Christ! Sitting at His Feet, the priest hears what Plato could not teach and what Socrates never learned.

Why do the few who are rich rarely support the missions? Why does the Church so often have to struggle against poverty, and why do conversions multiply more rapidly in poor countries, like Vietnam, than in prosperous countries? The reason is that there is a kind of balance struck beneath the wealth of heaven and the wealth of earth.

Thou didst receive thy good fortune in thy life-time, and Lazarus, no less, his ill fortune; now he is in comfort, thou in torment.

(Luke 16:25)

Heaven, too, has its economics. The cruelest words in Scripture will be pronounced on the last day against those who got all the worldly things they wanted:

They have their reward already.

(Matthew 6:16)

Appealing to his brethren everywhere, St. James confirms that rich pockets often have poor hearts, that poor pockets have hearts full of the riches of faith:

Listen to me, my dear brethren; has not God chosen the men who are poor in the world's eyes to be rich faith, to be heirs of that kingdom which he has promised to those who love him?

(James 2:5)

Our Blessed Lord insisted that His love of the poor and His efforts to save them were evidence of the truth of His claim to be the Messiah:

The poor have the gospel preached to them.

(Matthew 11:5)

But woe upon you who are rich; you have your comfort already. Woe upon you who are filled full; you shall be hungry. Woe upon you who laugh now; you shall mourn and weep. Woe upon you, when all men speak well of you; their fathers treated the false prophets no worse.

(Luke 6:24-26)

Poverty of spirit draws the priest to a closer union with the Person of Christ. A function of all ownership is to extend personality. A man is free on the inside because he has a soul; he is free on the outside, or economically, because he owns property. The human personality becomes enriched through things.

The priest, however, has another way to extend his personality: not by acquiring stocks and bonds, but by a greater reproduction in himself of the Hypostatic Union. He crushes his ego and its desires, so that in him there are two "natures" in one person: on the one hand, his human nature; on the other, his "participation in the Divine Nature" through grace and the losing of his human personality in the Person of Christ. Being less dependent on things, he becomes more and more an *instrumentum Divinitatis.*

It is Christ that lives in me.

(Galatians 2:20)

Crucified to the external extension of personality, the priest grows internally and becomes the extension of the Person of Christ. The less staffs the priest has to lean on — and staffs which pierce his hands — the more the Lord leans on him. Poor in himself, he is rich in Christ. The parishioners then do not see the human person in him: they see Christ, living, teaching, visiting, consoling, renewing Calvary. The instinct of parishioners is infallible: they know in whom Christ lives. Of one priest, they say: "He's a good Joe"; of another, "He is another Christ."

To the extent to which the wealth of a priest consists in the things of the Spirit, to the same extent the need for an outside complement to perfect his personality is reduced. The priest's confidence, as he confronts life, is derived less from the power of what he holds in reserve, than from his total reliance on Providence and on the Goodness of the Heavenly Father.

Prosperity unfavorable to Priestliness

Yet another reason for being poor in spirit is that temporal prosperity is unfavorable to spiritual advancement. Take the case of Solomon. He stepped downward, Scripture informs us, through multiplication. First, he multiplied gold and silver for himself; then he multiplied horses which he bought from Egypt; next, he multiplied wives. There is here a definite hint that carnality followed a love of wealth. Finally, he adored the false gods of his concubines. Confucius says that lust is the sin of youth, power the sin of middle age, and avarice the sin of old age. Avarice in the old can even represent the sublimation of the lusts of their youth.

So the Lord was angry with Solomon for playing Him false.

(3 Kings 11:9 [1 Kings 11;9, RSV])

The suggestion is that God was angry precisely because of the great blessings He conferred on Solomon, for every sin is aggravated by the mercies we have received. How much more, therefore, is sin aggravated after the gift of a vocation? Our Lord said that if He had not come and spoken to His people, they would have been comparatively without sin (John 15:22).

Hoarding, on one occasion recorded in the Bible, received a terrible punishment. After the Jews had crossed over the Jordan, Joshua won a victory and then set out for Hai where he was ignominiously routed. The defeat threw Joshua and his people into despondency, and Joshua complained to the Lord:

Better had we remained at our old post beyond the Jordan. O Lord my God, that I should see Israel turn their backs before their enemies!

(Joshua 7:7,8)

Thereupon the Lord explained the reason for the reverse. They were being punished because of the violation of a Divine command that no Jewish soldier should take for his own use any of the spoils of Jericho. One man, however, had violated the command; tempted by the sight of a costly Babylonian garment, some silver, and a bit of gold, he secreted them for his own use.

Though only one man in the entire army was guilty, the whole army was punished with defeat. The sin was imputed to and visited upon the entire nation:

But the Lord said to Joshua, Rise up; why dost thou lie there, face to ground? Guilt rests on Israel; they have transgressed My Covenant, by taking forfeited plunder for their own use; it has been stolen away secretly, and hidden among private goods.

(Joshua 7:10,11)

If the sin of one, who was not even a priest, affected all of Israel, will not the greed of a priest affect the parish? If the army was defeated at Hai because of such avarice, will not building projects and social organization suffer defeat because of the material aggressiveness of a servant of God? The guilt of one, even personal and hidden, can bring down Divine judgments on the whole parish. Did not Saul's violation of the agreement he made with the Gibeonites occasion much later a famine that lasted three years (2 Kings 21:1 [2 Samuel 21:1, RSV])? Did not David's obstinacy in taking a census which he had been warned not to take, occasion a pestilence to the destruction of seventy thousand of his subjects (2 Kings 24:10-15 [2 Samuel 24:10-15, RSV])?

The greed of Joshua's soldier, Achan, was hidden, but God. had witnessed the sacrilegious robbing of gold and silver He had ordered appropriated to His own use in the sanctuary. The crime had, moreover, been committed immediately after the celebration of the Passover, relating it even more closely to the altar and cult. To appropriate what belongs to the altar of God is more serious in God's eyes than the sinner always realizes.

Without naming the person, God revealed the fact and left it to the church of Israel to discover the offender. Justice took its course, and the sentence was executed. Achan with his children and his cattle were stoned to death; afterwards his tent, the stolen property and all his belongings were consumed by fire.

The Priest not only Begs but also Gives

When the priest in the pulpit asks the people to contribute to a diocesan expansion plan, does he first reach into his own pocket? When on Mission Sunday he urges the parishioners. to make a sacrifice to spread the Church in Africa, Asia or elsewhere, does he play his primary role in sacrifice? It is not fitting to ask others to give to a cause without setting the example. Can the Lord look on us with more favor than He looked on Achan, if we hide our bank accounts when the needs of the world are so pressing? And what blessings does He bestow on priests who give until it hurts, and then a little more? Fortunately, such priests are more numerous than is sometimes recognized. The Achans make the headlines, the scandalous hoarders become notorious; but there is a great army of priest-victims whose identity will become public only on the day of the great revealing.

Poverty of spirit does not begin with an act of the will to do with less; it begins with the Spirit of Christ in us. External poverty follows the internal. Indifference to the accumulation of possessions follows zeal for Christ. The greater the concern with material things, the lesser is the dedication to the spirit. Some priests may exhibit the externals of poverty, or what passes for such. They may be careless about the way they dress and act, soup on the vest, torn cassock, unswept aisles in the church but these things have no relation to poverty of spirit. They may reflect simply a lack of dignity and culture, a lust for saving, or a general carelessness about the dignity of one's person. To be unconcerned about being dirty impairs personality; poverty of spirit exalts it.

Three aspects of priestly poverty can be distinguished. In his personal life, poverty directs the priest to limit himself to the strictly necessary. In his apostolate, poverty of spirit inspires him to use spiritual means to attain his apostolic goals. In his use of resources, poverty obliges him to count only on God. As St. Augustine said, the poor in spirit are those who have hope only in God.

The priest can convince an incredulous, perverse and luxurious generation only by the acts of virtue opposed to those vices. That is why of all the virtues, the virtue of poverty seems the one most needed in our days. Pius XI stated that its practice was essential to defeat Communism.

The American priest lives at a level of material comfort higher than that of his brother priests anywhere in the world, but it does not necessarily follow that every American priest is attached to his comforts. Many would leave them tomorrow if circumstances made it necessary. The growth of the missionary spirit among priests in the United States demonstrates this fact. But the temptation is always present, and the priest who allows his soul to become possessed of a desire for wealth, can cause the gravest scandal. The danger of giving scandal is particularly great in the case of the diocesan priest. He cannot hide his lust behind a corporation, a society, or a group. Violations of the individual vow of poverty can sometimes be hidden behind a corporate selfishness. But the diocesan priest has no such façade. If he loves luxury, it shows, it shocks, and it scandalizes. On the other hand, his example is all the greater when he shows the detachment demanded by his station and office.

Poverty of Time and Talent

But the spirit of poverty is not to be understood merely in terms of material things. The Spirit beckons us to seek other, not less important goals. The priest must seek in particular a spirit of poverty in regard to time and in regard to self-satisfaction.

Time can become an object of hoarding, just like stocks and bonds. The priest may set up a schedule for rest, siesta, sleep and recreation, and routine can become a habit to the extent that anyone who disturbs it is in danger of judgment. But the neighbor has claims; hunger has claims; bereavement has claims. Our Lord had His rest disturbed, for He could not be hid. Two of His outstanding converts were made when He was tired, another conversion resulted from an interruption. Siesta time is not sacred; the "day off" is not sacred.

These legitimate recreations are expendable, if a soul can be saved. As St. Paul said, we are to redeem the time,

> *... hoarding the opportunity that is given you, in evil times like these.*

(Ephesians 5:16)

Many priests have taken a resolution never to waste a minute of time, particularly when the welfare of a soul is concerned. Keeping visitors waiting in the parlor, delaying a sick call, complaining because a penitent is late-these are all forms of avarice.

> *Let us practice generosity to all, while the opportunity is ours, and above all, to those who are of one family with us in the faith.*

(Galatians 6:10)

The pastor who believes that being made a shepherd of souls dispenses him from hearing confessions or administering the Sacrament of the Sick, shows that greed of time which St. Peter felt came on with age, and against which he warned:

> *Look anxiously, then, to the ordering of your lives while your stay on earth lasts.*

(1 Peter 1:17)

God insists on "*Today*" (Hebrews 3:13). The devil says: "*No more of this for the present*" (Acts 24:25), as Felix put off listening to Paul.

The lazy priest always has less time than the zealous priest because the former is thinking in terms of the interruptions to his leisure, while the latter seeks the opportunity to be another Christ. The priest's time is not his own; it is Our Lord's. The more we enrich ourselves with time, the more we impoverish the Kingdom of God.

The virtue of poverty is too rich in content to be limited to money. The saying that time is money takes on a new meaning when we understand what is meant by poverty of time. No priest was

124

ordained for an eight-hour day or for five days a week. He is ordained for the Kingdom of God, which is "opened to force" (Matthew 11:12). Time is for pardon.

> *We are careful not to give offence to anybody, lest we should bring discredit on our ministry; as God's ministers, we must do everything to make ourselves acceptable. We have to shew great patience, in times of affliction, of need, of difficulty; under the lash, in prison, in the midst of tumult; when we are tired out, sleepless, and fasting. We have to be pure-minded, enlightened, forgiving and gracious to others; we have to rely on the Holy Spirit, on unaffected love, on the truth of our message, on the power of God.*

(2 Corinthians 6:3-7)

Poverty of Self-Satisfaction

Not less important for the priest than poverty of time is poverty of self-satisfaction. There is no such thing in priestly spirituality as being satisfied because we have done our duty. It is not enough to perform the most essential activities, to work in the chancery, to administer cemeteries, to make converts, to fulfill one's hours "on duty." On one occasion (Matthew 25:30; Luke 17:10) the Apostles were looking for a crown of merit before their work was done, seeking applause before their orchestration was finished. Our Lord had to remind them that they were not entitled to sit down at the banquet of life simply because they had fulfilled their duties. Even when they had done all they were supposed to do, they had still to regard themselves as "unprofitable servants." A special reward requires more than merely to do one's duty.

> *If any one of you had a servant following the plough, or herding the sheep, would he say to him, when he came back from the farm, Go, and fall to at once? Would he not say to him, prepare my supper, and then gird thyself and wait upon me while I eat and drink; thou shalt eat and drink thyself afterwards? Does he*

hold himself bound in gratitude to such a servant, for obeying his commands? I do not think it of him; and you, in the same way, when you have done all that was commanded you, are to say, we are servants, and worthless; it was our duty to do what we have done.

(Luke 17:7-10)

Our service is an arduous one; it involves not only labor in the fields in the daytime, but serving tables at night. It is the mere duty of the priest to work both morning and evening. When he is exhausted, he cannot say: "Well, I already did my Boy Scout duty today." Rather must he tell himself: "I am worthless, an unprofitable servant." The less there is of self-satisfaction, the more zeal there is in His service. Counting the converts we have made may eventually make us believe that we, rather than the grace of God, made them. "I built three rectories; now I can retire; I heard confessions three hours today; I have done my duty." Labor union rules might regard that as sufficient; but we belong to a different union, where love, not hours, is the standard. When we think of all the Lord has done for us, we can never do enough. The word 'enough' does not exist in love's vocabulary. It is like telling the mother tending her sick child that she has done her duty and should take it easy.

In the parable about the unprofitable servant (Matthew 25:14-30), Our Lord describes a frequently ignored element of the priesthood. The priest is used to hearing himself being called an ambassador. He is reminded that he is an unprofitable servant as seldom as he is reminded that he is a victim. But the servitude which Christ describes is one of love, not one of duty. Our Lord refuses to distinguish between "work" and "extra work," between "on duty" and "standing by," between eight hours and eighteen hours. No airs of self-complacency are Divinely permitted to the priest. No self-pity, no pluming ourselves on our administrative talent, no such thing as saying: "I built a high school; now the bishop should make me a monsignor." The moment we become self-complacent about our achievements, the work spoils in our hands.

We are worthless servants when we have done our best. What are we then when we fail to do our best? We become unworthy even to be His servants, His priests. To our Redeemer alone belongs the merit and glory of our services; to us belongs nothing but the gratitude and humility of being pardoned rebels.

✠ J.M.J. ✠

~ 8 ~

The Spirit and Preaching and Praying

Preaching is not the act of giving a sermon; it is the art of making a preacher. The preacher then becomes the sermon.

It is from the heart's overflow that the mouth speaks.

(Luke 6:45)

The preacher without the Spirit of Christ is like Gehazi whom Elias sent to revive a dead man. Although he brought with him the prophet's staff, no miracle happened, for the virtue of the staff was negated by the hands that held it (4 Kings 4:25-38 [2 Kings 4:25-38, RSV]). One may hold the Scriptures of the Lord in the pulpit, as Gehazi held the staff in his hand, but no souls are saved. The absence of an inner spiritual life makes sermonizing dull, stale, flat and unprofitable.

It is possible for the priest to experience a *hardening* as a result of his intimate contact with the spiritual, without becoming spiritual. Sacristans are privileged to work close to the Eucharistic Lord, but that does not prevent some sacristans from being perfunctory in their genuflections. Jewelers become used to jewels. Husbands grow bored with beautiful wives, if there is no "stirring up of the first zeal." Contact with the Divine is a privilege that can similarly turn into indifference, unless each day one tries to get a step closer to the Lord. Trafficking with the Word of God one Sunday after another, without prayer and preparation, does not leave a priest the same; it leaves him worse. Failure to climb means to slide backward. There is no defense against *acedia,* against the tragic loss of Divine reality, except a daily renewal of faith in Christ. The priest who has not kept near the fires of the tabernacle can strike no sparks from the pulpit.

What answer to judgment shall the priest give who squanders hours a day on newspapers, television and magazines, yet cannot spare half an hour of the Lord's time to prepare his soul for the pulpit? No wonder if he produces shoddy, cheap moralizings and ulcerous scoldings which do damage to his espousal with the Spirit and dishonor the Christ Whose ambassador he is. Is he not rather like the hireling who "takes to flight because... he has no concern over the sheep" (John 10:13)? What right have we to preach to others who "labour and are burdened" (Matthew 11:28), if we ourselves shirk the burden of our calling? Is being caught up in the whirling machinery of "busy-ness" an adequate excuse for what is in reality laziness?

> *But what if sentry, when he sees the invader coming, sounds no alarm to warn his neighbours?*

(Ezekiel 33:6)

And yet to each priest the Lord has said:

Thou are My watchmen; the warning thou hearest from My lips, to them pass on. Sinner if I threaten with death, and word thou give him none to leave off his sinning, die he shall, as he deserves to die, but thou for his death shalt answer to Me.

(Ezekiel 33:7,8)

The priest at ordination was told to preach. The office is to be taken so seriously as to make every priest cry out with Paul:

It would go hard indeed with me if I did not preach the Gospel.

(1 Corinthians 9:16)

If a pastor fails to feed his parishioners with the Word of God, they may well be the first on the day of judgment, to demand his punishment for having left them spiritually starved. Do we repay our redemption, our vocation and our other blessings from the Lord by such disregard for His commands? How shall we call on the rocks and mountains to cover us from His merited indignation!

How much more our words would burn as we preach, if we prepared our sermons before the Eucharistic Lord; if our meditation each morning was on the subject of next Sunday's sermon; if before preaching, we prayed for five minutes to the Holy Spirit for Pentecostal fire; if we kept the Scriptures ever open near us, that we might gird ourselves with their truth when mounting the pulpit? Every person to whom we preach we shall meet again on the judgment day. How great our joy then, if we have rectified their consciences and elevated them to the embrace of the Sacred Heart. No wonder that Moses, Elias and Jeremiah all tried to run away from the crushing burden of delivering the Word of the Lord.

And shall we substitute the ledger for the Bible, the begging sermon for the penitential summons, tawdry platitudes for the scandal of the Cross? In the Old Testament, God ordered that the fire on the altar should never go out. Are not we ministers of the High Priest Who cast fire on the earth and willed that it be enkindled?

The Scriptures Our Inspiration

What inexhaustible subjects for sermons the Spirit gives us in the Scriptures. There is no occasion for which the Bible lacks a fitting theme, a pertinent application. There is, for example, the judgment on men who defy God, such as Balaam (Numbers 23:7-24:25; 31:8), Goliath (1 Kings 17:10-55 [1 Samuel 17:10-55, RSV]), Sennacherib (2 Paralipomena 32:1-21 [2 Chronicles 32:1-21, RSV]).

Then there are the parables of the Old Testament, for example, Balaam's seven parables (Numbers 23:7,18; 24:3; 15:20-23); Samson's (Judges 14:12); the ewe Lamb (2 Kings 12:3 [2 Samuel 12:3, RSV]); the wise woman of Tekoa (2 Kings 14:6 [2 Samuel 14:1-20, RSV]); the trees choosing a king (3 Kings 20:39 [Judges 9:7-15, RSV]); the parable of old age (Ecclesiastes 12:1-7); the poor wise man in a little city (Ecclesiastes 9:14).

Wonderful indeed would be the preacher who could improve on the five cries for mercy in the Gospel: Blind Bartimaeus (Mark 10:46,47); ten lepers (Luke 17:11-13); the woman of Canaan

(Matthew 15:21,22); the father of a demon-possessed boy (Matthew 17:14,15); and the rich man in hell (Luke 16:23,24).

What more applicable today than the story of Rahab (Joshua 2:21 and Hebrews 12:27), whose red string typified the long current of blood clamoring for Redemption; the woman full of good deeds — the only person Peter ever raised from the dead (Acts 9:36-42); or Naaman the Leper (4 Kings 5:1-14 [2 Kings 5:1-14, RSV]) who ridiculed the idea that God should use "sacraments" to manifest His saving power?

The lesson of the seven great intercessors is similarly pertinent to our times: Abraham for Sodom (Genesis 18), Judah for Benjamin (Genesis 44:18), Moses for Israel (Exodus 32:11), Jonathan for David (1 Kings 20:32 [1 Samuel 20:32, RSV]), Joash for Absalom (2 Kings 14 [2 Samuel 14, RSV]), Esther for the Jews (Esther 5), and Christ for His priests (John 17).

Preaching Repentance

But of all possible subjects for sermons, study of the Bible inevitably leads to the conclusion that the most important is repentance. It was the subject of John the Baptist's preaching (Matthew 3:8). Our Lord's first sermon was on repentance (Matthew 4:17). Our Lord gave it as the reason of His coming (Luke 5:32). It was the subject of Peter's first sermon to his fellow Jews (Acts 2:38) and of his first sermon to the Gentiles (Acts11:28). It was the subject Paul said he never failed to preach before Jew and Gentile (Acts 20:21); it was the theme of Peter's last message (2 Peter 3:9) in which he asserted that the only reason God gave us more time to live, was to repent. It was the subject both of Our Lord's first sermon and of His last. "Repentance and remission of sins should be preached to all nations" (Luke 24:47).

The message of Our Lady at Lourdes was "Do penance"; the same words were repeated at Fatima: "Do penance. But how often is penance preached? The current tendency is rather to downgrade the need for penance, to reduce the severity of the fast and the number of days of obligatory fasting. To make religion comfortable, however, is enough to make the Angel cry out again to any church like Ephesus:

Repent, and go back to the old ways.

(Revelation 2:5)

To the church of Pergamum, the same warning was sounded:

Do thou... repent; or I will come quickly to visit thee.

(Revelation 2:16)

Why repentance? Because it is the first act of a soul which turns back to God, the first stroke that severs sin from the heart. The Scriptures contain no expressions of vengeance against other sinners as terrifying as those directed by the Spirit of God in Deuteronomy (29:20,21) against those who obstinately delay repentance.

But the preaching of terror is not essential for repentance. Souls need not be like Dante, who went through Hell before he reached Paradise. The lighting of sulfurous coals in the pulpit is not Our Lord's path to repentance. St. Paul told Timothy how to woo souls from an evil life, and meekness was the approach he urged.

A servant of the Lord has no business with quarrelling; he must be kindly towards all men, persuasive and tolerant, with a gentle hand for correcting those who are obstinate in their errors.

(2 Timothy 2:24,25)

Before the thunder, we see the light. But to thunder against souls without bringing to them the light of God's truth and the love revealed through the Sacred Heart may bring a smile to their lips. It will not, however, bring them to their knees in repentance.

The Priest at Prayer

Three kinds of prayer in the Spirit should be of special concern to every priest: his unsaid prayers; his prayers made up of crosses; and his Breviary.

1. The Priest's Unsaid Prayers.

Because the priest is never free from the infirmities of a fallen nature, despite his sublime calling, Scripture often bids him to pray. But little help is found in weak human nature or in spiritual books, or even in the will itself, to inspire the necessary prayer. For one of the most neglected aspects of priestly prayer is the role which alone the Holy Spirit can play in its fructification.

Bad habits, acedia and lukewarmness may all conspire to prevent an increase in the level of prayer, but the Divine Spirit can enlighten the darkest soul and cleanse the foulest heart. The Holy Spirit is not indifferent to the obstacles created by man's carnal nature. As a nurse gently lifts a patient in his bed, so does the Holy Spirit sustain the priest in his weakness.

> *... when we do not know what prayer to offer, to pray as we ought, the Spirit Himself intercedes for us, with groans beyond all utterance: and God, who can read our hearts, knows well what the Spirit's intent is; for indeed it is according to the mind of God that He makes intercession for the saints.*
>
> (Romans 8:26,27)

Often, we do not even know what we should pray for. St. Paul himself was in this condition, when he asked for the removal of the thorn in the flesh. When James and John asked for the right and left places alongside the Savior, Our Lord told them that they knew not what they asked. But to recognize that we do not know what to pray for, is already an indication that we are on the path to be guided by the Spirit. Too often our prayers tend to be mere blueprints which we bring to God to rubberstamp. But when the Holy Spirit guides, prayer immediately rises above the level of petition.

Our Two Intercessors

We have two intercessors: one is Christ Himself; the Other is the Spirit. Christ speaks on our behalf. The Spirit intercedes in us that we may pray. He puts our hearts in a praying mood. He increases our boldness to draw nigh to the throne of grace. He suggests the things that we should pray for, multiplies our prayers, and gives us His Power.

What is meant by the groans of the Holy Spirit (Romans 8:26)? Very likely the secret workings of the heart toward God in a prayer that is without speech or vocal utterance. Very often, in deep affliction and distress, the human heart speaks not, but rather groans. As Christ intercedes for us in Heaven, so does the Holy Spirit, in afflictions and trial intercede in us on earth, revealing to us our need, creating holy aspirations, searching our hearts to expose what is wanting to our priesthood.

The Holy Spirit turns the dissatisfaction which each priest contains within himself into an inarticulate prayer. While creation longs for development, the priest — feeling his weakness — sighs for salvation. His very groaning proves a longing for the Infinite. With Augustine he knows that he was made for the Divine High Priest and is restless until he rests in Him. Very often we pray with the illusion that we know best what we should pray for. St. Paul suggests that, on the contrary, we often are ignorant of what we should pray for; hence the need of the illumination and guidance of the Spirit.

Pythagoras forbade his disciples to pray for themselves, because they did not know what was expedient for them. Socrates more wisely taught his disciples to pray simply for good things, for God knows best what sort of things are good. Our ignorance and our feebleness are alike grounds for asking the illumination of the Spirit to bring us into harmony with God's Will, whether in peace or in trial. The showers of Heaven are not less fertilizing because they fall at night; neither are the promptings of the Spirit less real and beneficial, when they reach the soul during seasons of spiritual gloom and ignorance. How consoling it is to know that Christ deputes the Spirit to intercede in us on earth, while He Himself intercedes for us in Heaven!

There is no priest in the world who does not at some time experience in an unutterable form this longing for greater communion with Christ. It defies all petition. In the unutterable cry, the Spirit reads a desire for communion with Him fuller than that which has yet be satisfied. When He makes intercession for us, it is not by direct supplication from Himself to the Father; it is by becoming the Spirit of supplication in us. When the Breviary becomes hard, when we struggle in prayer and the soul seems to lose touch with God, we have reached the point where we must pray for the Spirit of prayer. Finally, the Spirit makes us so intimate with God that we scarcely pass through any experience before we speak to Him about it, whether we visit the sick, preach, hear confessions, begin the office, or listen to the woes of a caller in the parlor.

The Undertones of Priestly Prayer

Priests are often reluctant to reveal their inner spiritual life even to their brother-priests. They tend to hide it from others and perhaps even from themselves, with the result that few know what goes on in their hearts. Yet even the weakest have aspirations toward goodness unsuspected by their critics. And many of the best hesitate to be seen in prayer by their brethren. But all the while, thoughts of holiness, or a sadness for not being more holy, flood their hearts. These undertones need articulation, these burdens need a wing, these mumblings need utterance; and that is the work of the Holy Spirit.

The effort to hide saintliness from others may often arise from an awareness of one's imperfections, so that we leave them to the Holy Spirit to define in our solitude. Few priests like verbal or vocal prayers. This is a fact. This is not because good priests are unprayerful. But because their prayers are sighs, their aspirations are inspirations. They have no sense of shouting to God across an abyss.

Always conscious of their mission, they feel the deep silent work of the Spirit within them. They have few petitions. They rarely make a novena for something they want; they set the people to make the novenas. Their best prayers are unspoken; their prayers are within their prayers — the talking to the Father, as does the Son through the Spirit Who inspires them what to say.

Thus we have the Father to Whom we pray and Who hears prayer. We have the Son through Whom we pray, *per Christus Dominum Nostrum,* and we have the Holy Spirit in Whom we pray, Who prays in us according to the Will of God with such deep, unutterable sighings. The intercession of the Holy Spirit within us is as Divine as the intercession of Christ above. Our very weakness, our humiliation and the grossness of our flesh provide the sphere of operation for the Holy Spirit, Who awakens the soul to come out and meet its Lord. As we grow in the knowledge of the Spirit dwelling within us, in the reality of His breathing within us, we begin to recognize how much beyond all our theology is that divine hunger by which He draws us heavenward.

How different the priesthood becomes when we start with the principle that we do not know what we want! Then we pray to the Spirit that we may properly understand our needs. Before a school or convent is built, before the parish makes plans for a social affair, the first prayer is to ask the Holy Spirit if the project is in conformity with God's Will. We often lose the benefit of prayers by proposing to ourselves improper ends. As St. James said:

> *What you ask for is denied you, because you ask for it with ill intent.*
>
> (James 4:3)

Scripture assures us that the true mark of participation in the divine Nature is the following of the Spirit:

> *Those who follow the leading of God's Spirit are all God's sons.*
>
> (Romans 8:14)

As Christ carries on His intercessory work in Heaven, He applies it through the Spirit Who could not come until He was glorified (John 7:39). The work that the Blood of Our Lord effected in Heaven when He entered beyond the veil, now continues to be applied through His Spirit, so that Christ's prayers become ours and ours are made His. But His Spirit is ours not only in time of prayer but in every moment of life.

2. Our Crosses

The priest devoted to the Spirit has an answer when trials, injustices, betrayals, disappointments, broken health or temptations assail him: he knows that the Spirit has prepared them. He immediately recalls that

> *by the Spirit, He was led on into the wilderness, where He remained forty days, tempted by the devil.*

> (Luke 4:1)

The grouchy old pastor to whom an assistant has been assigned, the indolent television-viewer whom the zealous pastor has no choice but to accept — these and other such apparently diabolical trials are permitted by the Spirit, just as the Spirit led Our Lord to the devil. Under the guidance of the Spirit every trial enriches the soul of the priest. He best heals wounds who has felt a similar wound.

The priest never complains against either his bishop, his brother-priests, or his people, if he sees that the Spirit is the author of his trials. Look at poor Jonah, and yet see how much God had to do with his mission to preach penance! His trials seemed to arise from purely natural causes, and yet the Lord had decreed each and every one of them: "*But now the Lord sent out a boisterous wind over the sea....*" (Jonah 1:4); "*At the Lord's bidding, a great sea-beast had swallowed him up....*" (Jonah 2:1); "*And now, at the Lord's bidding, the sea-beast cast Jonah up again....*" (Jonah 2:11); "*... at God's bidding a worm... struck at the plant's root and killed it*" (Jonah 4:7); "*... at the Lord's bidding the sirocco came...*" (Jonah 4:8).

Once we understand that all trials come from the Lord, they lose their bitterness, and our heart is at peace. When such trials arise, we must beg the faithful to fight with us through their prayers. A measure of the value we set on prayer is the insistence with which we ask the flock entrusted to our care to pray for us. St. Paul in prison wrote the Philippians that he will have no further worry over his soul's health if he has them "to pray for me, and Jesus Christ to supply my needs with his Spirit" (Philippians 1:19). He knew he could not work without the intercession of his converts. He valued Lydia's prayers and those of her household; he valued the jailer's prayers; he desired the prayers of Euodia, Syntche and Clement; and to the Ephesians he wrote:

> *Pray for me too, that I may be given words to speak my mind boldly, in making known the Gospel Revelation, for which I am an ambassador in chains.*

(Ephesians 6:19,20)

The priest may claim the prayers of his people, for through their prayers he receives from the Spirit whatever he needs. Yet how few are the parishes which place primary stress on prayer when a high school is being built or a mission being preached! Fund-raising campaigns are organized to get the money and telephone canvassers are enlisted; but are prayers presented as the first priority in order to draw down the blessing of God? The priest can save souls without eloquence, but he cannot move them without prayer and the Holy Spirit. To build a church we need "stones that live and breathe" (1 Peter 2:5), but what are the "living stones compacted in charity" if not the Christian community united in prayer? To build a church we need holiness, but whence comes holiness save from the Spirit? How many parishioners ever pray for the pastor or his assistants? If some do not, may not the reason be that from our prison cells of spiritual need, we priests have not urged them to pray for us, as did Paul the Philippians?

3. The Breviary

Few like to admit that they are bored by something they are expected to enjoy. The Breviary belongs in this category. Priests are expected to rave about their love of it, but many of us are like those affected people who pretend to love the opera, when they neither enjoy nor understand it. Why not admit the truth about the Breviary: many of us find it "strange talk" (John 6:61). But when asked if we will go away, we have the courage to refuse, and to repeat with Peter: "Lord, to whom should we go?" (John 6:69).

Maybe the Breviary was meant to be difficult for the average priest. Could it not be a wrestling with God like that of Jacob (Genesis 33:24)? If we learn to see it in this light, it may still be a constant struggle, but it will fall into the category of incessant and prolonged intercession. We pray it then as Our Lord prayed in the Garden, with drops of blood crimsoning the earth, as the friend who kept knocking at the door in the night for a loaf of bread, as the widow who was resistless in her pleading to the judge, as the Syro-Phoenician woman who would settle for the crumbs that fell from the Master's table. Importunity means not dreaminess, but sustained work. If *laborare est orare,* then is it not sometimes true of the Breviary that *orare est laborare?*

Our faith clings to the Breviary as the poor woman from the land of Tyre and Sidon clung to the Lord (Matthew 15:21-28). She had three handicaps to overcome: Christ's silence; the resistance of the disciples; and finally Christ's seeming rejection of her as unworthy to share His glory. Are not these our three common difficulties with the Breviary? Our High Priest seems to be silent; the Church makes us use a tongue which is hard; and all too often we let ourselves become convinced that Our Lord is not very pleased with us. Yet we struggle along, day by day, inspired by a sense of duty and faith. And if we do, will not Our Lord say to us in the end, as He said to that woman:

For this great faith of thine, let thy will be granted.

(Matthew 15:28)

The Breviary is Weighted

May not the Breviary also be difficult because in it we gather up not only all the intentions of the Church, but also the unpraying, the sinners, those who turn their backs on God, those who delay repentance? It is not easy for us to do this anymore than it was easy for Our Lord, Who was sinless, to be "made... into sin" (2 Corinthians 5:21). Everyone would like to have a feeling of devotion when he prays, but what if we pray for those who have only sensibility and no devotion?

Whenever we pick up that book, we pick up Japan and Africa, two billion unbelievers, fallen-aways, the burden of the churches throughout the world. If millions are reluctant to pray, do we not feel their reluctance? If the unconverted drag their feet, how can we take wings and fly? Three times during His Agony Our Lord came back to His three Apostles seeking consolation. The Breviary is not a personal prayer; it is an official prayer and therefore is weighted down "with the burden of the Churches." And until we realize that we are vocalizing the prayer of the Church, will we understand both its beauty and its burden?

Our Lord poured forth His personal prayers to His Father on the mountain top, but when He prayed for His enemies, He was bleeding on a gibbet (Luke 23:34). The more His prayer was related to redemption, the more He suffered. Easy indeed it is for us to love God solitary and alone, but suppose we have to pray for those who do not love? Do we not take on their lovelessness? And is this not good for us, for if all our prayers were personal, would they not be selfish? Then we might try to bargain with God as Jacob did:

If God will be with me, he said, and watch over me on this journey of mine, and give me bread to eat and clothes to cover my back, till at last I return safe to my father's house, then the Lord shall be my God.

(Genesis 28:20,21)

Jacob loved God while loving himself. But in the Breviary, we are making an act of love, not only for the Church but also for her enemies. The Breviary, like the angel, is the test of our strength; as the angel shook Jacob and made him reel and roll, so the Breviary tests our endurance. If the Breviary be approached as a work, as a wrestling with God, as an intercession on the cross, as something intended to bring us not consolation but struggle, we shall eventually learn to enjoy the battle and turn it to the glory of God.

Despite all our complaining, we love the Breviary. Our life has two principal "gripes": one, the food in the seminary before we are ordained; two, the Breviary after we are ordained. But we grow fat on the meals, and we advance in holiness with the Breviary. We expect too much from it, at first, as does a bride of her groom. But once we realize that when we pick up the "book," we are not mockingbirds singing for ourselves alone, that our melody is rather the song of the angels rising to the throne of God on behalf of the Mystical Body and the world, it becomes easier. We may not understand every word, but God understands what we do not.

While it is true that it is only the Spirit who can make our reading of the Breviary fruitful, there are many things we can do to prepare ourselves for the soft caress of His breath.

Aids to the Breviary

1. Read the office of the day in the presence of Our Lord in the Blessed Sacrament, a practice for which a plenary indulgence is granted. Furthermore, since the Breviary is the Body of Christ praying, it is read with more faith when closely united with the Head Who "lives on still to make intercession on our behalf" (Hebrews 7:25).

2. Advert to the fact that most of the Psalms confront us with two figures: one is the Sufferer; the other is the King. It helps us to interpret the suffering psalms as the Church, and the kingly psalms as Christ. That long Psalm 118 [RSV 119] would thus become the Church pleading its love for Christ, the New Law. And when we

come across "cursing psalms," it may be well to remind ourselves that of all bad men, religious bad men are the worst, and that the Judge takes sin seriously.

3.   Often appeal to the Holy Spirit during the recitation. As a mother first prays for her child even before he can know what she is doing, then teaches him to pray so that later she may pray with him, so does the Spirit pray in the Breviary first in us and then through us.

> *Go on praying in the power of the Holy Spirit; to maintain yourselves in the love of God, and wait for the mercy of Our Lord Jesus Christ, with eternal life for your goal.*

(Jude 20,21)

4.   Offer certain hours of the office for specific intentions. How often is a priest not asked to pray for someone: a boy taking an examination, a mother before childbirth, a father going on a trip, or a young couple about to be married? The Breviary, the Church's prayer, gathers up all these intentions of the parish, the diocese, the nation, and the world. It helps to offer a particular psalm for a determined person.

5.   The Breviary can never be properly read while listening to the radio or watching television, or with one ear and half the mind concentrated on a baseball game. *Magna abusio est habere os in Brevario, cor in foro, oculus in televisifico.*

> *No need for Me to prove thee a guilty man, thy words prove it; thy own lips arraign thee.*

(Job 15:6)

> *This people does Me honour with its lips, but its heart is far from Me.*

(Matthew 15:8)

Moments of mental soaring may occasionally accompany the recital of the Breviary, but in general the vision of the Mount of the Transfiguration is followed by the descent to the plain. Moments of exaltation are few and far between. We must be content to go on like pilgrims, usually on foot, sometimes with broken boots.

The Breviary is, however, not only a yoke and a burden; it is also a duty — a duty of love. The two aspects seem almost contradictory, but the test of love is self-sacrifice, not emotion. Besides, the duty itself is a good. When we lose faith, we lose a sense of duty. How this duty is performed will depend upon the level of behavior. If a priest is egotistic, the Breviary will be said out of duty alone; if he is conscious that it is the prayer of the Church, the duty will have love in it; if he is a priest-victim, love will fan duty into an ardor which feels no obligation. Jacob had to toil seven years for Rachel, yet *"they seemed to him only a few days, because of the greatness of his love"* (Genesis 29:20).

✠ J.M.J. ✠

~ 9 ~

The Spirit and Counselling

Not all who visit a psychiatrist have need of his services, as some who come to the priest have need of a psychiatrist. Catholics who are not emotionally disturbed will sometimes consult a psychiatrist because the pastor and the clergy have given up counselling. It used to be that the two regular advisers, each with his own area of action, were the family physician and the pastor. Today the doctor is often more interested in diseases than in sick people, while too many priests rely more on their index cards than on the Gift of Counsel. Psychiatrists occasionally fill the void created by the want of genuine concern for the ills and woes of people on the part of the clergy. The state has largely taken over education; now psychology would take the soul away from the priest.

To permit this to happen would be a failure in respect to a major duty. Yet how preserve this side of our ministry except by the Holy Spirit? Abundant treatises on psychological counselling are of course available; but while much assistance is to be gleaned from them, in the same way that a loudspeaker aids the preacher, they still remain in the natural order. Unless they are used under the guidance of the Spirit, they will avail naught.

Not every person who is disturbed emotionally or spiritually, falls within the province of the priest-counsellor, but the number whom he could help is greater than generally suspected. Two major causes of mental unhappiness are a want of purpose in life and an unrequited sense of guilt. The Holy Spirit alone can reveal the full purpose of life in Christ, and the Holy Spirit alone can convict us of sin. It is surprising how few Catholic books on counselling have references to the supernatural order, to grace, faith, mortification and prayer. The stress on such aids as "keeping your chin up," "self-confidence," "lifting yourself by your bootstraps," tends to make the Christian overlook the unseen influences which alone are ultimately capable of giving lasting rest to weary souls.

The concern of the priest as counsellor is solely with those souls who do not belong in the domain of medicine and psychiatry. However, this does not restrict him to the care of normal souls, for those who are abnormal because of a denial of guilt, fall equally under his jurisdiction. It is the task of the priest, and he enjoys the power of the Spirit, to regenerate and progressively remould all such souls into the Divine Image. And once restored to the heavenly inheritance, they can say with Paul:

We, after all, were once like the rest of them, reckless, rebellious, the dupes of error; enslaved to a strange medley of desires and appetites, our lives full of meanness and of envy, hateful, and hating one another. Then the kindness of God, our Savior, dawned on us, His great love for man. He saved us; and it was not thanks to anything we had done for our own justification.

(Titus 3:3-5)

No Carnal Wisdom in Counselling

The aim of all counselling is to move the person from the realm of flesh to that of the Spirit:

To live the life of nature is to think the thoughts of nature; to live the life of the Spirit is to think the thoughts of the Spirit.

(Romans 8:5)

The therapy of the Spirit seeks "a renewal in the inner life of your minds".

(Ephesians 4:23)

Where does the priest get the gifts of counsel, the discernment of spirits, the wisdom to understand human hearts? Partly from study, but principally from prayer to the Holy Spirit:

146

Is there one of you who still lacks wisdom? God gives to all, freely and ungrudgingly; so let him ask God for it, and the gift will come.

(James 1:5)

The Spirit comes to the aid of our weakness.

(Romans 8:26)

The attitudes, judgments and values of people are determined by the spirit that moves them. Their spirit is either of Christ or of the world (1 Corinthians 2:12). What spirit is it that leads the young into lust, a slavery to pleasure and rebellion against authority, that causes the middle-aged to be immersed in cares, and the old to grow avaricious?

Our century may well witness a phenomenon of alarming proportions: a growth in diabolical possession and a renewed interest in Satan. Plays, novels, books and movies can be expected to use his name more and more, not as something evil, but as something fascinating, to play with the flames of hell as children will play with fire.

The Goal of the Priest Counsellor

Priestly counsel based on natural knowledge alone cannot deal with such an enemy. Diabolical possession must be met by Christ-possession in the priest, so that he is restless to open to hearts the treasures of God's goodness; to disclose sin that it may be redeemed; to leave the ninety-nine just to seek the one that is lost; to ferret out leaders and train them in the apostolate and the making of conversions; to wrap about them the mantle of the Sacred Heart; to listen without interruption to the distressed, recognizing the dignity of the person who speaks; to reconcile husband with wife by revealing to them how they can sanctify one other, as St. Paul did for the unhappy couples of Corinth (1 Corinthians 7:14); to act in such a way that two tides meet in his priestly heart as they met at Bethlehem: the tide of human need and the tide of Divine fulfillment; to look at the fallen-aways as Our Lord looked on Peter and drove him to tears (Luke 22:61); to have the same Pauline patience which restored Mark to usefulness; to oppose himself everywhere to the awful waste and wear and tear of sin; to pray for those who seek him out (for prayerlessness is the insomnia of the soul); to make people think as they leave the parlor, that they have been with Christ; to understand that the Holy Spirit gives strength to those who spend it; to realize that as there is no beauty in the slothful animal, so there is no power in the slothful priest; to pray daily to the Holy Spirit to teach him to find enjoyment only in souls; to be convinced that he cannot reach a sinner with the fingertip of parochial organization, or raise one soul to sanctity with a lavish expenditure of cheap advice; never to hesitate to receive a visitor for the sake of his own comfort, knowing that God gives him no reward without the dust of toil; in a word, to be "another Christ" and not just "another Joe."

It is all very well to tell the poor and the hungry of the parish to register with Catholic Charities, but the priest will be held personally responsible before God for his compassion for the poor. One may never use a social agency to escape a priestly duty. One wonders what was in the mind of the Jewish priest who passed by the wounded man on the road from Jerusalem to Jericho (Luke 10:31). As he continued on his way, did he tell himself, to use modern equivalents, that he would tell the social center in the next town to send an ambulance? But he is eternally recorded in the Gospel as the one who failed his fellow man in his hour of need. In neglecting our neighbor, we turn away our "own flesh and blood" (Isaiah 58:7). It is not only the purse that must be drawn out to help the poor; the purse means nothing without the heart.

The merciless will be judged mercilessly.

(James 2:13)

Saintly Priests are Sought Out by The Distressed

The best counsellors are not the worldly wise with tape recorders, or those who know all the psychological tricks of interviewing, more concerned with congenial surroundings than the presence of the Spirit. The best guides of souls are saintly priests and priests who have suffered in union with Christ. Through such does the Holy Spirit pour His seven gifts. Those who live close to Christ impart Christ. As St. Augustine said: "What I live by, I impart." Suffering brings wisdom, but books bring only natural understanding. The priest who has been crucified and endured his passion with patience will always be found to be the merciful priest. If there is a long line outside one confessional on Saturday and only one or two outside another, it is time for a priest to ask himself some questions. Holiness draws penitents to holy priests. The attraction of such priests is the attraction of Christ Himself.

> *If only I am lifted up from the earth, I will attract all men to Myself.*

(John 12:32)

No priest sees problems so sympathetically as the priest who is standing on the watch tower of Calvary. Like the sun, it cannot be seen, and yet it illumines all else.

How many souls say of that great army of saintly priests: "He showed me my heart," or "He showed me the loveliness of Christ," or "It was like talking to Our Lord." It is not possible for a priest, at one and the same time, to be clever and to show that Our Lord is mighty to save. With noble iteration, no less than thirty-three times does St. Paul use the expression "in Christ." To him it is the secret of "*encouragement, loving sympathy, common fellowship in the Spirit*" (Philippians 2:1). The priest imbued with this concept, because he has "*crucified nature with all its passions and all its impulses*" (Galatians 5:24), always directs others in the shadow of the Cross and the light of the Spirit.

Counselling and the Conscience

Priestly counselling is basically the application of the Redemption to the individual. It is not just preaching to one person instead of preaching to a crowd; for in counselling, the individual

149

presents his problem as does a patient to a doctor. The priest establishes the facts, as the doctor does; then he presents his diagnosis and treatment, always mindful of the words of Our Lord:

Only the Spirit gives life; the flesh is of no avail; and the words that I have been speaking to you are Spirit and Life.

(John 6:64)

The Spirit is particularly important when the priest is dealing with a problem of behavior rather than an intellectual one. In almost nine cases out of ten, those who have once had the Faith but now reject it, or claim that it does not make sense, are driven not by reasoning but by the way they are living. Catholics usually fall away not from any difficulty with the Creed, but from some difficulty with the Commandments. When this happens, the priest's task is to arouse the conscience through the Spirit. There is not much reference to the conscience alone in Scripture, but there is abundant testimony that the conscience is aroused by the Holy Spirit. St. Paul tells us that it was his conscience that was illumed by the Holy Spirit, making him ready to be doomed in order to save his brethren:

I am telling you the truth in Christ's name, with the full assurance of a conscience enlightened by the Holy Spirit.

(Romans 9:1)

It is the work of conscience to witness to our fulfillment of our duty toward God; but it is the work of the Spirit to witness to God's acceptance of our faith in Christ and our obedience to Him. Thanks to the Spirit, the testimony of conscience and the declaring of Christ, in our life become identical. Conscience alone in a person may be likened to a room that is very poorly lighted, and in which the Commandments are printed on the wall in small characters. When the Holy Spirit illumines the conscience, a brilliant light is shed upon those characters. The Holy Spirit restores consciences, so that they accept the guidance of the law of Christ. The Holy Spirit also shows the conscience the relationship between sin and its purging by the Blood of Christ, so that there is no more a consciousness of sin (Hebrews 9:14; Hebrews 10:2-22).

It is never enough for a priest to tell his people that they must follow their conscience; he must constantly seek the illumination of their conscience by the Spirit.

The end at which our warning aims is charity, based on purity of heart, on a good conscience, and a sincere faith.

(1 Timothy 1:5)

One never understands the enormity of sin except through the Spirit, a truth which Our Lord explained to His priests the night of the Last Supper. Sin is best treated and overcome, not solely in relation to the breaking of a commandment, but in terms of the breaking of our bonds with the Father, Son and Holy Spirit. Sin disrupts our ties with the Heavenly Father because it alienates us as sons. Such is the message of the parable of the prodigal son (Luke 15:11-32). Sin also re-enacts Calvary:

Would they crucify the Son of God a second time, hold Him up to mockery a second time, for their own ends? (Hebrews 6:6)

A personal equation must be established between the soul and the crucifix. Sins of pride are understood through the crown of thorns; sins of lust through the torn flesh; sins of avarice through the poverty of nakedness; and sins of alcoholism through thirst. Moreover, sin must be seen as resisting the Spirit of Love (Acts 7:51); as stifling the Spirit of Love (1 Thessalonians 5:19); and as distressing the Spirit of Love (Ephesians 4:30).

Conscience is always enlightened when sin is seen as hurting someone we love. No sin can touch one of God's stars or silence one of His words, but it can cruelly wound His Heart. Once the penitent understands this truth, he can see why he has such emptiness and desolation in his soul: he has hurt one he loves.

Many who approach a priest still try to conceal their conscience. They offer spurious reasons to explain their actions. The priest who remains on a purely psychological level cannot always see through such deceits, and in consequence he cannot help the one who has come to him. It takes a spiritual X-ray to penetrate such a mind:

151

Who else can know a man's thoughts, except the man's own spirit that is within him? So no one else can know God's thoughts, but the Spirit of God. And what we have received is no spirit of worldly wisdom; it is the Spirit that comes from God, to make us understand God's gifts to us; gifts which we make known, not in such words as human wisdom teaches, but in words taught us by the Spirit, matching what is spiritual with what is spiritual. Mere man with his natural gifts cannot take in the thoughts of God's Spirit; they seem mere folly to him, and he cannot grasp them, because they demand a scrutiny which is spiritual. Whereas the man who has spiritual gifts can scrutinize everything, without being subject, himself, to any other man's scrutiny. Who has entered into the mind of the Lord, so as to be able to instruct him? And Christ's mind is ours.

(1 Corinthians 2:11-16)

Thousands would flock to us every year, mail from frustrated souls would reach our doors, the young would seek us out, hearts unnumbered would seek comfort in our confessional, did we but realize the extraordinary powers of direction, counselling and guidance that come from living in the Spirit of Christ.

Counselling Through Sympathy

Compassion is identification with others, whether they be laughing or weeping:

Rejoice with those who rejoice, mourn with the mourner.

(Romans 12:15)

Such heart-unity with the woes of others, as the parable of the Good Samaritan teaches, is independent of our natural feelings. The Psalms also inspire us to a like sympathy for everyone we meet.

Time was, when these were sick; what did I then? Sackcloth was my wear; rigorously I kept fast, prayed from my heart's depths. I went my way sadly, as one that mourns for brother or friend, bowed with grief, as one that bewails a mother's loss.

(Psalm 34:13,14 [35:13 – 14, RSV])

When Elizabeth, after being long childless, finally brought forth John the Baptist,

her neighbors and her kinsfolk, hearing how wonderfully God had shewed His mercy to her, came to rejoice with her.

(Luke 1:58)

Did not the woman who had lost her piece of money and found it, call in her neighbors to rejoice, as did the shepherd who found the lost sheep? Did not Our Blessed Lord weep over His enemies whom He knew were about to stain their hands with His Blood (Luke 19:41)? Did He not say also that the angels in heaven are not indifferent spectators at the conversion of sinners (Luke 15:7-10)? When Our Blessed Lord saw the tomb of His friend, Lazarus, did He not weep so that the Jews exclaimed: "*How he loved him*" (John 11:37)?

The weddings and the funerals in the parish, the converts and the fallen-aways, the faithful youths and the juvenile delinquents, the bigots and the men of good will to all of these the sympathy of Christ goes out in the priest as he fulfills the words of Paul:

Bear the burden of one another's failings; then you will be fulfilling the law of Christ.

(Galatians 6:2)

Everywhere in the Bible, the priest is pictured as binding up the broken, bringing back those that have been driven away, carrying lambs in his bosom, and gently leading those that are with young (Ezekiel 34:2, 4; Isaiah 40:11). This is a great worry to a good priest, and he may feel the burden so much as to cry out as Moses did:

Lord, he said, why dost Thou treat me thus? Must I carry a whole people like a weight on my back? I did not bring this multitude of men into the world; I did not beget them; and Thou wouldst have me nurse them in my bosom like a child.... I cannot bear, alone, the charge of so many; it is too great a burden for me.

(Numbers 11:11-14)

At other times, the spiritual priest full of anxiety for his converts, will compare his feelings with the pangs of a woman in childbirth:

My little children, I am in travail over you afresh, until I can see Christ's image formed in you.

(Galatians 4:19)

Such a priest will express a special sympathy on sick calls to those who suffer. No priest can sympathize who is "outside" the suffering of others. "Crucifixion with Christ" through zeal and work and self-denial, will enlighten others by reminding them that Our Lord carried His scars with Him to heaven. When therefore, He lays His hand affectionately on any heart, He leaves the impression of His nails. The sick will be assured that their sufferings are not a punishment for their own sins so much as an opportunity to join in reparation for the sins of the world.

The priest will show such souls that there are no accidents in life, that the Providence of God rules the fall of a sparrow or the loss of a hair, that He made the wind that caused Jonah to be caught, that He made the sea-beast which swallowed him, that all sufferings that come to us even from our friends are to be seen as coming from His hand. In the Garden did He not say to Peter:

Am I not to drink that cup which my Father Himself has appointed for Me?

(John 18:11)

Even the cup of sorrow which comes from those who should reach us the wine of friendship, must be seen as God's gifts bitter though it be.

154

The priest's own life may be full of a peculiar kind of suffering "from false brethren" (2 Corinthians 11:26) who ridicule his zeal, criticizing him if he interrupts a deserved rest in order to help a tortured soul, or if he pays two visits in one week to a dying mother of seven children. But none such barbs will make him bitter. His patient bearing of those who break bread with him will arm him with sympathy for others. His attitude will be like that of David when Shimei took up stones to throw at David and cursed him. One of David's generals asked if he should cut off his head. David replied:

Let him curse as he will; the Lord has bidden him curse David, and who shall call him to question for doing it?

(2 Kings 16:10 [2 Samuel 16:10, RSV])

All things, all people, even our own brother priests, are sometimes used for our chastening, that we may better be able to console others. Thus will be verified in us, as in another Christ, the words of Simeon:

... to be a sign which men will refuse to acknowledge; and so the thoughts of many hearts shall be made manifest....

(Luke 2:34,35)

Counselling the Sinner

A woman is said to have gone to confession after an absence of thirty years. The confessor, a priest who in thirty years had never made a meditation before Mass, barked a bitter question at her: "Why have you stayed away from the Church for thirty years?" Her reply was a logical one. "Because, Father, thirty years ago I met a priest just like you."

A Spanish story has it that a priest who showed little mercy to a penitent heard a voice from the crucifix: "I, not you, died for her sins."

So jealous is God of His mercy that sometimes He permits priests to fall into the very sins they unjustly and inordinately condemn. If there is anything devotion to the Sacred Heart brings home to the priest, it is His mercy and His love of sinners.

No matter how strong the grip of vice, the penitent must still be assured that no mountain of guilt is so great as not to be removable by the Blood of Christ. Ever mindful of the treasures of mercies he has received from the Sacred Heart, the confessor will assure every sinner that "even lame folk shall carry plunder away" (Isaiah 33:23), as the people of Jerusalem were told when victory seemed impossible.

Many sinners, particularly those guilty of sins which cause excessive introversion, are prone to adopt the language of Cain:

Guilt like mine is too great to find forgiveness.
(Genesis 4:14)

They may even curse the day of their birth, as did Job (3:1; 27:2) and Jeremiah (20:1-18), or even ask God to take away life as did Elijah (3 Kings 19:4 [1 Kings 19:4, RSV]). But did not Our Lord Himself on the Cross, shutting out the consolations of Divinity, cry out (as He suffered for the darkness of atheists and agnostics):

My God, my God, why hast Thou forsaken Me?

(Matthew 27:46; Mark 15:34; Psalm 21:2 [22:1, RSV])

Such souls must be assured:

Was there ever such a God, so ready to forgive sins, to overlook faults?... He loves to pardon.
(Micah 7:18,19)

And after all, if they had never sinned, or we had never sinned, how could we all call Jesus "Savior"?

We come from a world where God is ever working in love, where His sympathy never grows cold, where His mercy never tires, where His tenderness never wearies.

My Father has never ceased working, and I too must be at work.

(John 5:17)

He makes use of every faintest hope, waterpots at a marriage feast, loaves and fishes in a boy's basket, a Matthew at a desk, a man sitting under a tree, a student with Isaiah in his hands — He notes them all in compassion. The key to his apostolate is not "the human touch," but the Christ-touch.

He held out His Hand and touched him.

(Mark 1:41)

Close, intimate, personal contact with affliction and grief is the key to counselling in the Spirit. The spontaneous impulse of pity breaking through the barriers of disease and disgust is the Christ-touch continued in the priest. He touches the leper and is unpolluted, as He took on sin and was without sin; so the priest, like a sunbeam, passes through a fouled humanity without stain.

Counselling is touching where there is disease or misfortune; it is not the simple giving of advice. A shake of the hand could be more of an occasion of grace than a meal sent superciliously from an agency. The priest takes the hand of the diseased whom he wishes to help; he goes down to their level, sees the old with their eyes, and the cancerous with their thoughts, knowing all the while that he can make them holy only to the extent to which Christ has already touched him.

✠ J.M.J. ✠

~ *10* ~

The Priest as Simon and Peter

No other Apostle arouses as much sympathy as Peter in the priest's heart. He seems very close to each of us in his conflicts and emotions, his strength and his weakness, his resolve to be heroic and his disastrous failure to live up to his aspiration. At one moment he is humble, at another proud. He affirms fidelity to his Lord, then denies Him. He is so supernatural, yet so very weak and natural. He extols as Divine the Master he loves, only to be frightened by a servant girl into saying that he does not know "the man." No chain is stronger than its weakest link, and the weakest link in the entire apostolic chain was the first link, Peter — and the Son of God holds on to that. Hence the "gates of hell shall not prevail."

Two "Natures" of Every Priest

Like Peter, every priest has two "natures": a "human nature" which makes him another man, and a "priestly nature" which makes him another Christ. The Epistle to the Hebrews identifies these two aspects. The priest is *different* from ordinary men as the one who offers sacrifice in their name.

The purpose for which any high priest is chosen from among his fellow men, and made a representative of men in their dealings with God, is to offer gifts and sacrifices in expiation of their sins.

(Hebrews 5:1)

Nevertheless, the priest is like every man in his weakness.

He is qualified for this by being able to feel for them when they are ignorant and make mistakes, since he, too, is all beset with

159

humiliations, and, for that reason, must needs present sin offerings for himself, just as he does for the people.

(Hebrews 5:2-4)

An angel would not make a fitting priest to act on behalf of men. He does not possess a body subject to temptations, nor has he experiential acquaintance with human suffering. He would lack the weakness which makes for sympathetic understanding. But though a priest is like men, he must also be unlike them. He is withdrawn from among men, so that he may act in Christ's name and appear as Christ to men.

It is significant that the first one chosen by Jesus to be a Christian priest was given a new name to represent his new character. He did not, however, lose his old name. Instead, he now had two names. He was at one and the same time, Simon and Peter. Simon was his natural name; Peter was his vocation. As Simon, he was the son of Jonah. As Peter, he was the priest of the Son of God. Peter never entirely got rid of Simon. But once called, Simon never ceased to be Peter. Sometimes it is Simon that rules; at other times it is Peter.

It might parenthetically be noted that Peter's brother, Andrew, was the one who was constantly making introductions. He introduced his brother Simon to Our Lord (John 1:41). When a group of Gentiles approached Philip and asked to meet Jesus, Philip consulted Andrew and together they went to Jesus (John 12:20-22). Andrew also introduced the lad who had the loaves and fishes (John 6:8). Andrew began his work of witnessing within the family circle.

He, first of all, found his own brother Simon, and told him, we have discovered the Messiah (which means, the Christ), and brought him to Jesus. Jesus looked at him closely, and said, Thou art Simon the son of Jona; thou shalt be called Cephas (which means the same as Peter).

(John 1:41-42)

Maybe someone in our family circle, a parent or a teacher, brought us to Christ, who by vocation changed our name. However great the dignity of our Christ-like office, we still bear with us the human nature descended from our own Jona. Even as Our Lord made Peter the rock on which He built His Church, He reminded him that he was taken from among weak men:

Blessed art thou, Simon son of Jona.

(Matthew 16:17)

We drag our physical inheritance, our congenital weaknesses, our temperament and our body to the altar. The Simon element never leaves us, even when we take on the role of Peter. The sinful and the sinless, the human and the divine, the old Adam and the new, our bond to an earthly mother and our filiation to a heavenly Mother — under both of these aspects we ascend the altar steps, carry the Eucharistic Lord to a bedside, and sit long tedious hours dispensing mercy and hope to sinners.

On ordination day, we wrongly imagined that the Simon-nature had disappeared. But reality soon reasserted itself. The Simon-Peter conflict reappeared.

The impulses of nature and the impulses of the Spirit are at war with one another; either is clean contrary to the other, and that is why you cannot do all that your will approves.

(Galatians 5:17)

Of this I am certain, that no principle of good dwells in me, that is, in my natural self; praiseworthy intentions are always ready to hand, but I cannot find my way to the performance of them.

(Romans 7:18)

The passage of the years and the growth in spiritual maturity cause certain kinds of temptations to decline, but others take their place. The demon of the noonday gives way to the demon of night. When Peter toward the close of his apostolate wrote his first epistle, he suggested by the opening words that he believed the Simon in him to be dead, for he identified himself as "Peter, an apostle of Jesus Christ" (1 Peter 1:1). However, in his second and last epistle, shortly before his martyrdom, he acknowledged the continuing struggle of the man of the flesh against the man of God: "Simon Peter a servant and apostle of Jesus Christ" (2 Peter 1:1).

In every priest either Simon has the mastery or Peter. In the prototype, in Simon Peter himself, Peter gradually achieved dominion over Simon thanks to the Holy Spirit. After Pentecost, one hears less of Simon, and when the name is mentioned, there is a reason for it. Thus, Cornelius is directed to send for "Simon, who is surnamed Peter" (Acts 10:5), because outsiders would know him best by the one name, Christians by the other. James, at the Council of Jerusalem, uses the name Simon out of an old and familiar friendship. Elsewhere, the word is Peter. The impulsive daring that was Simon's is changed into steadfast, bridled courage. In that last Epistle, nevertheless, he himself repeats the name so long unused, that it must have vanished from all but the most retentive memories. But if he reverted to it, he did so with a purpose, to recall humbly from out the mist of years his old unsanctified self.

The turning point in the spiritual life of a priest is not only his vocation, his calling. It is also that moment when he becomes obedient to the Spirit. This is a kind of second ordination, a crisis which carries him from being a priest merely by office, into the possession and manifestation of the Spirit of Christ.

Before Peter possessed the Spirit of Christ, the tug of war between his earthly and his priestly nature was revealed at Caesarea Philippi, when he confessed the Divine Christ but denied the suffering Christ. The Father had illumined his mind to recognize and proclaim that

Thou art the Christ, the Son of the living God.

(Matthew 16:16)

But when Our Lord announced that He would be crucified, Peter, drawing Him to his side,

> *... began remonstrating with Him; Never, Lord, he said; no such thing shall befall Thee.*

(Matthew 16:22)

Here in a vignette we have the entire paradox, which has proved for many a stumbling stone, a scandal, of infallibility and peccability. We have Christ's vicar Divinely guided in his office as key-bearer to the gates of heaven and earth. We have also this same Peter, the rock, the bearer of the keys, left to himself and without guidance, stigmatized as Satan. Paradox it is, but also fact. What Simon-Peter is there in all the priesthood who has not seen this scene re-enacted a thousand times in his own person: at this moment, another Christ; at that, another Satan?

Peter was willing to confess Christ the priest, but not Christ the victim. Men called to be rocks can become stones of stumbling. The Lord himself, however, defined His terms of service in clear language. The priesthood means imitation of Christ, and imitation means self-crucifixion. An unwillingness on the part of a priest to follow Him to Calvary, can sound to Our Blessed Lord only like the voice of the devil himself, that is to say, the voice of Simon repeating the sentiments with which Satan at the very start of His public life had tried to tempt Him away from the Cross. Our Lord did not take away Peter's vocation. He contented Himself with warning him that the flesh was with him and that in a moment of overconfidence he would fall. Peter is thus set forth by Our Blessed Lord as a constant reminder that it is in their strongest qualities, unless they are periodically renewed by Divine grace, that men are most liable to fail.

The Compromising Priest

No man can serve two masters. The priest nevertheless, will sometimes try to make the best of both the Simon and the Peter in him. Christ does not want it that way. In His priest there is no place for calculated less or more. Our Lord requires unmeasured love, but sometimes our nature asks for a compromise. It was such a spirit Our Blessed Lord had in mind when He urged His followers not to be satisfied with merely doing what they are obligated to do.

If a man...compels thee to attend him on a mile's journey, go two miles with him of thy own accord.

(Matthew 5:41)

Our Lord may have been referring here to the forced transport of military baggage, not just to forced attendance on or company of someone. The supreme example would be Simon of Cyrene, who was compelled to carry the Cross (Mark 15:21).

St. Luke gives a vivid picture of the priest who is unwilling to do all the Lord requires of him, of the attempt at compromise and the half-obedience to the Divine Will. It is noteworthy that in the opening presentation, the protagonist is described by the sole name of Simon. Here is the passage (Luke 5:1-6):

It happened that He was standing by the lake of Genesareth, at a time when the multitude was pressing close about Him to hear the Word of God; and He saw two boats moored at the edge of the lake; the fishermen had gone ashore, and were washing their nets. And He went on board one of the boats, which belonged to Simon, and asked him to stand off a little from the land; and so, sitting down, He began to teach the multitudes from the boat. When He had finished speaking, He said to Simon, Stand out into the deep water, and let down your nets for a catch. Simon answered Him, Master, we have toiled all the night and caught nothing; but at Thy Word I will let down the net. And when they had done this, they took a great quantity of fish.

After being rejected in His own home town of Nazareth, Our Blessed Lord directed His steps to Capharnaum, which would henceforth be His base of operations. He found Himself so pressed by the crowds that He took refuge in a boat belonging to Simon. Floating off a little from the land, He began to teach the people.

Then, when He had finished speaking, He turned to Simon and told him to launch out into the deep. "Let down your nets for a catch," He directed him.

Simon, however, was far from convinced. He was not prepared to challenge Him, but neither would he obey wholeheartedly. Even the word he used in answering Jesus reflected the ambivalence of his attitude. "Master," he said. It was the same word that Judas would use when betraying Him, a word without hint of recognition of the Divine, at most an admission of His status as a teacher, a rabbi. Simon's words reveal his thoughts. "What does He, coming from Nazareth, know about the way to fish at Capharnaum," he was surely thinking. "At this time of day who would dream of catching fish? The professional fisherman knows that night is the time to fish, and we have worked all night yet found nothing."

Peter knew all about fishing on the lake of Genesareth. It was accordingly as a mark of respect to the Master, as one might say, to humor Him, that he agreed to go part way: "but at Thy word I will let down the net." Our Lord had asked for nets; Peter compromised with a net. Our Lord asks for complete obedience; the servant gives a begrudging response. The flesh is not spirit; reason is not faith. Peter, relying on reason, let down a net. He flung into the Lord's face the bitter cry of life's unfruitful hours. But when the net caught a quantity of fishes so great that it was near breaking, suddenly there appeared from behind the bulk of Simon the priestly form of Peter:

Simon Peter fell down and caught Jesus by the knees; Leave me to myself, Lord,... I am a sinner.

(Luke 5:8)

Notice the double changes of name. Christ is no longer "Master"; He is "Lord." Simon is no longer Simon; he is Simon Peter. The priest's nature asserts itself over that of the man under the impact of the miracle wrought by the High Priest for the benefit of Simon's unworthy self. It was more than fish that Simon caught; it was the Lord. As Coventry Patmore puts it:

In strenuous hope I wrought,
and hope seem'd still betray'd
Lastly I said,
"I have labor'd through the night, nor yet
have taken aught;
But at Thy word I will cast forth the net!"
And lo, I caught
(Oh, quite unlike and quite beyond my thought,)
Not the quick, shining harvest of the sea
For food my wish,
But Thee.

So long as we think of Our Lord as "Master," we feel that what we are doing is enough, that we can settle for a net when He calls for nets. The moment, however, the Holy Spirit makes us realize His Lordship, makes us understand we are His priests through the Spirit, there comes over us the terrifying awareness of sin. The more we recognize the holiness of the High Priest, the more conscious we are of our own failings. The condition of all our priestly success is not in us the workers, nor in the nets of our schools and clubs. The worker failed, the net was near breaking. Our sufficiency is from God. The failure to catch souls must not be ascribed to God. We fail rather because we look upon Him only as Master, and not as Lord, or because we render less than complete obedience to His will.

The moment that Simon Peter was struck by his unworthiness, it is likely that Our Lord took him by the hand. So at least the last words of the account suggest.

> *But Jesus said to Simon, do not be afraid; henceforth thou shalt be a fisher of men.*

> (Luke 5:10)

Our Blessed Lord seems paradoxically to draw priests closest to Him, when they are most conscious of the distance which separates them from Him. We preach the Word of God effectively only when we have trembled at the Word. The priests and the missionaries who make the most converts are those with the deepest and most overwhelming sense of personal unworthiness.

If a priest complains that he cannot make converts in his parish, his city or his mission, it is time to ask if he is relying on his own resources. There is always a reason if the Divine guarantee, "Thou shalt be a fisher of men" (Luke 5:10), is not effective. I recall a parish in South America in which only eight of the eight thousand faithful attended Sunday Mass. A new pastor in six years raised to eighteen hundred the number of Holy Communions on weekdays. He preached eighty closed retreats a year, and he had the joy of seeing over 98 per cent of his people fulfill their religious duties. Our Lord did not say that we would be fishers for men, but fishers of men. Success comes through our union with Him.

Peter and Judas

Every bad priest is close to being a good one; every good priest is in danger of being a bad one. The line between sanctity and sin is a fine one. It is easy to cross, and the one who crosses can quickly gain momentum in either direction. St. Thomas Aquinas said that everything increases its motion as it nears its proper place or home. Saints grow rapidly in charity; wicked men rot quickly. We can see the truth of the point if we compare Peter and Judas. There seemed to be little difference in them for a long time, and then suddenly all the difference between being a saint and a devil.

The two of them were called to be priests, but that was only the first of the many points of similarity between them. Our Lord called them both devils. He called Peter "Satan" (Matthew 16:23; Mark 8:33) for tempting the Priest not to be a Victim on the Cross. Judas he called a "devil" one day at Capharnaum (John 6:71), referring to the future betrayal, when "Satan entered into him" (John 13:27) at the Last Supper.

Our Lord warned both Peter and Judas that they would fall. Peter rejected the warning. Though others might deny the Master, he asserted with bravado that he never would. Judas was similarly warned.

The man who has put his hand into the dish with Me will betray Me.

(Matthew 26:23)

Putting this into terms meaningful to us, it means that Judas would accept a "toast" from Our Lord and still "lift up his heel against Him." Judas also knew enough Scripture to understand that his act of betrayal was being likened to the betrayal of David by Ahithophel (2 Kings 15:31 [2 Samuel 15:31, RSV]).

Both Peter and Judas carried out the betrayals which Christ had foretold. Peter fell when challenged by a maidservant during the night of Christ's trial. Judas performed the nefarious deed in the Garden when he delivered Our Lord to the soldiers.

Our Lord made a positive effort to save both from their own weakness. He gave Peter a look.

The Lord turned, and looked at Peter.

(Luke 22:61)

He addressed Judas as "friend" and accepted his kiss.

Wouldst thou betray the Son of Man with a kiss?

(Luke 22:48)

The Lord only looked at Peter, but he spoke to Judas. Eyes for Peter, lips for Judas. There is nothing that Jesus will not do to save His priests.

Both Peter and Judas repented, though in a crucially different sense.

And Peter went out, and wept bitterly.

(Luke 22:62)

And now Judas, His betrayer, was full of remorse at seeing Him condemned, so that he brought back to the chief priests and elders their thirty pieces of silver; I have sinned, he told them, in betraying the blood of an innocent man.

(Matthew 27:3,4)

Why is one at the head of the list and the other at the bottom? Because Peter repented unto the Lord and Judas unto himself. The difference was as vast as that between Divine reference and self-reference; as the difference between the Cross and the psychoanalytic couch. Judas recognized that he had betrayed "innocent blood," but he never wanted to be washed clean in it. Peter knew he had sinned and sought Redemption. Judas knew he had made a mistake and sought release the first of the long army of escapists from the Cross. Divine pardon presupposes but never destroys human freedom. One wonders if Judas, as he stood beneath the tree that would bring him death, ever looked across the valley to the Tree that would have brought him life. On this difference of repenting unto the Lord and repenting unto self, as did Peter and Judas respectively, Paul would later on comment in these words:

Supernatural remorse leads to an abiding and salutary change of heart, whereas the world's remorse leads to death.

(2 Corinthians 7:10)

Both lived in the same religious environment, heard the same words of the Word, were swept by the same winds of grace, and yet the internal reaction of each made the difference:

One man taken, one left, as they work together in the fields; one woman taken, one left, as they grind together at the mill.

(Matthew 24:40,41)

Judas was the type who said, "What a fool I am"; Peter, "Oh, what a sinner." It is a paradox that we begin to be good only when we know we are evil. Judas had self-disgust which is a form of pride; Peter had not a regrettable experience, but a *metanoia*, a change of heart. The conversion of the mind is not necessarily the conversion of the will. Judas went to the confessional of his own paymaster; Peter to the Lord. Judas grieved for the consequences of his sin, as a single girl might sorrow over her pregnancy. Peter was sorry for the sin itself because he wounded Love. Guilt without hope in Christ, is despair and suicide. Guilt with hope in Christ, is mercy and joy. Judas took the money back to the temple priests. So is it always. When we give up Our Lord for any earthly thing, sooner or later it disgusts us; we no longer want it. Having loved the best, we can be satisfied with nothing less. Divinity is always betrayed out of all proportion to its due worth. And the tragedy is that he might-have-been St. Judas.

Peter and Judas illustrate how two called to the priesthood through the same spiritual experience of falling away from the Lord can end in a totally different way because of the response to or neglect of grace when the chips are down. Sometimes a reconciliation is sweeter than an unbroken friendship. Peter was always grateful for his grace. It shone in his Epistles. Each letter a man writes is characteristic of him. The Epistles of Paul to Timothy are notes of exhortation to be holy in his priesthood. The Epistles of John are a call to brotherhood. The Epistle of James is a plea for practical religion. What was the dominant note of the Epistles of Peter? It was the value of the pardon he had received, reminding us that our redemption was bought and paid for not "*in earthly currency, silver or gold; it was paid in the precious Blood of Christ; no Lamb was ever so pure, so spotless a Victim*".

(1 Peter 1:18,19)

Causes of the Priest's Fall and Resurrection

During a retreat, and often in the quiet hours of meditation, a priest grows discontent with his mediocrity, and wonders how he slipped into spiritual indifference. A study of the history of Peter shows that the decline can be due to number of causes.

1. Neglect of Prayer

First in time and importance in the fall of Peter and in the fall of every priest is surely a neglect of prayer. Entering Gethsemane, Our Lord said: "Pray that you may not enter into temptation" (Luke 22:40). While Our Blessed Lord was experiencing His agony in the garden, He who had no sin began to feel the penalty of sin, as if it were His own. He saw the betrayal of future Judases, the sins of heresy that would rend His Mystical Body, the militant atheism of the Communists, who (though they could not drive Him from the heavens) would drive His ambassadors from the earth. He saw the broken marriage vows, slanders, adulteries, apostasies, all the crimes that were thrust into His hands as if He Himself had committed them. While all these things were drawing the Blood from His Body, the Apostles were sleeping in the Garden. Men do not sleep when they are worried, but these slept.

Every soul can understand, at least dimly, the nature of the struggle that took place on the moonlit night in the Garden of Gethsemane. Every heart knows something about it. No one has ever come to the twenties — let alone the forties, the fifties, the sixties or the seventies of life without reflecting on himself and the world round about him, and without knowing the tension that sin causes in the soul. Faults and follies do not efface themselves from the record of memory; sleeping tablets do not silence them; psychoanalysts cannot explain them away. While the sun of youth shines bright, it may blind the eye momentarily so that the outline of sin is obscure. But then comes a time of clarity — a sick bed, a sleepless night, the open sea, a moment of quiet, the innocence in the face of a child — when our sins, like spectres or phantoms, burn their unrelenting characters of fire upon our consciences. Their full seriousness may not have been realized in the moment of passion, but conscience bides its time. It will bear its stern uncompromising witness sometime, somewhere. It will force a dread upon the soul, a dread designed to make it cast itself back again to God. Such a soul experiences indescribable agonies and tortures, yet they are only a drop of the entire ocean of humanity's guilt which overwhelmed the Savior as if they were His own in the Garden.

While the apostles slept, the enemies plotted.

Then He went back, and found them asleep; and He said to Peter, Simon, art thou sleeping? Hadst thou not strength to watch even for an hour?

(Mark 14:37)

Our Lord came to the one whom He called a Rock, but He did not address him as Peter. He spoke to him in his human character, in the weakness of his flesh. "Simon," He said. Simon was in a deep sleep, and that was the first step in the fall of Peter. He neither watched nor did he pray. But it was not that night that Peter lost the battle. His defeat had been prepared in previous weeks. What is thought of today is done tomorrow. What we are at twenty we are apt to be at forty. The only difference is that the real characteristics have become more apparent. Spiritual slackness prepares way for the wreck.

Our Blessed Lord chose His words to stress for Peter and the Church the double character of the priest — the spirit of the priest is of Christ, the flesh of the man.

The spirit is willing enough, but the flesh is weak.

(Matthew 26:41)

Peter and the other priests were placed in the world and trained to resist the forces of evil. If they were sheltered from evil, they would not need to be watchful. Faculties which are fully and frequently employed acquire the facility of the pianist's fingers. This is a law of nature. It applies equally in the spiritual world. Watchfulness against the forces of evil trains the spirit to resist. If salvation was completed by a single act, there would be no need of constant prayer. But danger is as long as life, and the Apostles and their successors find the strength to keep close to Him. One wonders if Peter did not recall the exact words Christ had used when years later he wrote:

... live wisely, and keep your senses awake to greet the hours of prayer.

(1 Peter 4:7)

St. Paul similarly insisted that watchfulness was a condition for keeping the Spirit of Christ against the inroads of the flesh:

... learn to live and move in the Spirit; then there is no danger of your giving way to the impulses of corrupt nature. The impulses of nature and the impulses of the Spirit are at war with one another; either is clean contrary to the other, and that is why you cannot do all that your will approves...... those who belong to Christ have crucified nature, with all its passions, all its impulses.

(Galatians 5:16-24)

A priest's life spent so much in public must be fortified within with prayer and vigilance:

Without Me you can do nothing.

(John 17:19)

The constant giving out of self needs replenishing from above. As the channel through which the waters of Life pass to the people, the priest must devote unceasing care and prayer to keep himself clean and holy. To recall St. Teresa of Avila, he who omits prayer needs no devil to cast him into hell; he casts himself into it. Peter slept when he was called to pray. That is the first step in the fall of a priest.

2. *Substitution of Action for Prayer*

Next in the spiritual decline of a priest comes the substitution of work for prayer. He now is too busy to pray; he has no time for meditation. He becomes so active that he loves the extraordinary. He immerses himself in endless visits, meetings, and conferences. Too busy to be on his knees, he is not too busy to swing swords, to blast out against public officials and bad politics. He does exactly what

Peter did in the Garden, when Judas and the soldiers came to arrest Our Blessed Lord (John 18:10,11):

Then Simon Peter, who had a sword, drew it, and struck the high priest's servant, cutting off his right ear; Malchus was the name of the servant. Whereupon Jesus said to Peter, Put thy sword back into its sheath. Am I not to drink that cup which My Father himself has appointed for Me?

As a swordsman, Peter was an excellent fisherman. The best he could do, in his wild use of secular means, was to hack off the right ear of the High Priest's servant. There was still a lot of Simon-nature in Peter. He presumably intended to slay Malchus, but Divine Power prevented him. The last recorded miracle of Our Blessed Lord before His Resurrection was the healing of that ear (Luke 22:51). It is possible that the healing of the wound was the reason Peter was not arrested.

Peter's action that night symbolizes all priests who avoid the obligations of their priesthood by being busy. Some lose themselves in a passion for buildings, others in organization, others in an endless round of banquets and speeches, committee meetings, and fund drives. Such are the swords which take the place of prayer. Administration, long hours in offices, theatrical presentations, social evenings, parish feasts — they are the marks of prosperity that can kill the Spirit.

In times of prosperity, the Church administers; but in times of adversity the Church shepherds. A $2 million church is no sign of a $2 million faith, nor is a poor rectory the mark of a poor priesthood. Often it is not zeal for Christ which draws the sword of action but an empty and lonely soul. Boredom can beget ceaseless unreflective activity.

Aristotle says one vice is the enemy of spirituality, the vice of doing too much. When the Christ-spirit leaves, the flesh-spirit produces the "practical priest," the "priest of action." It is then *labora,* but no *ora.*

Pius XI had an extremely appropriate comment on this spirit.

Attention must be called to the very great danger to which the priest exposes himself when, carried away by a false zeal, he neglects his own personal sanctification in order to devote himself unreservedly to the external works of his ministry, however admirable these may be. ... It will make him run the risk of losing, if not Divine grace itself, at least the inspiration and unction of the Holy Spirit which gives such wonderful power and efficacy to the external works of the apostolate.

Pius XII restressed the danger of sword-swinging in place of prayer:

We cannot refrain from expressing our worry and anxiety to those who all too often are so caught up in a whirl of external activity that they neglect the primary duty of the priest, the sanctification of self. Those who rashly assert that salvation can be brought to men by what is rightly and properly called, the "heresy of action," must be called to a more correct judgment.

3. *Giving Up Mortification: Lukewarmness*

After the priest gives up meditation and fills his day with "activism," the priest's next downward step is to give up mortification and become lukewarm.

> ... *Peter followed Him at a long distance.*
>
> (Matthew 26:58)

At the Last Supper, Peter had promised everything; quickly he begins to give up everything. When Our Blessed Lord set His face toward Jerusalem, Peter and the others "followed Him with faint hearts" (Mark 10:32), dreading the prospect of the Cross. Peter felt, it is true, the tug of the Passion of Christ, but a reluctance to become irrevocably involved made him stay far behind. As a commentator of the ninth century wrote: "Peter could not have denied the Savior if he had stayed by His side." He would have stayed by His side, if he had not drawn his sword without orders, and if above all he had known how to watch and pray with the Savior. Every priest undergoes the same experience. Neglect of watching, prayer and mortification produces an inner uneasiness about being too close to the Lord.

When this happens, the priest's heart is no longer in his work. He celebrates Mass and says his office, but he rarely makes a visit to the Blessed Sacrament. He keeps the Lord at a distance. He mounts the pulpit to plead for the missions, but gives nothing out of his own pocket. He no longer assists at a Mass after he finishes his own. He loses the taste of spiritual things. Saintly priests annoy him. He observes the days of fasting and abstinence, but cuts a lot of corners. He whispers to his conscience: "Well, if I have not done all the good that I could, at least I did no harm."

Instead of contemplating the evil of which he has been guilty, he glories in the sins he avoids; he compares himself not with those who are better, but with those who are worse. He gives up spiritual reading, substitutes the Book of the Month for the Book of Revelation. His sermons are unprepared. They are for the most part critical and complaining. All he achieves is to project his own mediocrity to others. His soul is empty. At most, it is confusedly aware that an ever increasing distance separates it from Our Lord. At night, when he awakens, the words of the Master ring in his ears:

If any man has a mind to come My way, let him renounce self, and take up his cross, and follow Me.

(Matthew 16:24)

Though Peter is following the Lord, he is actually walking toward a pit into which he will fall. He who does not advance in perfection, falls into imperfection. An untended garden becomes full of weeds. Things do not remain the same by being left alone. White fences do not stay white; they gradually become gray, then black. There are no plains in the spiritual life. We go up hill, or we go down. The moment we cease to row against the stream, the current carries us down the river.

What God said through Isaiah of His people, He may also say of the priests who follow behind:

This friend, that I love well, had a vineyard in a corner of his ground, all fruitfulness. He fenced it in, and cleared it of stones, and planted a choice vine there; built a tower too, in the middle, and set up a winepress in it, and it bore wild grapes instead.... I call upon you to give award between my vineyard and Me. What more could I have done for it? What say you of the wild grapes it bore, instead of the grapes I looked for? Let me tell you, then, what I mean to do to this vineyard of Mine. I mean to rob it of its hedge, so that all can plunder it, to break down its wall, so that it will be trodden under foot. I mean to make waste-land of it; no more pruning and digging; only briars and thorns will grow there, and I will forbid the clouds to water it.

(Isaiah 5:1-7)

The parable represents those who have consecrated themselves to the service of God. They are fenced in with sacerdotal graces, yet they end up neither hot nor cold, so that God would vomit them out of His mouth (Revelation 3:16). God takes away the talent from the slothful servant and gives it to the diligent one (Matthew 25:29).

4. *Satisfaction of Creature Wants, Emotions and Comforts*

Peter first gave up prayer, then action, then mortification. When the moment of crisis comes, he is making himself comfortable by a fire, at first standing and then sitting.

Peter followed at a long distance, right into the high priest's palace, and there sat down with the servants by the fire, to warm himself.

(Mark 14:54)

What a spiritual biography! Peter was the last man who should have followed the Lord at a distance. His seniority and his position of leadership both carried additional responsibilities. But when a man has little spiritual satisfaction within, when the tide of his devotion has ebbed, he has to find some compensation for his inner

177

loneliness. For Peter, this took the form of warming himself by a fire and of chatting with the servant girls. To compensate for internal poverty, one seeks to be rich on the outside. It was only after Adam and Eve had by sin lost the inner effulgence of grace that they became conscious of the fact that they were naked. They felt the need for clothes to cover their newfound shame; previously, their bodies had glowed with a mantle of charity woven by the fingers of God. It is almost universally true that excessive external display betrays an inner poverty and nakedness of soul.

To return to Simon Peter. It was the moment of crisis, and here he was making himself at home in an equivocal position. The Gospel narrative underscores the ironic contrasts. St. John (18:18) observes that it was cold, that Peter felt the need to warm himself by the fire. Peter by placing himself a distance from the Sun of Righteousness felt cold. His behavior was that which characterizes the bourgeois priest: comfortable, while others suffer; an armchair strategist on the missions, but himself doing nothing about them. Peter was now like the pastor who sits by his fire on Saturday while his curates hear confessions, instruct converts, take the sick calls. The warm glow of the fire in that courtyard was a "far better parish" to Simon than the garden of Gethsemane.

His love of luxury found him bad company. The warm fires of prosperity have overthrown many, who through want and troubles, had stood erect in grace. The outcome is that, withdrawn from the Lord, Simon encounters an occasion of sin. Lacking time for meditation, he yet has time for conversation. Though Jesus was at a distance, a girl was near. The lips of Peter which had but tasted the Eucharistic Banquet of Life already speak a lie. A short time ago, he was ready to die with Christ; now, without Him, he lacks the nerve to withstand a woman's curiosity. He had then asserted:

Thou art the Christ, the Son of God,

(John 6:70)

178

Now, juggling his theology, he protests like a coward:

I know nothing of the man.

(Matthew 26:72)

If Peter had stayed with Christ, no questioner could have wrung that shameful ambiguity from him. The subtlety of Satan creeps into the friendships of those who lack spirituality, causing them to hurt their friends more deeply than any enemy could. To sit by the fires of the ungodly may comfort the body, but it wrecks the Christ-principle within. Satan did not come to Peter *"roaring like a lion"* (1 Peter 5:8), but as a frivolous girl indulging her curiosity. This was the moment in which the automatic connection between watching and praying was demonstrated in the life of Peter, as it is at some unanticipated moment in every life. The man who fails to watch, cannot expect an answer to prayer. Admittedly, God has the power to save whoever is falling, lest his bones be broken; but to ask for safety without watching is to *"put the Lord thy God to the proof"* (Matthew 4:7). God's special protection for His friends cannot be presumed upon when we have become indifferent to His friendship. Jonah chafed against God's word when he was told to go to Nineveh and preach penance; instead, he set his heart on Tarshish and found a ship standing ready to take him away from his mission (Jonah 1:3). Once the spirit of a priest grows cold, the enemies of Christ, the world, the flesh and the devil, quickly find a way to provide the "fire," the comfort and the company.

For every priest there is a lesson in the Gospel's observation that the priest who follows a long distance from Our Lord calls Him "a man." It is as if he said: "I was never meant for that kind of life; I never had a vocation." He similarly gets angry when anyone tells him that he is not Christlike. In him, as in Peter, the tendency is strong to revert to the Old Adam nature. One's mind conjures up Simon in his early days as a fisherman. One can almost hear the picturesque curses whenever his nets got snarled. While he lived in the intimate companionship of Our Blessed Lord, such words would not so much as occur to him; yet in a few hours he has a throwback.

The curses pour from him, and this in the face of a young woman. Others have a better understanding of what the priest ought to do, than he himself has. The maid servant could tell Peter he was supposed to be with the Galilean. Even those whose office is (like Martha's) to be busy with profane things, are often scandalized at the priest's failure to recognize that his office is to be with Christ.

The summons to be God's ambassador is no guarantee against weakness. Moses became arrogant when God chose him to lead His people, and he struck the rock to draw water from it (Numbers 20:7-12). David, the tenderest of all hearts, is betrayed into committing murder (2 Kings 11:14-27 [2 Samuel 11:14 – 27, RSV]). Solomon, the wisest of all intellects, stoops to the folly of idolatry (3 Kings 11:4 [1 Kings 11:4, RSV]). Finally, when Peter had completed the triple denial, even nature protested. The first thing Our Lord did was to awaken Peter's memory, and He did it by the crowing of the cock. In that dark hour, when Peter had even forgotten to declare the Divinity of his Master, had forgotten his loyalty and his debtedness to the One Who called him to be the rock, one might have expected a lightning bolt, a thunderclap, to proclaim the enormity of the lapse. Christ settled for a sound Peter had heard a thousand times. A familiar sound, but with a new meaning, because it was the fulfillment of the Master's warning.

Nature is on God's side, not ours. It has in faith to Him... fickleness to me, traitorous trueness, and... loyal deceit ... (Francis Thompson, *The Hound of Heaven*)

The fall of the priest is completed by these steps: neglect of prayer, withdrawal to a distance from the Eucharistic Lord, dedication to a comfortable existence, negligence concerning occasions of sin; and finally, the substitution of a creature for the Christ.

✠ J.M.J. ✠

~ *11* ~

The Return to Divine Favor

Horrible as is this condition, it is not necessarily final. When Our Blessed Lord was led from the court, His face covered with spittle, He "turned and looked at Peter" (Luke 22:61). The Master is bound, is insulted, is abandoned, is rejected. Yet He does not give up. He turns and looks at Peter. With boundless pity His eye seeks out the one who had just failed Him. He spoke no word. He just looked! But for Peter, what a refreshment of memory, what an awakening of love! Peter might deny the "man," but God would still love the man, Peter! The very fact that the Lord had to turn to look on Peter meant that Peter's back had been turned on the Lord. The wounded stag was seeking the thicket to bleed alone, but the Lord came to Peter's wounded heart to draw out the arrow.

And Peter went out, and wept bitterly.

(Luke 22:62)

Peter was filled with repentance, as Judas in a few hours would be filled with remorse. Peter's sorrow was caused by the thought of sin itself or the wounding of the Person of God. Repentance is not concerned with consequences. This is what distinguishes it from remorse, which is inspired principally by fear of unpleasant consequences. The same mercy extended to the one who denied Him would be extended to those who would nail Him to the Cross, and to the penitent thief who would ask for forgiveness. Peter did not actually deny that Christ was the Son of God. He denied that he knew "the man," that he was one of His disciples. He did not abjure his faith. But he sinned. He failed the Master. And yet the Son of God chose Peter, who knew sin, rather than the beloved John as the Rock upon which to build His Church, that sinners and the weak might never have excuse to despair.

The Love of Christ for His Priests

And the Lord turned, and looked at Peter....

(Luke 22:61)

The incident probably occurred as Our Blessed Lord, after interrogation by Caiaphas, was being led to the Sanhedrin. Our Divine Lord may even have heard Peter raise his well-known voice, have heard the oaths and curses assuring the bystanders that he did not know Jesus of Nazareth. Our Lord did not say: "I told you so." No burning words of condemnation passed His lips. Just one glance, a single look of wounded love. Such is the mercy of Our Lord when we are unfaithful and disloyal to Him! He seeks to win us back through added privilege and multiplied mercy! It is not only the fevered, the paralyzed and the lepers who know the tender compassion in the eyes of the Son Incarnate; it is above all, priests and sinners. It is not just the glance of Christ that brings repentance; it is also our response. The sun that shines so warmly both softens wax and hardens mud. The Divine Mercy calling the fallen hardens them to hell, or softens them to heaven.

In the synagogue at Capharnaum, Our Blessed Lord cast blazing eyes of anger on His baffled enemies as He wrought a miracle. With His Divine knowledge He knew that they were not willing to believe, would not be convinced were He to rise a thousand times from the dead. But Peter's attitude was different. One look of sorrowful reproach brought sorrow to his soul. The rich man who came to Our Lord was not yet prepared to go the whole way, though he was a sincere seeker after God. The Gospel tells us:

Then Jesus fastened His eyes on him, and conceived a love for him.

(Mark 10:21)

The centurion recognized the Divine Majesty on the Cross and said:

No doubt but this was the Son of God.

(Mark 15:39)

It is the same Divinity which was recalled to Peter when Jesus turned and looked at him. John, who was privileged to look so often on that dear Face, was haunted by It on the Isle of Patmos after the lapse of half a century. He spoke of how all the earth would wither away as Christ would come in judgment:

And now I saw a great throne, all white, and One sitting on it, at Whose glance earth and heaven vanished, and were found no more.

(Revelation 20:11)

That Face, too, would be the reward of all who would love Him and return to Him as Peter did:

... God's throne (which is the Lamb's throne) will be there, with his servants to worship Him, and to see his Face....

(Revelation 22:3,4)

Like Peter, every priest at one time or another gets out of step with Christ, follows behind, communes with worldly company and secular fires. Christ, nevertheless, treats him as He treated Peter. He constantly turns to look upon him. It was not Peter who thought of turning, but the Lord. Peter, because he was guilty, would by preference have looked anywhere else, but the Lord looked at him. This is the essential point for every follower of Christ to keep in mind when he sins — *the Lord turns first.*

No man understands wrong fully until he sees it in the light of the Face of Christ. He may feel mortified at the fool he made of himself, but he will sorrow only when he sees the Beloved crucified. The man who says, "I am so stupid" instead of "Lord, be merciful to me a sinner" is still far from rebirth.

What a lesson of tenderness is revealed by Our Lord's refusal to blast Peter! At such a moment, when one is teetering on the tightrope, a breath or a glance makes all the difference. It starts the return to God instead of plunging into the abyss of evil. As Christina G. Rossetti wrote:

O Jesu, gone so far apart
Only my heart can follow Thee,
That look which pierced St. Peter's heart
Turn now on me.

Thou who dost search me through and through
And mark the crooked ways I went,
Look on me, Lord, and make me too
Thy penitent.

One look at Divinity convinces us of sin. Peter the denier, under the eye of the Son of God, became at once Peter the penitent. That one look in which Divinity searches the soul, is the beginning of personal responsibility to God. We do not sin against abstractions or even against Commandments only; as persons, we sin against a Person. The awfulness of sin is not exhausted in the breaking of a Commandment; it embraces the re-crucifying of Christ. That is why the ultimate sorrow is related to the Crucifix, where each of us can read his autobiography. We see our pride in the Crown of Thorns; our lust and carnality in the nails; our forgetfulness of God in the pierced Feet, and our thievery in the riven Hands. Penitence is to hold ourselves up in God's infinite Light and let Him shine our darkness away.

The difference between the sinner and saint is that one persists in sin, while the other weeps bitterly. The Greek word translated as "weeping" in the Gospel is one which implies a long and continued sorrow. Those who cannot find time to mourn for their sins also lack time to mend. The man gripped by remorse often takes to drink to dull his conscience. It is often not love of liquor, but hatred of something else, that makes a drunkard. The remorse of Judas led not to a striking of the breast in a Mea Culpa, but to the taking of a life.

He had no heart to pray. Neither did he seek God's face to sue for mercy. But Peter sorrowed. He was humbled, not hardened.

Once the tears wash the eyes, the spiritual vision becomes clearer; that is why tears are often associated with the true understanding of sin. The tears in Peter's eyes were a rainbow of hope after a black storm. In them shone the entire spectrum of the radiant forgiveness of Christ's glance. Peter's memory of that life restoring glance was surely still in his mind when he wrote in his first Epistle:

You had been like sheep going astray; now, you have been brought back to Him, your Shepherd, who keeps watch over your souls.

(1 Peter 2:25)

Christ still looks on us priests with sad but hope-filled eyes. He bids each of us, when the Simon is dominant, to resurrect our Peter vocation. No priest ever reaches a stage when "it is all up." David cried out in his misery and was heard. Peter, drowning after an act of rashness, was saved. When Thomas doubted, he was offered a pierced Heart to restore his faith. The Prodigal Son rose from swine and husks to a banquet in the Father's house.

Did priests but realize Infinite Love has need to communicate itself! One day a saintly soul prostrate before Jesus in the Tabernacle asked: "How dost Thou wish that I should call Thee?" And He replied: "Mercy." *If we had never sinned, we never could call Jesus our Savior.*

A religious accorded special revelations by the Sacred Heart declared that He spoke these words: "And now lastly I address Myself to My own consecrated ones, that they may make Me known to sinners and to the world. "Many as yet are unable to understand what My true feelings are. They treat Me as One from Whom they live apart, know only slightly, and in Whom they have little confidence. Let them re-enkindle their faith and their love trustfully in My intimacy and love."

All our Priestly Powers over Souls depend on our Love of our Lord

The next lesson Our Lord taught Peter was that love must constitute the basis of the pastoral office. It was the week after the Resurrection, and the Apostles were assembled by the Sea of Tiberias. Simon Peter, the established and accepted leader, said to Thomas, Nathaniel, James, John and two other disciples:

I am going out fishing.

(John 21:3)

The word Peter used implied a progressive or habitually repeated action. Was Peter telling them that he was going permanently to his fishing business? It seems hard to imagine, and yet it is implied in the tense. In addition, Peter's character for all its good points, was vacillating and impetuous. He it was who had told Our Lord he would not deny Him, only to insist that he knew not the man. Leave your boats behind you, the Lord told Peter and the others, henceforth you will be fishers of men (Luke 5:10). And here they are back at their old job.

On the Sea of Tiberias, night was the best time to fish. That night, nevertheless, they caught nothing. Work performed at the impulse of our own will, is futile. Then day broke and the morning light revealed the Risen Savior standing by the sea. No, they answered His question, they had caught nothing. Cast the net on the right side, He directed them; and there followed the catch of a multitude of fishes. Both Peter and John reacted characteristically.

As John was first to reach the empty tomb on Easter morn, so Peter was first to enter it; as John was first to believe that Christ was risen, so Peter was first to greet the Risen Christ; as John was first to see the Lord from the boat, so Peter was first to rush to the Lord, plunging into the sea in his enthusiasm.

Naked as he was in the boat, he cast a coat about him, forgot personal comfort, abandoned human companionship, and eagerly swam the hundred yards to the Master. John had the greater spiritual discernment, Peter the quicker action. It was John who leaned on the Master's breast the night of the Last Supper; he, too, was nearest the Cross, and to his care the Savior committed His mother; so now he was the first to recognize the Risen Savior on the shore. Once before, when Christ had walked on the waves toward the ship, Peter could not wait for the Master to come to him, but asked the Master bid him come upon the water. Now he swam to shore after girding himself out of reverence for his Savior.

The other six remained in the boat. When they came to shore, they saw fire, a fish laid on it, and some bread, which the compassionate Savior had prepared for them. The Son of God was preparing a meal for His poor fishermen; it must have reminded them of the bread and fishes He had multiplied when He had proclaimed Himself the Bread of Life. After they had dragged the net ashore and counted the one hundred and fifty-three fish they had caught, they were well convinced that it was the Lord. Nor did the symbolic significance escape them. Having called them to be fishers of men, He was offering a concrete anticipation of the size of the catch which would ultimately be drawn into the bark of Peter.

Christ had been pointed out by John the Baptist on the bank of the Jordan, at the start of His Public Life, as the "Lamb of God" (John 1:29); now that He was about to leave this earth, He applied the same title to those who would believe in Him. He who had called Himself the Good Shepherd appointed others also to be shepherds. They had just ended the meal He had Himself prepared for them on the seashore. As earlier He had given the Eucharist after the supper, and the power to forgive sins after He had eaten with them; so now, after partaking of bread and fish, He turned to the one who had denied Him three times, and demanded a triple affirmation of love. The confession of love must precede the bestowing of authority, for authority without love is tyranny: "Simon, son of John, dost thou care for Me more than these others?" (John 21:15).

One may properly wonder if the morning fire Our Lord had kindled reminded Peter of another fire some ten days before, when he denied the Master. Peter had denied by a fire; he was restored by a fire. Such is the scene of the conversation in which Christ commissions Peter to feed the lambs and the sheep.

Authority Inseparable from Love

Authority must never be without love. Love of Our Lord precedes any fruitful service in His Name. Such is the lesson which Christ once more inculcates as he reinstates Peter to the Apostolic office, from which he had fallen. Once again He addresses him as Simon, reminding him of the critical moments when Christ had first given him a new name and new authority (Matthew 16:17), and when He had warned him of his impending fall while promising restoration through His love (Luke 22:31). Though authority in the Church is based on love, love in its turn is inseparable from obedience:

> *If you have any love for Me, you must keep the commandments which I give you.*

> (John 14:15)

The Gospel account of Christ's triple question to Peter introduces a curious detail. The Greek text uses two different words, both of which are translated into English as "love." The first of these words is *agapao*, a word which implies a knowledge of the preciousness of the one who is loved. It is the word John uses to express God's love for fallen man, whom He so loved "that he gave his only-begotten Son, that those who believe in Him may not perish" (3:16). The other Greek word is *phileo*, indicating the response of the human spirit to anything that appears as pleasurable, a love implying some kind of friendship.

Loving and Liking

The first two times that Christ asks Peter to proclaim his love for Him, He uses the word *agapao*, whereas the third and final question

188

contains the word *phileo*. But each time Peter in his answer uses the same word, the word *phileo*. In the New Testament, it is the less frequently used word to describe love. *Agapao,* implying an awakened and higher sense of value, occurs about 320 times; *phileo*, indicating a love of friendship and mutual attraction, only 45 times. To recreate the scene in the terms and form of a playwright might produce a result something like this:

CHRIST: Simon, son of John, do you love Me more than do these others, with a Divine, sacrificial, victim-like and self-surrendering love?

PETER: You know, Lord, that I love You with a deep, human, instinctive, personal affection, as my closest friend.

CHRIST: Simon, son of John, do you love Me more than do these others, with a divine, sacrificial, victim-like and self-surrendering love?

PETER: I have already told You, Master. You know that I love You, with a deep, human, instinctive, personal affection, as my closest friend.

CHRIST: Simon, son of John, do you love Me, with a human, instinctive, deep, personal affection, as a very close friend?

PETER: How often, Lord, must I repeat my answer? For the third time, I love You with the human, instinctive, deep, personal affection one has for one's closest friend.

Peter's answer shows that he was hurt. He was grievously hurt. Yet the reason is not quite as simple as might appear on the surface. It was not just the thrice-repeated question that upset him. It was rather that the change from *agapao to phileo* indicated a scaling down of Our Lord's demands. He was no longer calling for the victim-kind of love for which He had first asked. It is as if Our Lord were putting His hands under that poor, weak, fragile love of Peter, just as He in fact starts with our poor, weak, human love as a beginning of a rich apostolate. The Lord asked for a love of devotion, and all He got was a love of emotion. But even that He does not reject. It is not enough, He says, but it is enough to start.

During the Public Life, when Our Blessed Lord had told Peter that he was a rock upon which He would build His Church, He prophesied also that He Himself would be crucified and would rise again. Peter then tempted Him away from the Cross. In reparation for that temptation which Our Lord called Satanic, He now notified Peter that He was not only commissioning Him with full authority to rule over His lambs and sheep, but that He was arranging for him yet another parallel with Himself, that Peter too would die upon the cross. "You will have a cross like that to which they nailed Me," He told Him in effect, "the cross you would have denied me and thus precluded My glory. Now you must learn what it really means to love. My love is a vestibule to death. Because I loved you, they killed Me; for your love of Me, they will kill you. I once said that the Good Shepherd gives His life for His sheep; now you are My shepherd in My place; you will receive the same reward for your labors as I have received — crossbeams, nails, and then ... life eternal."

> *Believe me when I tell thee this;*
> *As a young man, thou wouldst gird*
> *thyself and walk where thou hadst the will to go,*
> *But when thou hast grown old,*
> *Thou wilt stretch out thy hands,*
> *And another shall gird thee, and carry thee*
> *where thou goest, not of thy own will.*

(John 21: 18)

Impulsive and self-willed in the days of his youth, Peter would in his old age glorify the Master by a death on the cross. From the day of Pentecost, the Spirit made Peter's decisions. He was led where he would not go. He had to leave the Holy City, where imprisonment and the sword awaited him. Next, his Divine Master directed him to Samaria, to the house of the Gentile, Cornelius; then to Rome, the new Babylon, where he was strengthened by the strangers of the Dispersion whom Paul had brought into the fold; finally, he was led

190

to a cross to die a martyr's death on the hill of the Vatican. At his own request, he was crucified with his head downwards, deeming it unworthy to die like the Master. Inasmuch as he was the rock, it was fitting that he himself be laid in the earth as an impregnable foundation of the Church.

The man who had tempted the Lord away from the Cross was the first apostle to embrace it himself. His acceptance of the cross redounded to his Savior's glory more than all the zeal and impetuosity of his youth. When Peter did not yet understand that the cross was the means of redemption from sin, he offered his own death rather than that of the Master, asserting that even if all the others failed to defend Him, he would stand alone to protect Him. But after the illumination of Pentecost, he saw that it was the Cross of Calvary that gave meaning to the cross he would embrace. Toward the end of his life, when the cross was already in clear view ahead of him, Peter would write:

> *I am assured, by what our Lord Jesus Christ has made known to me, that I must fold my tent before long. And I will see to it that, when I am gone, you shall always be able to remember what I have been saying. We were not crediting fables of man's invention, when we preached to you about the power of our Lord Jesus Christ, and about His coming; we had been eye-witnesses of His exaltation.*

(2 Peter 1: 14-16)

Humans seek the friendship of those who are above them in character and in power, but Our Lord condescends to ask our love. He will accept it even when it has little capacity for sacrifice and surrender. The trial of love is ultimately between the soul and Christ. When a priest is ordained, the bishop asks him searching questions; but the real examination is in the heart, and the interrogator is the ever-present and ever living Savior. It is not recorded that Peter never again went fishing, but it is certain that all of his life he retained a live sense of the difference in his priesthood, between the joy of knowing the Lord and the sadness of falling away from Him.

Love alone can make easy the pastoral task of feeding lambs and sheep. Love it was that turned the seven years of Jacob's hard bondage for Rachel into so many pleasant days. Even the falls can be incorporated into sanctity. Peter is more glorious in heaven for his recovery, as Paul is more glorious for his renewed friendship for Mark after they quarreled. The wrath of Moses, the lying of Abraham, the drunkenness of Noah, all are swept away in the great and final affirmation of love.

Our Lord often complains in the Scriptures. He expresses disappointment and surprise at the conduct of some of His followers. Yet, like Peter, He finds us on some shore, and with quick forgiveness asks us again to love.

As the physician feels his patient's pulse to judge his heart, so Our Lord tests the pulse of each priest's soul by his love. The test can sometimes be wounding, but that is because our sins have been wounds to Him. There is no mention of Our Lord having ever applied this test to anyone before His Passion and Death, of His having challenged an individual with the question if he loved Him. Now He acted with the assurance of one who has earned a claim on man's affection, a claim that the sinner's heart cannot resist.

After each affirmation of love, Our Blessed Lord committed Peter to apostolate and to service. These are the elements which keep love from degenerating into an indulgence of sentiment. He sent Mary Magdalen from the tomb to make an announcement to Peter, and He sent Peter from his confession to do the work of the Church. We may not separate ourselves from others even in the moment of the consciousness of our greatest self-distrust. The lesson is one for all priests: it was to Peter, in spite of his notorious betrayal, that Our Blessed Lord gave the keys of the Church.

Sympathy is the way to self-knowledge. Our own penitence deepens as we know our brother's sins. Every brother's fall reminds us of our need of vigilance. Nothing deepens our love for Christ like the larger knowledge of His grace which we gain as we see souls saved by Him. Peter could bear the better with the inadequacies of the flock, because of his recognition of himself as a sinful brother. St. Thomas Aquinas says that God sometimes permits people to sin in order to take them out of their pride, to awaken in them a sympathetic love for others.

The decision was and is a very personal one. There are no multitudes in the eyes of God. Just as He singled out from the crowd the woman who touched the hem of His garment (Luke 8: 43,44), so He singled out Peter. He had acted similarly before: "Adam; Where art thou?" (Genesis 3:9); "Abraham, Abraham" (Genesis 22: 1); "Samuel, Samuel" (1 Kings 3:10 [1 Samuel 3:10, RSV]); "Martha, Martha" (Luke 10:41); "Saul, Saul'; (Acts 9:4); "Simon, Son of John" (John 21: 15).

Three Forms of Love

The measure of our priesthood is the level of our love. Love exists in three forms: unawakened, penitent, and believing. The first stage includes very little love of Christ, because of an excessive love of the world; the second kind is not so much love, as "*fear which has torment,*" because of sin; the third is the love that is "*poured out in our hearts by the Holy Spirit, Whom we have received*" (Romans 5:5). The unawakened man performs acts of obedience, but they are more apparent than real. The penitent's obedience is that of a slave. But in the true lover, obedience is filial. It produces prayer and holiness.

Rising above the multitudinous cares of the priest as pastor, his concern over schools, convents, finances, buildings and administration, the priest as another Christ must ultimately get back to the sublime truth that the one reality is the soul. For this does he sanctify himself. Pere Jean-Baptiste Lacordaire, in *Letters to Young Men*, wrote:

I am of your opinion about the mountains, the sea and the forest; they are the three great things in nature, and have many analogies, especially the sea and forest. I am as fond as yourself of them; but as old age creeps on, nature takes less hold upon us, and we feel the beauty of the saying of the Marquis de Vauvenargues, "Sooner or later, we enjoy only souls." This is why we can always love and be loved. Old age withers the body but to the soul that is not corrupted it gives a new youth. And the moment of death is that of the blossoming of our minds.

When love goes out of our heart, we hate the things we are obliged to do, or at least we cover up our deep feelings with the metallic ring of formalism. Our sermons become scoldings. Lost sheep become interruptions to our leisure. To minister at the altar of love with an unloving heart; to belong to a profession of self-sacrificing love, while seeking our own comfort; to offer but hollow words of love to suffering souls: these things bring their own punishment.

Even if one has not yet reached the level of love which permits performance of the duties of the apostolate without disturbing one's interior happiness, one can always follow the advice of St. Francis de Sales:

If you cannot pray like a soul enjoying the gift of contemplation, you can at least make a spiritual reading and reflect on it; if not strong enough to fast, you may at least deprive yourself of a delicate morsel; if you cannot quit the world, you may at least guard against its spirit; if you cannot love God with a pure love, you may love Him at least out of gratitude; if you do not experience a lively sorrow for your sins, you can try to get it by asking it of God; you cannot bestow many alms, but you can give at least a drink of water; you cannot bear great insults, but you may bear at least a little reproach without murmuring; to be despised is beyond what you can endure, but you may bear with that little coldness manifested by your neighbor in his behavior toward you; the sacrifice of your life is not required of you, but you can put up with some inconvenience and preserve patience under some little trying circumstance.

Peter, restored, is close to a fire. That other fire at which he denied Christ is one the world made; but this fire Christ prepared. The enthusiasm, the effort, the passion lighted by the fires of the world leave but ashes and dust. Not so, however, when enkindled by Him Who came to cast fire upon the earth (Luke 12: 49).

~ 12 ~

Melchizedek and Bread

Why are we called priests "in the line of Melchizedek"? Why are we not priests in the line of Aaron, to whom the priesthood belonged in the Old Testament? The Epistle to the Hebrews (7:11) indicates the reason, namely, that the Levitical priesthood did not represent the perfection of the priesthood. Now, there could be no need for a fresh priest to arise, accredited with Melchizedek's priesthood, not with Aaron's, if the Levitical priesthood had brought fulfillment."

The reasons for the inadequacy of the Levitical priesthood were many.

1. The priesthood of Aaron was carnal, temporal, successive and perishing. The priesthood of Melchizedek, as symbolic of that of Christ, is eternal. The Levitical priests were personally unclean, in the liturgical sense of the word. They had to offer sacrifices for their sins, and death for each of them put an end to his ministrations.

But Melchizedek is eternal. This aspect of his priesthood is expressed in symbolic terms in the Bible:

No name of father or mother, no pedigree, no date of birth or of death; there he stands, eternally, a priest, the true figure of the Son of God.

(Hebrews 7:3)

The omission of any reference to Melchizedek's ancestry, birth or death, is the Holy Spirit's way of presenting him as the type of Our Lord.

Summarizing the difference between the two priesthoods, Scripture continues:

Of those other priests there was a succession since death denied them permanence; whereas Jesus continues forever, and His Priestly office is unchanging; that is why He can give eternal salvation to those who through Him make their way to God; He lives on still to make intercession on our behalf.

(Hebrews 7:23-25)

2. A second reason is that Our Lord combines within Himself both Kingship and Priesthood, and this was true also of Melchizedek.

Melchizedek, too, was there, the king of Salem. And he, priest as he was of the most high God...

(Genesis 14: 18)

Melchizedek was in his person king and priest, thereby foreshadowing the adorable Lord, in whom justice and peace would kiss each other (Psalm 84:10). Our Lord would not have peace without justice; hence He made "peace with them through His Blood, shed on the cross" (Colossians 1:20).

3. The "greatness" of Melchizedek was a foretelling of the greatness of Christ. Abraham acknowledged that Melchizedek was greater than he was, by paying him tribute:

To him, Abraham gave tithes of all he had won.

(Genesis 14:20)

This the Epistle to the Hebrews (7:4-8) applies to Our Lord:

Consider how great a man was this, to whom the patriarch Abraham himself gave a tenth part of his chosen spoil. The descendants of Levi, when the priesthood is conferred on them, are allowed by the provisions of the law to take tithes from God's people, although these, like themselves, come from the privileged stock of Abraham; after all, they are their brothers; here is one who owns no common descent with them, taking tithes from Abraham himself. He blesses him, too, blesses the man to whom the promises have been made; and it is beyond all question that blessings are only given by what is greater in dignity to what is less. In the one case, the priests who receive tithe are only mortal men; in the other, it is a priest (so the record tells us) who lives on.

4. The priesthood of Melchizedek was sacramental and unbloody, not the offering of bullocks and goats.

And he, priest as he was of the most high God brought out bread and wine with him...

(Genesis 14: 18)

Each day in Mass we mention the sacrifice of Melchizedek as *sanctum sacrificium immaculatam hostiam*. The sacrifice was a peaceful one, offered after Abraham had won the war against the four kings.

5. Our Lord Himself was of an ancestry distinct from that of the Levitical priesthood. He belonged to the tribe of Judah; not, like Aaron's sons, to the tribe of Levi. His line was different, not only because He is eternal, but also because, as the Epistle to the Hebrews (7: 14-18) insists, His temporal generation was different:

Our Lord took His origin from Juda, that is certain, and Moses in speaking of this tribe, said nothing about priests. And something further becomes evident, when a fresh priest arises to fulfill the type of Melchizedek, appointed, not to obey the law, with its outward observances, but in the power of an unending life; (Thou art a priest in the line of Melchizedek, God says of him, forever).

The historical setting of the meeting between Abraham and Melchizedek is significant. All we know about Melchizedek is found in brief passages in Genesis (14: 18-20) and Psalm 109, and in the Epistle to the Hebrews (5:6-10; 6:20; 7:17,21). Genesis reports that while Lot, Abraham's nephew, was living in Sodom, the city was attacked and taken by the armies of four powerful kings. It is the first war recorded in the Bible. In addition to capturing the king of Sodom, they seized Lot and his family. When Abraham learned of Lot's misadventure, he mustered a small army of 318 servants and gained a mighty victory. He not only recovered the spoils seized by the invaders, but he also freed Lot and his family.

Abraham had a right to everything gained by his victory. Would he avail himself of his right, ignoring the misfortune of others? Knowing that Abraham might have been tempted to have enriched himself materially, God sent help in the person of Melchizedek.

Melchizedek, too, was there, the king of Salem. And he, priest as he was of the most high God, brought out bread and, vine with him, and gave him this benediction, On Abram be the blessing of the most high God, Maker of heaven and earth, and blessed be that most high God, Whose protection has brought thy enemies into thy power.

(Genesis 14: 18 – 20)

God won the victory for Abraham. The spoils therefore belonged not really to Abraham but to God, who in addition now promised Abraham an even greater reward. The help was accepted, and Abraham gave his tithe to the priest.

Later, when the king of Sodom came and told Abraham to keep the spoils for himself, Abraham was able to answer:

By this hand, which I lift up to the Lord God, the Prince of heaven and earth, I will take nothing of thine, though it were but a thread from the woof or the strap of a shoe. Never shalt thou say, Abram got his wealth from me.

(Genesis 14:22,23)

What noble words! He would keep nothing for himself. Because he had not sought wealth, as Solomon did not pray for it, he was given a special reward:

Have no fear, Abram, I am to protect thee.

(Genesis 15: 1)

Thus does the heavenly High Priest bless those who do not seek the material spoils of earth.

We then are priests according to the line of Melchizedek. When the Levitical priesthood proved to be inadequate in the days of Eli and his sons (1 Kings 1:4,5; 2:12-17,22 [1 Samuel 3;2:12-17,22, RSV]), God said:

Afterwards, I will find Myself a priest that shall be a faithful interpreter of my mind and will.

(1 Kings 2:35 [1 Samuel 2:35, RSV])

The fulfillment is found in Christ, whose priests we are:

So it is with Christ. He did not raise Himself to the dignity of the high priesthood; it was God that raised Him to it, when He said, Thou art My Son, I have begotten thee this day, and so, elsewhere, Thou art a priest forever, in the line of Melchizedek.

(Hebrews 5:5,6)

Since Melchizedek offered bread and wine, it is fitting to look for the Eucharistic Bread anticipated in the Old Testament.

Bread of Presence

God has always been present to His Church in a way different from His presence elsewhere. The Church of the Old Testament already enjoyed a prototype, show or symbol of the Eucharistic Presence. The ancient sanctuary contained two items of particular significance: the lampstand, and the bread of presence. St. John applies both to Christ, the Light of the World (John 8:12) and the Bread of Life (John 6).

The Old Testament

The Epistle to the Hebrews (9:2) records that "there was an outer tabernacle, which contained the lampstand and the table and the loaves set out before God; sanctuary was the name given to this." The so-called table of the show-bread was important not so much for the table itself, as for the bread placed upon it. It was the Bread of Presence, literally "Bread of the Face." It was to this Bread of Presence that Christ referred in Matthew (12:4) as "the loaves set out there before the Lord." The bread was meant as a memorial placed continually in God's presence.

The bread is to be a token-sacrifice to the Lord.

(Leviticus 24:7)

Each Saturday a fresh supply of bread was substituted for the old, twelve loaves — one for each of the twelve tribes. All were thus represented, little Benjamin no less than royal Judah, Dan as well as the priestly Levi, and just as much for one tribe as for another. No part of God's family was forgotten. Each was fully represented, and they were always before Him.

The table is to hold the loaves of bread which are to be set out continually in My Presence.

(Exodus 25:30)

The bread of the Old Testament was thus the presence of the people before the Lord, but the Bread of the New Testament is the Presence of the Lord before the people. In the Old Testament there was never a moment when they were out of His sight. Bread was a continuous reminder to Him of His covenant relation to them, and of His promises to them of a Savior and Redeemer. As the twelve tribes were made one in His Presence, so also, His ecclesia, His Church, so by "the one bread is made one body, though we are many in number; the same bread is shared by all" (1 Corinthians 10:17).

The Bread of Presence was before His Face; that is why it was called the continual bread.

...keep hallowed loaves set forth continually....

(2 Paralipomena 2:4 [2 Chronicles 2:4, RSV])

...the bread set forth there as always...

(Numbers 4:7)

The bread was to be made of the finest flour and upon each row incense was placed to indicate that the offering was a sacrifice to the Lord.

Put grains of fine incense upon them; the bread is to be a token sacrifice to the Lord.

(Leviticus 24:7)

Thus was prefigured the union of the sacrament and sacrifice under the New Law.

Even a "sanctuary lamp" was provided — not that the Bread was the substance of the Body and Blood of Christ, but only a shadow, an anticipation.

Never must the altar be empty of this perpetual fire.

(Leviticus 6:13)

From that day to this, a lamp announces the Presence.

The Holiness of The Sanctuary

For the Christian who lives in the realm of grace, the demands of the holiness of God are not less demanding than they were for the Jew under the Old Testament. If those who rebelled in the desert did not escape judgment, much less shall we who are privileged to live in the fullness of revelation.

Beware of excusing yourselves from listening to Him who is speaking to you. There was no escape for those others, who tried

*to excuse themselves when God uttered His warnings on earth;
still less for us, if we turn away when He speaks from heaven.*

(Hebrews 12:25)

The Old Testament contains seven instances of sudden judgment in connection with the tabernacle or the temple, its liturgy, its worship, or its vessels. Three of them had to do with the offering of incense, three with the Ark, and one with the candlestick.

Probably the first to die in the desert were Aaron's two sons who had just been ordained priests. God had sent down fire from heaven upon the altar of sacrifice and directed that it be always kept burning, like a sanctuary lamp before a tabernacle (Leviticus 9:23,24). What their sin is uncertain, but it may have been drinking alcohol in forbidden circumstances (Leviticus10:9), but in any case, they offered a strange fire. They may have lighted a fire themselves instead of taking it from the altar, and they may also have mixed a strange incense which was expressly forbidden (Exodus 30:9,10): "whereupon the Lord sent down fire which devoured them and they died there in the Lord's presence" (Leviticus 10:2). To approach the tabernacle with the spirit of the world in our soul, instead of the spirit of Christ is to offer foreign fire. But whatever the sin of those Old Testament priests was, we are bidden to "worship God as He would have us worship Him, in awe and reverence; no doubt of it, our God is a consuming fire" (Hebrews 12:28,29).

The Ark fell into the hands of the Philistines (1 Kings 4 [1 Samuel 4, RSV]), because the Jews had used it as a magical charm to protect them in time of war. The Philistines put it in the Temple of Dagon, and the statue of the god fell prostrate before the Ark, as those who came to arrest Our Blessed Lord fell down at the mention of His Name (John 18:6).

When the Philistines refused to acknowledge the power of God, great numbers of them died with the plague (1 Kings 5:6 [1 Samuel 5:6, RSV]). As the Ark was a source of blessings to those who reverenced it, it was similarly a source of affliction to those who refused to recognize the power of God Who dwelt symbolically in it. The same is true of Christ.

We are Christ's incense offered to God, making manifest both those who are achieving salvation and those who are on the road to ruin; as a deadly fume where it finds death, as a life-giving perfume where it finds life. Who can prove himself worthy of such a calling?

(2 Corinthians 2: 15,16)

Everywhere the Ark went, while it was in the hands of the Philistines, there went the punishment of God:

No city was free from the fear of death, and God's heavy visitation; even those who survived had shameful sores to tend, and everywhere cries of anguish went up to heaven.

(1 Kings 5:12 [1 Samuel 5:12, RSV])

Though we see no such manifestations of this power when the Eucharist is profaned, may it not be that God is reserving His judgment for those who approach it without faith? Men may plead that they have eaten in His Presence and done wonderful works in His Name and cried "Lord, Lord," but He will say that He knows not such workers of iniquity (Matthew 7:21-23; Luke 12:25-27).

The Philistines finally became penitent, returned the Ark, and offered tokens of reparation for their sins; but how much more mercy they would have obtained, if they had acknowledged God's Presence, not in terror, but in appeal to His Mercy!

If God punished the Philistines so harshly for keeping the Ark, which was only a promise and prototype of the Eucharist, then what reverence should the Eucharist itself not awaken in those who have the reality and the substance! How terrible a thing it is to fall into the hands of the Living God! (Hebrews 10:31) How feeble Nabuchodonosor seemed when he fed on grass (Daniel 4:30)! What a contemptible "god" did Herod appear when worms were devouring his vitals (Acts 12:21-23)! How Belshazzar trembled with fear, his knees shaking at the sight of the handwriting on the wall (Daniel 5:6)! How Felix fled from enlightenment when Paul reasoned with him about righteousness and judgment (Acts 24:25)! Persons who are filled with slavish fear seek to banish what causes them terror, rather than part with the sin which alone makes God an object of dread. But to us has been given the power to call down the Lord on our altars! Our greater privileges should make us tremble at knowing how God punished those with fewer talents and less light.

Another Old Testament incident which helps the priest to see how much reverence God demands for His Sacrament is seen in the punishment that was given to the people of Bethshemesh. They were happy to receive the Ark back from the Philistines, but they failed to show respect. Rather, manifesting an unlawful curiosity, they looked into it and were smitten by God (1 Kings 6: 19 [1 Samuel 6:19, RSV]).

Some things are too holy to be looked upon with curious eyes. Moses was not allowed to approach the burning bush to see why it was not consumed (Exodus 3:5). The Old Testament had a very strict prohibition against any rude curiosity in relationship to sacred symbols. As Moses was told, "Do not come nearer" (Exodus 3:5), so in relationship to the Ark, which was to be carried by Aaron and his sons: "None must pry into the secrets of the shrine while they are yet uncovered on pain of death" (Numbers 4:20).

For their sinful curiosity, "the Lord smote some of the Bethsamites themselves, for prying into the ark of the Lord (1 Kings 6:19 [1 Samuel 6:19, RSV]). The Bethsamites being Israelites and having Levites among them, knew the laws regarding the Sacred Ark and the reverence with which it should be treated. Probably the reason they pried into it was to see if the Philistines had put any gold into it, in addition to the gold offerings which they had placed in a separate coffer, when they brought it back. So doing, they broke the law which forbade the ordinary people even to approach the Ark, and directed the priest to cover it with a veil.

For irreverence to what was a mere figure of the Blessed Sacrament, the Philistines were afflicted with diseases, the Israelites visited with death. If the penalty seems to us severe, it is because our minds have fallen short of the reverence due to either what symbolizes His Presence, or what is the Presence Itself. After the disaster had fallen upon them,

Who can stand his ground, the Bethsamites asked, before a God so Holy as this?

(1 Kings 6:20 [1 Samuel 6:20, RSV])

After the Ark had been kept in the house of Abinadab for some time, his two sons, Oza and Ahio, were appointed as its drivers to prepare the way while the oxen were driven by Oza. They had reached the threshing floor of Nachon, when the oxen began to kick, thus tilting the Ark to one side. Oza put out his hand and caught hold of it. The act seemed a natural one in the circumstances, yet it was punished as a rash deed, it "provoked the Divine anger; the Lord smote him, and he died there beside the Ark" (2 Kings 6:7 [2 Samuel 6:7, RSV]).

Such was the Lord's displeasure when any irreverence was shown to the Ark. The Law was clear as to who might touch the Ark, and how it should be carried. It was not proper to put it in a wagon as had been done, nor was it to be touched by anyone except the priest:

Then when Aaron and his sons have wrapped up the sanctuary and all its appurtenances ready for the march, the sons of Caath [Kohath] will enter and carry them away in their wrappings; they are not to touch the things of the sanctuary, on pain of death.

(Numbers 4:15)

The Ark should have been carried by two staves, held by priests. Oza was not a priest and was accordingly not authorized to touch the holy thing. This violation of God's command may have been the fruit of an habitual irreverence induced by long familiarity with the Ark.

206

God's action showed that no service was acceptable to Him unless regulated by strict adherence to His revealed Will. The utmost reverence was demanded of all who approached Him (Leviticus 10:3).

How strictly the Lord enjoins His priests:

Keep yourselves unsullied, you that have the vessels of the Lord's worship in your charge.

(Isaiah 52: 11)

The privilege of belonging to the Mystical Body of Christ implies both tremendous privileges and equal responsibilities.

Nation is none I have claimed for My own, save you; and guilt of yours is none that shall go unpunished.

(Amos 3:2)

Such are the judgments falling upon men in connection with the tabernacle, or the temple, its worship, its holy vessels, or its priesthood. When all these are taken together, one trembles at the reverence God demands for the things that are His, and the punishment He metes out sometimes for the least infraction of what is dedicated to His service. The altar at which the priest stands is holy.

If the angels tremble, shall we not quake? But the Presence must not enkindle a fear born of sin or impiety, but a holy fear begotten of love for One who dwells amongst us. As Leo XIII put it:

Our Lord instituted It to call to mind the supreme Love whereby Our Redeemer poured forth all the treasures of His Heart, in order to remain with us until the end of time.

The Real Presence

It is a common experience to be stopped on the street by a stranger who asks: "Where does so and so live?" That same question through the centuries has been asked of those who believe in God:

Daily, I must listen to the taunt, Where is thy God now?

(Psalm 41:4 [42:3, RSV])

To the one who is suffering, it may seem that God has vanished. But, in the calmer moments of the New Testament, His disciples one day asked Our Lord:

Where dost Thou live?

(John 1:38)

John and Andrew had already heard Him speak; they had learned their theology, namely, that He is the "Lamb of God" (John 1: 36, 37), and therefore, the Redeemer. There, bodily present, was the One for whom all the ages had breathlessly panted. They began to follow Our Lord, and He spoke the first words of His public Messianic life:

What would you have of Me?

(John 1:38)

Man? Teacher? Savior? Esteem? Advancement? Power? What do each of us seek in Christ? Is it something He has, or is it He?

The response of the disciples was a simple question:

Where dost Thou live?   (John 1:38)

Where is His permanent Presence? Where His dwelling? We know His Power is in the mountains; His Wisdom in the laws of nature; His Love in gravitation pulling all things to a center. But this is not presence. These are but effects. But Body, Blood, Soul and Divinity — "Where dost Thou live?"

We know the answer in theory. He dwells in the Eucharist. But in practice, do we know it? Ah! that requires a special search, an extra effort, maybe an hour to find out. That is why in answer to their question, He answered:

Come and see.   (John 1:39)

The "come" is a visit; to "see" is to enjoy. The first words that fell from the lips of Him Who is the Bread of Life were an invitation to seek greater union with Him. John and Andrew called Him "Master, when they first saw Him, but now they were urged to discover that He was the "Lord." At the Last Supper, He was still "Master" to Judas, but to the others, He was "Lord."

From that day to this, first-hand knowledge of Him as Lord is given to priests who "come and see." Priests can follow, like John and Andrew. Eucharistic devotion is something added, something extra, something special in the understanding of Our Lord. One can know all the theology of the Lamb of God and Redemption, and still not walk that "extra" mile to know where He "dwells." To "come" demands leaving the rectory or the magazine; to "see" requires being in His Presence. But once before His tabernacle we can say with Job:

I have heard Thy Voice now; nay, more, I have had sight of Thee.

(Job 42: 5)

A newly ordained French priest received a visit from a strange priest of another nationality. The visitor being unkempt, he was given a poor room in the attic. The French priest lived to see that visitor canonized, as Don Bosco. On learning of the canonization, he reflected: "If I knew he was a saint, I would have given him a better room." What will be our thoughts on the day of judgment when we reflect on the thousands of times we passed our church or a chapel without even a quick prayer, a greeting? The innkeeper at Bethlehem did not "see" that it was He. The capitalists of the Gerasenes did not know it was He. The Samaritans, who refused to receive Him, did not know it was He.

Now as we ask the question: "Where dost Thou dwell?' He points to the tabernacle and says, "Come and see." We should do ill not to love Him when He brings Himself so close. John and Andrew set the example:

They went and saw where He lived, and they stayed with Him all the rest of the day, from about the tenth hour onwards.

(John 1 :39)

The "went and saw" balanced the "come and see." But there was more: "and they stayed with Him." No priest who has ever risen from such an hour in His Presence will ever have any other words on his lips than those of Andrew:

We have discovered the Messiah.

(John 1:41)

Immediately after that visit, Andrew brought his brother Peter to the Lord. The work of conversion is inseparably connected with long visits to Jesus in His dwelling.

~ *13* ~

Judas and the First Crack in His Priesthood

Where does a spiritual decline begin? What is the first symptom of a train of sins? The traditionally listed enemies of spirituality are the world, the flesh, and the devil. But are not these secondary? Is there not first a detachment from something, before an attachment to anything, is possible? It is often said that Judas, the supreme example of the fallen apostle, was first corrupted through greed. The Gospel does not support this view. Greed could conceivably have been his intent when he accepted the call of Christ to follow Him. As it appeared in his life, it required a certain watchfulness to avoid detection. How he must have squirmed as Our Blessed Lord unfolded the parables of the vanity of wealth! Surely, he realized that they applied to him.

Later, greed became bold. Judas protests the wastefulness of Mary for anointing the Feet of the Savior with costly ointment. Knowing the price of everything and the value of nothing, Judas calculated that the cost of the unguent would enable a man to live comfortably for a year. How disappointed must Judas have been when earlier he had heard Zacchaeus of Jericho tell Our Lord:

Here and now, Lord, I give half of what I have to the poor; and if I have wronged anyone in any way, I make restitution of it fourfold.

(Luke 19:8)

Judas must also have wondered why Matthew gave up a profitable post as collector of customs to follow the poverty of the Savior. Matthew may himself have been surprised that he was not made treasurer, because of his familiarity with monetary transactions. Love of money was present in Judas; this is obvious. It showed itself clearly when he saw the perfume broken over the Lord's Feet.

What is the meaning of this waste? ... It would have been possible to sell this at a great price, and give alms to the poor.

(Matthew 26:8,9)

Mary obeyed the instinctive impulse of uncalculated love only to be charged for not having calculated. Lovers on earth concern themselves little about the usefulness of their gifts. True lovers of Christ do not measure their gifts. They break alabaster and give all. But to Judas, the cold-blooded spectator, it was useless waste. Avarice, indeed, can be one of the great sins of the priest, and perhaps the most insidious. It is a kind of "clean" sin, because it parades under the guise of prudence, of "caring for old age." Simon Magus, for example, very quickly got the idea that the laying on of hands was a good way to make money (Acts 8:19).

The good priest lives for his vocation; the avaricious priest lives on his vocation. When he attends a pastoral conference, he ignores every reference to the sanctification of the clergy, to moral and spiritual discipline, to visitation of the sick. But when the Bishop talks about salaries, stole fees, promotions, then he sits up and listens. He is always out to get a "better" parish, but for him "better" simply means more lucrative.

The words of the Lord to the contrary, the avaricious man believes that he can serve both God and Mammon. What Our Lord meant was that a man cannot divide his heart between God and money; and if he could, God wants no part of a divided heart. St. Paul said:

You know well enough that wherever you give a slave's consent, you prove yourselves the slaves of that master; slaves of sin, marked out for death, or slaves of obedience, marked out for justification.

(Romans 6:16)

It often happens that those who are fond of amassing wealth are sometimes sinless in other respects. They are celibates, they may even be meticulous about the external laws of the Church, but so were the Pharisees, *"the Pharisees, who were fond of riches"* (Luke 16:14). It was to them that the Lord told the parable of the rich man and Lazarus (Luke 16:19-31).

Was Avarice the Beginning of the Fall of Judas?

But was avarice the cause of the fall of Judas? No! His fall began with lack of faith and trust in the Lord, which became evident when, at the time of the second Passover mentioned in St. John's Gospel, Jesus promised the Eucharist to the crowd that had followed Him to Capharnaum (John 6). Peter believed and confessed his faith. But Jesus knew that not all of the Twelve were faithful:

Have I not chosen all twelve of you? And one of you is a devil. He was speaking of Judas, son of Simon, the Iscariot, who was one of the twelve, and was to betray Him.

(John 6:71,72)

It was Judas's lack of faith that hardened his heart and confirmed him in his greed. A year later, again at Passover time, Our Lord reprimanded Judas for his money-madness. St. John opens his account of the tragedy of Calvary with the words: "Six days before the Paschal feast Jesus went to Bethany" (John 12:1). There, in the house of Lazarus, Mary anointed Jesus. But he "who was to betray Him" (John 12:4) protested that the money should have been given to the poor. By now it was clear that Judas "was a thief" (John 12:6) and, at once reprimanding him and predicting His own death, Jesus answered,

Let her alone; enough that she should keep it for the day when my body is prepared for burial. You have the poor among you always; I am not always among you.

(John 12:7,8)

Thus the story of Judas's fall is told in relation to the Passover. It was at a Passover that Our Lord first announced the Eucharist, and at another Passover He instituted it. The first rupture in the soul of Judas was when Our Lord said He would give man His Body and Blood as their food. The total collapse came the night of the Last Supper, when Our Blessed Lord fulfilled this promise. Here is unmistakable evidence that fidelity and holiness on the one hand, and betrayal and disloyalty on the other, are linked to the Eucharist, the Bread of Life. The first crack in the priesthood comes in our attitude to the Eucharist: the holiness with which we offer Mass, the sensitiveness of our devotion to the Blessed Sacrament.

The first mention in the Bible that Judas was a betrayer was not when he revealed his greed, but when Our Lord declared Himself the Bread of Life. On that occasion, Our Lord lost the support of three distinct types of follower; He lost the masses, because He refused to be a Bread King, giving the Eucharist instead of plenty; He lost various disciples who "*walked no more in His company*" (John 6:67), because the Eucharist was to them a scandal; finally, He lost Judas.

Two who had been called by Christ to be priests are contrasted by St. John: Peter and Judas. When the wholesale desertions followed Christ's announcement that He would give His Flesh for the Life of the world, Our Lord asked Peter if he, too, would leave. Peter answered:

Lord, to whom should we go? Thy words are the words of eternal life; we have learned to believe, and are assured that Thou art the Christ, the Son of God.

(John 6:69, 70)

The Heart of Our Lord now becomes sad because of what happened to His twelve. The number was symbolic, dating from the

214

twelve patriarchs and the twelve tribes, and so often used with reference to the Apostles. (Was not each of the twelve Apostles from one of the twelve tribes?) There is, therefore, something tragic about the Divine complaint:

Jesus answered them, Have I not chosen all twelve of you? And one of you is a devil. He was speaking of Judas son of Simon, the Iscariot, who was one of the twelve, and was to betray Him.

(John 6:71, 72)

Avarice later! But now, long before the meal in Simon's house, long before his exchange with the Temple priests, Judas is first described as a betrayer, as Our Lord gives us His Flesh to eat and His Blood to drink. What did the thirty pieces of silver add to the selling of that Body and Blood? He had already denied it! He is yet a thief; then a traitor; later, an open ally of the enemy. He stole from the apostolic purse, developed a neurotic hatred both of money and of himself; finally, took his own life. But when did the fissure first show? When began the unseen collapse — so unseen that the Apostles at the Last Supper did not know of it? It began when he who was called to be a priest and victim, refused to accept the words of his Lord:

As I live because of the Father, the living Father Who has sent Me, so he who eats Me will live, in his turn, because of Me.

(John 6:58)

The flesh! Certainly, it explains certain aspects of priestly weakness. Worldliness! Love of stocks and bonds! Luxury! Alcohol! Mention any sin that comes to mind. These are the tails on the falling kites of the priesthood. But there was already a rent in the garment of holiness before these other forms of nakedness and shame appeared. Our Lord knows where all such overt and scandalous sins started. Maybe they started in a "fifteen-minute Mass," a "one-minute thanksgiving," a flight from the night shirt to the alb, a failure to visit the Eucharistic Savior except "officially" when one "had" to

215

celebrate Mass or conduct devotions. But somewhere, somehow, the man who is a priest because of the Eucharist, failed to be a Eucharistic priest. If a surgeon stayed away from human body and blood, would he not lose his proficiency? Is he not licensed precisely for body and blood? But we, who are not "licensed" but "ordained" for Body and Blood, how shall we retain our power, our holiness, our priestly skill, except by that lively faith in the Body and Blood of Christ?

The Betrayal and The Passover

The Gospels seem to make a point about associating Judas with the Passover. Avarice, one of the effects of his failure to be Eucharistic, is first mentioned in this connection:

Six days before the paschal feast, Jesus went to Bethany.

(John 12:1)

Such are the words with which the Beloved Disciple raises the curtain on the tragedy of Calvary. And who is first mentioned? Judas! As Mary, the sister of Lazarus, shows devotion to the Body and Blood of the Savior, anointing Him "for burial" (John 12:7, 8), so does Judas betray his greed and prepare to sell that Body and Blood.

The hypocrisy of Judas in expressing concern for the poor is stressed by Our Lord's identification of Himself that same week with the poor (Matthew 25:35 ff). When Jesus reprimanded Judas and told him to "let her alone" (John 12:7), the false apostle resolved to consummate the betrayal.

And at that, one of the twelve, Judas who was called Iscariot, went to the chief priests and asked them, what will you pay me for handing Him over to you? Where upon they laid down thirty pieces of silver, And he, from that time onwards, looked about for an opportunity to betray Him.

(Mathew 26: 14-16)

The cross united not only Our Lord's friends but also His enemies. The Saduccees and Pharisees, Judas and the Sanhedrin, Rome and the Temple priests, Herod and Pilate — all those who had lesser enmities united in the greater hostility to Jesus, the Savior of the world. The Church, which is the continuing Christ, must always expect such hostile coalitions in time of crisis. Evil is hypersensitive to goodness. It detects a challenge to its existence, long before good men are awake to the signs of the times.

Judas at The Last Supper

Now comes the Passover of Our Lord's Death when the true Lamb of God is sacrificed for us pilgrims to eternity. The twelve Apostles are gathered around Our Lord. Where did Judas sit at this first Mass? John was certainly on His Heart's side. Who was on the Lord's other side? Possibly Peter, though one detail suggests the contrary:

> *Jesus had one disciple, whom He loved, who was now sitting with his head against Jesus' breast; to him, therefore, Simon Peter made a sign, and asked him, Who is it He means?*

(John 13:23, 24)

If Peter was on the other side, he would hardly make a sign as here described.

Could Judas have been next to Our Lord? It is conceivable, for Our Lord makes many attempts to save those He has chosen. Matthew seems to suggest it, for how else could Christ have told Judas that He knew his intentions, while the others continued under the impression that he went out to help the poor (Matthew 26:22,25)? Betrayers and traitors rarely know they are discovered. If then, Judas was given that place as a sign of Divine Love, how, in his hardened heart, he must have thought: "If He knew what I am going to do, He would never have given me this place."

At this point Our Lord again referred to the Passover:

217

I have longed and longed to share this Paschal meal with you before My Passion.

(Luke 22: 15)

Was Judas reminded of the other Passover when Our Lord had promised the Eucharist?

Also significant for Judas, though ignored by him, was the stress on humility at this solemn moment of the institution of the Eucharist. Our Lord insisted that in a certain sense, His apostles were kings. He did not deny their instinct for aristocracy, but He told them that theirs was to be the nobility of humility, the greatest becoming the least. To drive the lesson home, He reminded them of the position He occupied among them as Master and Lord of the table and yet free of every trace of superiority. Many times He repeated that He had come not to be served but to serve. To bear the burden of others and particularly their guilt was His reason for becoming the "Suffering Servant" foretold by Isaiah (52:13-53:12). And not content with words, He reinforced them with example.

And now, rising from supper, He laid His garments aside, took a towel, and put it about Him; and then He poured water into the basin, and began to wash the feet of His disciples, wiping them with the towel that girded Him.

(John 13:4)

The minuteness of John's description is striking. It lists seven distinct actions: rising, laying His garments aside, taking a towel, putting it about Him, pouring water, washing the feet, and wiping the feet with a towel. One can imagine an earthly king, just before he returns from a distant province, rendering a humble service to one of his subjects; but one would not say that he was doing it because he was about to return to his capital. Yet Our Blessed Lord is described as washing the disciples' feet because He is to go back to the Father. He had taught humility by precept: "He that humbles himself shall be exalted" (Luke 14: 11); by parable, as in the story of the Pharisee and the Publican; by example, as when He took a child in His arms; and now by condescension.

The scene was like a re-enactment of His Incarnation. Rising up from the Heavenly Banquet in intimate union of nature with the Father, He laid aside the garments of His glory, wrapped about His Divinity the towel of human nature, which He took from Mary; poured the laver of regeneration which is His Blood shed on the Cross to redeem men, and began washing the souls of His disciples and followers through the merits of His Death, Resurrection and Ascension. St. Paul expressed it beautifully:

His Nature is, from the first, Divine, and yet He did not see, in the rank of Godhead, a prize to be coveted; He dispossessed Himself, and took the nature of a slave, fashioned in the likeness of men, and presenting Himself to us in human form; and then He lowered His own dignity, accepted an obedience which brought Him to death, death on a cross.

(Philippians 2:6-8)

Once Peter's protests are stilled, the other disciples are motionless, lost in mute astonishment. When humility comes from the God-man as it does here, it is obvious that it will be through humility that men will go back to God. Each one would have withdrawn his feet out of the basin were it not for love which pervaded their hearts.

But Our Lord was still not willing to abandon Judas. Once more He tried to arouse him to a realization of what he planned.

And you are clean now; only, not all of you.

(John 13: 10)

It was one thing to be selected as an apostle; it was another to be elected to salvation through observance of the corresponding obligations. But that the Apostles would realize that heresy or schisms or treachery in their ranks was not unexpected, Jesus cited Psalm 40 to show that it had been anticipated by the prophets:

The man who shared My Bread has lifted his heel to trip Me up. I am telling you this now, before it happens, so that when it happens you may believe it was written of Me.

(John 13:18, 19)

The reference was to David's sufferings at the hands of Ahithophel, a disloyalty now identified as a prefigurement of what David's royal Son would suffer. The lowliest part of the body, the heel, was described in both instances as inflicting the wound. In Genesis (3:14) God told the serpent that the woman would crush him while he lay in ambush at her heels. It now seemed that the devil would have a momentary revenge, by using the heel to inflict a wound on the seed of the woman — the Lord. On another occasion Our Lord said:

A man's enemies will be the people of his own house.

(Matthew 10:36)

Only one who has suffered such betrayal from within the household can even faintly grasp the sadness of the Savior's soul that night. All the good example, counsel, companionship and inspiration are fruitless with those who will to do evil. One of the strongest expressions of sorrow expressed by Jesus now fell from His lips to describe His love of Judas and to lament the renegade apostle's free decision to sin.

Jesus bore witness to the distress He felt in His Heart; Believe me, He said, believe Me, one of you is to betray He.

(John 13:21)

There were twelve questions in all. Ten of the apostles asked:

"Is it I, *Lord?*"

They were all full of sorrow, and began to say, one after another, Lord, is it I?

(Matthew 26:22)

One, however, asked:

Lord, who is it?

(John 13:26)

This was John himself. The twelfth had little choice but to continue his pretence.

Then Judas, he who was betraying Him, said openly, Master, is it I?

(Matthew 26:25)

Notice that eleven called Him Lord; but Judas called Him Master. It is a perfect illustration of St. Paul's insistence that it is only through the Holy Spirit that anyone can say, Jesus is the Lord" (1 Corinthians 12:3). Because the spirit that filled Judas was satanic, he called Him Master; the others called Him Lord, in full confession of Divinity.

Throughout the first part of the Passover meal, both Our Lord and Judas had been dipping their hands in the same dish of wine and fruit. The very fact that Our Lord chose bread as a symbol of the betrayal, might have reminded Judas of the Bread promised at Capernaum. Humanly speaking, it would seem that Our Lord should have thundered out His denunciation of Judas, but rather in a last attempt to save him, He used the bread of fellowship.

He answered, the man who has put his hand into the dish with Me will betray Me. The Son of Man goes on His way, as the scripture foretells of Him; But woe upon that man by whom the Son of Man is to be betrayed; better for that man if he had never been born.

(Matthew 26:23-25)

In the presence of Divinity, who can be sure of his innocence? It was reasonable for every disciple to ask if it was he. Man is a mystery even to himself. He knows that within his heart there lie, coiled and

221

dormant, serpents that at any moment can sting a neighbor, or even God, with their poison. None of them could be sure that he was not the traitor, even if none was conscious of a temptation to betray Him. Judas alone knew where he stood. Even though Our Lord revealed His knowledge of the treason, Judas remained fixed in his determination to do the evil. The revelation that the crime was uncovered and the evil stripped naked did not shame him into withdrawal.

Some recoil in horror when their sins are put bluntly before them. But though Judas saw his treachery described in all its deformity, he in effect declared in the language of Nietzsche: "Evil, be thou my good." Our Lord gave a sign to Judas. In answer to the question of the apostles ("Is it I?") He declared:

It is the man to whom I give this piece of bread which I am dipping in the dish. Then He dipped the bread, and gave it to Judas the Son of Simon, the Iscariot.

(John 13:26, 27)

That Judas committed his sin freely is evidenced by his subsequent remorse. So too was Christ free to make His betrayal the condition of His Cross. Evil men seem to run counter to the economy of God, to be an errant thread in the tapestry of life, but they all fit into the Divine Plan. If the wild wind roars from the black heavens, there is somewhere a sail to catch it and yoke it to the useful service of man.

When Our Lord said: "It is the man to whom I give this piece of bread which I am dipping in the dish," He was actually offering a gesture of friendship. The giving of the morsel seems to have been traditional among both Greeks and Semites. Socrates said that it was always a mark of favor to give a morsel to a table neighbor. Our Lord held open to Judas the opportunity to repent, as He later did once again in the Garden of Gethsemane. But though Our Lord held the door open, Judas would not enter. Rather would Satan enter in.

The morsel once given, Satan entered into him; and Jesus said to him, Be quick on thy errand.

(John 13:27)

Satan possesses only willing victims. The marks of mercy and friendship extended by the Victim should have moved Judas to repentance. The bread must have burned his lips, as the thirty pieces of silver would later burn his hands. Only some minutes previously the Hands of the Son of God had washed the feet of Judas; now the same Divine Hands touch the lips of Judas with a morsel; in a few hours, the lips of Judas will kiss those of Our Lord in the final act of betrayal. The Divine Mediator, knowing all that would befall Him, directed Judas to open wider the curtain on the tragedy of Calvary. What Judas was to do, let him do quickly? The Lamb of God was ready for sacrifice.

The Divine Mercy did not identify the traitor, for Our Lord hid from the others the identity of the betrayer. The practice of the world which loves to spread scandals, even those which are untrue, is here reversed in the hiding of what is true. When they saw Judas leave, the others assumed that he went on a mission of charity.

None of those who sat there could understand the drift of what He said; some of them thought, since Judas kept the common purse, that Jesus was saying to him, Go and buy what we need for the feast, or bidding him give some alms to the poor.

(John 13:28)

But Judas had gone out to sell, not to buy. He would minister not to the poor, but to the rich in charge of the temple treasury. Though Our Blessed Lord knew the evil intention of Judas, He still continued to behave kindly. He would bear the ignominy alone. In many instances, Jesus acted as though the effects of the deeds of others were unknown to Him. He knew that He would raise Lazarus from the dead, even when He wept. He knew who believed Him not, and who would betray Him, yet this did not harden His Sacred Heart. Judas rejected the last appeal, and thus despair remained in His heart.

Judas went out, "and it was night" (John 13:30), an appropriate setting for a deed of darkness. It perhaps was a relief to be away from the Light of the World. Nature is in sympathy at times, at times in discord with our joys and sorrows. The sky is gloomy with clouds when there is melancholy within. Nature was suiting itself to the evil deeds of Judas. When he went out, he found not the fact of God's smiling sun but the Stygian blackness of night. It would also be night at midday when the Lord was crucified.

Judas is intelligible only in terms of the Body and Blood of Christ. Clawing at money was the effect, not the cause of a ruined priesthood.

Judas and The Priesthood

1.   Those who have been cradled in the sacred associations of the priesthood know best how to betray Our Lord. Judas knew where to find Our Lord after dark.

Here there was a garden, into which He and His disciples went. Judas, His betrayer, knew the place well; Jesus and His disciples had often forgathered in it.

(John 18:1, 2)

2.   Divinity is so holy, that all betrayal must be prefaced by some mark of esteem or affection.

It is none other, he told them, than the Man whom I shall greet with a kiss.

(Matthew 26:48)

3.   No bishop or priest knows the ultimate depth of spiritual sorrow and grief, until he has felt the hot blistering kiss of a brother in Christ who is a traitor.

4.   A priest can always sell Our Lord, but no priest can buy Him.

Whereupon they laid down thirty pieces of silver.

(Matthew 26:15)

5. Any pleasure, profit or gain that one receives through rejecting the Eucharistic Lord proves so disgusting, that the beneficiary is impelled, like Judas, to throw it back in the face of those who *gave it to us.*

> *And now Judas, His betrayer, was full of remorse at seeing Him condemned, so that he brought back to the chief priests and elders their thirty pieces of silver; I have sinned, he told them, in betraying the Blood of an Innocent Man.*
>
> (Matthew 27:3,4)

Could not the money have been given to the poor? Judas never thought of that then.

6. Many psychoses and neuroses are due to an unrequited sense of guilt. The Lord would have pardoned Judas as He pardoned Peter, but Judas never asked for it.

When a man hates himself for what he has done and is without repentance to God, he will sometimes pound his breast as if to blot out a sin. There is a world of difference between pounding a breast in self-disgust, and pounding it with the *mea culpa* of one asking for pardon. Self-hatred can become so intense as to pound the life out of a man, leading him to suicide. Though death is a penalty of original sin and naturally feared by any normal person, some rush into its arms.

The conscience of Judas warned him before the sin. After the sin it gnawed, and the rending was such that he could not bear it. Down the valley of Cedron he went, that valley of so many ghostly associations. Jagged rocks and gnarled and stunted trees he chose as the proper place to empty himself of self. Everything around proclaimed his destiny and his end. Nothing was more revolting to his eyes than the gilded roof of the temple, for it reminded him of the Temple of God he had just sold. Every tree seemed the gibbet to which he had sentenced Innocent Blood. Every branch was an accusing finger. The very hill on which he stood overlooked Calvary, whereon the One he had sentenced to death would unite heaven and earth, a union he would now exert his final efforts to prevent. Throwing a rope over a limb of a tree, he hanged himself (Matthew 27:5).

The lesson is clear. We are Eucharistic priests. Watch a priest read Mass and you can tell how he treats souls in a confessional, how he ministers to the sick and poor, whether or not he is interested in making converts, whether he is more concerned about pleasing the Lord Bishop than the Lord God, how effective he is in instilling patience and resignation in those who suffer, whether he is an administrator or a shepherd, whether he loves the rich, or the rich and the poor, and whether he gives only money sermons or Christ words. The moral rot of the priesthood starts with a want of lively faith in the Divine Presence, and the sanctity of the priesthood starts there too.

~ 14 ~

Why Make a Holy Hour?

What good does a medical convention achieve if the doctors agree on the need for good health, but take no practical steps to implement their argument? So with a book on the priesthood. What concrete recommendations may be given to the priest to make him worthy of the supernal vocation to which he is called? One immediate and essential answer is the Holy Hour. But why make a Holy Hour?

1. Because it is time spent in the Presence of Our Lord Himself. If faith is alive, no further reason is needed.

2. Because in our busy life it takes considerable time to shake off the "noonday devils," the worldly cares which cling to our souls like dust. An hour with Our Lord follows the experience of the disciples on the road to Emmaus (Luke 24:13-35). We begin by walking with Our Lord but our eyes are "held fast," so that we do not "recognize Him." Next, He converses with our soul, as we read the Scriptures. The third stage is one of sweet intimacy, as when "He sat down at table with them." The fourth stage is the full dawning of the mystery of the Eucharist. Our eyes are "opened" and we recognize Him. Finally we reach the point Where we do not want to leave. The hour seemed so short. As we arise we ask:

Were not our hearts burning within us when He spoke to us on the road, and when He made the Scriptures plain to us?

(Luke 24:32)

3. Because Our Lord asked for it.

Had you no strength, then, to watch with Me even for an hour?

(Matthew 26:40)

The word was addressed to Peter, but he is referred to as Simon. It is our Simon-nature which needs the hour. If the hour seems hard, it is because... *the spirit is willing enough, but the flesh is weak.* (Mark 14:39)

4. Because, as St. Thomas Aquinas tells us, the priest's power over the *corpus mysticum* follows from his power over the *corpus physicum* of Christ. It is because he consecrates the Body and Blood of Christ, that the priest can teach, govern and sanctify the members of the Church. Practically, this means that he walks into the confessional from the foot of the altar; that he mounts the pulpit after having enacted the mystery of redemption. Every sick call, every word of counsel in the parlor, every catechism lesson taught to children, every official act in the chancery, flows from the altar. All power resides there, and the more "short-cuts" we take from the tabernacle to our other priestly duties, the less spiritual strength we have for them.

The Eucharist is the *fans et caput* of all the spiritual goods of the Church. (Urbi Et Orbi, May 8, 1907)

It is from the Eucharist that all other Sacraments receive their efficacy. (Catechism of the Council of Trent, Part II, Chapter 4, No. 47.)

If all the sacraments, if all our preaching, confessing, administrating, and saving start with that Flame of Love, then how can we refuse to be sparked by it an hour a day?

5. Because the Holy Hour keeps a balance between the spiritual and the practical. Western philosophies tend to an activism in which God does nothing, and man everything; the Eastern philosophies tend to a quietism in which God does everything, and man nothing.

The golden mean is *Surgite postquam sederitis:* action following rest; Martha walking with Mary*; contemplate aliis tradere*, in the words of St. Thomas. The Holy Hour unites the contemplative to the active life of the priest.

Thanks to the hour with Our Lord, our meditations and resolutions pass from the conscious to the subconscious and then become motives of action. A new spirit begins to pervade our sick calls, our sermons, our confessions. The change is effected by Our Lord Who fills our heart and works through our hands. A priest can give only what he possesses. To give Christ to others, one must possess Him.

6. Because revelations made by the Sacred Heart to saintly souls indicate that still unexplored depths of that Heart are reserved for priests. There are veils of love behind which only the priest may penetrate, and from which he will emerge with an unction and power over souls far beyond his own strength. The "house" of the priest is not the rectory. He is "at home" only where Christ is present. There alone he learns the secrets of love. To St. Margaret Mary, the Sacred Heart complained that so few priests answer His cry: "*I am thirsty*" (John 19:28). His words to her were: "I have a burning thirst to be honored in the Blessed Sacrament, and I find hardly anyone who endeavors according to My desires to quench that thirst by making some returns to Me."

7. Because the Holy Hour will make us practice what we preach. It grieves the Sacred Heart to see a scandalous disparity between the high ideal of the priesthood and its poor realization.

> *Here is an image, He said, of the kingdom of heaven; there was once a king, who held a marriage feast for his son, and sent out his servants with a summons to all those whom he had invited to the wedding; but they would not come.*
>
> (Matthew 22: 2,3)

It was written of Our Lord that He "set out to do and to teach" — *facere et docere* (Acts 1: 1). The priest who practices the Holy Hour will find that when he teaches, the people will say of him as of the Lord:

All ... were astonished at the gracious words which came from his mouth.

(Luke 4:22)

8. Because the Holy Hour makes us obedient instruments of Divinity. In the Eucharist there is this double movement; first, of the priest to the Eucharistic Heart; and secondly, of the priest to the people. The priest who has given himself to the Heart of Our Blessed Lord, is known by Our Lord as "expendable" for His purposes. The priest becomes endowed with an extra power because of his suppleness in the hands of his Master. God gives some graces directly to souls, as a man gives alms to the poor man he happens to meet. But the Sacred Heart wishes great graces to be distributed to souls through the hands of His priests.

The effectiveness of priests has little or nothing to do with their natural endowments. A Eucharistic priest will be a better instrument of the Lord among souls than a learned one who loves Him less. One of the promises made to priests who love the Sacred Heart is: "I will give such priests the power of touching the most hardened hearts."

9. Because the Holy Hour helps us make reparation both for the sins of the world and for our own. When the Sacred Heart appeared to St. Margaret Mary, it was His Heart, and not His Head, that was crowned with thorns. It was Love that was hurt. Black Masses, sacrilegious communions, scandals, militant atheism — who will make up for them? Who will be an Abraham for Sodom, a Mary for those who have no wine? The sins of the world are our sins, as if we had committed them. If they caused Our Lord a bloody sweat, to the point that He upbraided His disciples for failing to stay with Him an hour, shall we with Cain ask:

10.

Is it for me to watch over my brother?

(Genesis 4:9)

The priest who asks what he can do about Communism knows that battles are won when his hands are lifted, like those of Moses, in prayer.

11. Because it will restore our lost spiritual vitality. Our hearts will be where our joys are. One reason why many fail to progress after many years in the priesthood, is that they shrink from casting the whole burden of their lives upon Our Lord. They fail to seek their joy in the union of their priesthood with the victimhood of Christ. They will sometimes remain stubborn, clinging to the things of sense, forgetful that the Eucharistic door is really not a door at all; it is not even a wall, for there we have the "breaking down the wall that was a barrier between us" (Ephesians 2: 14).

The Sacred Heart promised through St. Margaret Mary to "make His priests like two-edged swords, which will make the holy fountain of penance spring up in them." Our lives at best are weak, perhaps broken like fragmented china. So we go to the Sacred Heart and ask *ut congregata restaures, et restaurata conserves*: that "Thou wouldst bring together and mend, mend and forever preserve, what now lies broken." We need to be cemented again by love into unity, and where can such love be found except in the Sacrament of unity?

12. Because the Holy Hour is the "Hour of Truth." Alone with Jesus, we there see ourselves, not as the people see us — always judging us to be better than we are — but as the Judge sees us. If we take praise seriously, nothing so deflates our pomposity as the realization of the helplessness to which the Lord of Heaven has reduced Himself, under the species of Bread. Our failings, our want of charity to other priests, our too hasty responses to those whose appearance offends us, our sugary kindness to the well dressed, our seeking out the rich, our avoiding the poor, our hurried Mass, our impatience in the confessional — all these the Eucharistic Lord draws out of our conscience.

Living in sin, grievous or venial, becomes intolerable for the priest who practices the Holy Hour. It is like having a doctor at hand to warn us of a growing cancer. Eventually, we are driven to ask the

Divine Physician to heal us. No sin is a hidden sin in meditation; no excuses are given. We take sin out of its lair and lay it before God. We always knew that *God saw it;* but in the Holy Hour we see it. Our sins are placed before our eyes not as a human weakness, but as a re-crucifying of Our Lord:

> *Scrutinize me, O God, as Thou wilt, and read my heart; put me to the test, and examine my restless thoughts. See if on any false paths my heart is set, and Thyself lead me in the ways of old.*

> (Psalm 138:23-24 [139:23-24, RSV])

But there is no need to fear, because during the Hour, we enter into the private chambers of the Judge. We make friends with Him before the trial while making reparation for our sins.

13. Because it reduces our liability to temptation and weakness. Presenting ourselves before Our Lord in the Blessed Sacrament is like putting a tubercular patient in good air and sunlight. The virus of our sins cannot long exist in the face of the Light of the world.

> *Always I can keep the Lord within sight; always He is at my right hand, to make me stand firm.*
> (Psalm 15:8 [16:8, RSV])

Our sinful impulses are prevented from arising through the barrier erected each day by the Holy Hour. Our will becomes disposed to goodness with little conscious effort on our part. Satan, the roaring lion, was not permitted to put forth his hand to touch righteous Job, until he received permission (Job 1: 12). Certainly, then will the Lord withhold serious fall from him who watches (1 Corinthians 10: 13). With full confidence in his Eucharistic Lord, the priest will have a spiritual resiliency. He will bounce back quickly after a falling:

Fall I, it is but to rise again, sit I in darkness, the Lord will be my light. The Lord's displeasure I must bear, I that have sinned against Him, till at last He admits my plea, and grants redress.

(Micah 7:8,9)

The Lord will be favorable even to the weakest of us, if He finds us at His feet in adoration, disposing ourselves to receive Divine favors. No sooner had Saul of Tarsus, the persecutor, humbled himself before his Maker, than God sent a special messenger to his relief, telling him that "even now he is at his prayers" (Acts 9:11). Even the priest who has fallen can expect reassurance, if he watches and prays.

They shall increase, that hitherto had dwindled, be exalted, that once were brought low.

(Jeremiah 30: 19,20)

14. Because the Holy Hour is a personal prayer. The Mass and the Breviary are official prayers. They belong to the Mystical Body of Christ. They do not belong to us personally. The priest who limits himself strictly to his official obligation and adoration, is like the union man who downs tools the moment the whistle blows. Love begins when duty finishes. It is a giving of the cloak when the coat is taken. It is walking the extra mile.

Answer shall come ere cry for help is uttered, prayer find audience while it is yet on their lips.

(Isaiah 65:24)

Of course, we do not have to make a Holy Hour — and that is just the point. Love is never compelled, except in hell. There love has to submit to justice. To be forced to love would be a kind of hell. No man who loves a woman is obligated to give her an engagement ring; and no priest who loves the Sacred Heart ever has to give an engagement Hour.

"Would you, too, go away?" (John 6:68) is *weak* love; "Art thou sleeping?" (Mark 14:37) is *irresponsible* love; "He had great possessions" (Matthew 19:22; Mark 10:22) is *selfish* love. But does the priest who loves His Lord have time for other activities before he performs acts of love "above and beyond the call of duty"? Does the patient love the physician who charges for every call, or does he begin to love when the physician says: "I just dropped by to see how you were"?

15. Meditation keeps us from seeking an external escape from our worries and miseries. When difficulties arise in the rectory, when nerves are made taut by false accusations, there is always a danger that we may look outwards, as the Israelites did, for release.

From the Lord God, the Holy One of Israel, word was given you, Come back and keep still, and all shall be well with you; in quietness and in confidence lies your strength. But you would have none of it; To horse! you cried, We must flee! and flee you shall; We must ride swiftly, you said; but swifter still ride your pursuers.

(Isaiah 30: 15,16)

No outward escape, neither pleasure, drink, friends or keeping busy, is an answer. The soul of a priest cannot "fly upon a horse"; he must take "wings" to a place where his "life is hidden away ... with Christ in God" (Colossians 3:3).

16. Finally, because the Holy Hour is necessary for the Church. No one can read the Old Testament without becoming conscious of the presence of God in history. How often did God use other nations to punish Israel for her sins! He made Assyria the "rod that executes My vengeance" (Isaiah 10:5). The history of the world since the Incarnation is the Way of the Cross. The rise of nations and their fall remain related to the Kingdom of God. We cannot understand the mystery of God's government, for it is the "sealed book" of Revelation. John wept when he saw it (Revelation 5:4). He could not understand why this moment of prosperity and that hour of adversity.

What we often forget is that all the judgments of God begin with the Church, as they began with Israel. Not politics, but theology is the key to the world. We bemoan the wickedness of men, but is not the Lord all the while looking at our own failures? Judgment begins with us:

> *Make thy way, the Lord said to him, all through the city, from end to end of Jerusalem; and where thou findest men that weep and wail over the foul deeds done in it, mark their brows with a cross. To the others I heard Him say, Yours it is to traverse the city at his heels, and smite. Never let eye of yours melt with pity; old and young, man and maid, mother and child, all alike destroy till none is left, save only where you see the cross marked on them. And begin first with the temple itself.*
>
> (Ezekiel 9:4-6)

Amos gave the same lesson. The more unmerited the favors, he insisted, the greater the punishment:

> *Nation is none I have claimed for my own, save you; and guilt of yours is none that shall go unpunished.*
>
> (Amos 3:2)

God speaks through Jeremiah and says that punishment begins with the holy city, *in civitate mea.*

> *Here am I beginning my work of vengeance with that city which is the shrine of My Name, and shall you be acquitted, you others, and go scot-free? That shall never be, says the Lord of hosts; to the sword if I appeal, it is for a whole world's punishment.*
>
> (Jeremiah 25:29)

Lest we think that we do not share responsibility for what comes upon the world in the New Testament, let Peter reaffirm the warning:

235

The time is ripe for judgment to begin, and to begin with God's own household; and if our turn comes first, what will be its issue for those who refuse credence to God's message?

(1 Peter 4:17)

The Hand of God will strike first the Church, then the world. We who are the watchmen set on the walls, are the first to be judged. Jerusalem was destroyed only after Our Lord purged the Temple. Jacob's house felt the famine before the Egyptians did. The Jews were carried into captivity before the Assyrians fell to the Medes and Persians.

If then of dire things a *sanctuario meo incipite,* shall not we priests atone for the sins of the world, keep our priesthood holy for the sake of our country and the world, and be faithful? If judgment thus starts with the sanctuary, then so shall mercy. Thus, can the world be saved. What a contribution could the 55,000 priests in the United States make to the peace of the world, if each spent an hour daily in the sanctuary! And how blessed for each would be the moment of death:

Blessed is that servant who is found doing this when his Lord comes.

(Luke 12:43)

A priest ending his Holy Hour will say with John the Baptist:

He must become more and more, I must become less and less.

(John 3:30)

The alleged superiority of being "in the chancery" or the alleged inferiority of being "only an assistant" dissolves before the tabernacle. What ultimate difference does it make if one is passed over for a "good" (rich) parish, or if the "second best" man in the diocese is made *officialis?* Self-assertiveness gives way to Christ-assertiveness in the presence of the tabernacle. The priest who makes the Lord everything for an hour each morning is not seriously wounded by an episcopal "pass-over" when the promotion was logically his. The "littleness" of the Lord in the Eucharist makes "bigness" in the priest an absurdity.

Instead of being the "best man" in the nuptials of Christ and His Church, we sometimes act as if we sought to be the bridegroom-and that office the Lord will not surrender. In the Holy Hour, the priest learns to be concerned only with furthering the beauty of the Bride which is the Church, so that it may be presented with "no stain or wrinkle" (Ephesians 5:27) on the day of the Wedding of the Lamb.

To our parish, as Paul to the Corinthians, we say:

I have betrothed you to Christ, so that no other but He should claim you, His bride without spot.

(2 Corinthians 11: 2)

An inflexible law governs the influence of the priest on others: the more he is inflated, the less are the Lord and His Church glorified. Meditation on the "emptying" of the Savior in the Eucharist will keep the priest always conscious, that he is the moon receiving his light from the sun.

No Eucharistic bishop will ever say or even think: "I built twenty-one high schools, forty-three new parishes and six convents in nineteen years." He knows too well who provided the money — the people! He knows too well who gave the authority — the Church! He knows too well who supplied the help — his priests! Daily will he hear the Lord from the tabernacle whisper:

After all, friend, who is it that gives thee this pre-eminence? What powers hast thou, that did not come to thee by gift? And if they came to thee by gift, why dost thou boast of them, as if there were no gift in question?

(1 Corinthians 4:7)

If the Lord had not given us a vocation, what would we be: insurance clerks, truck drivers, school teachers, doctors, farmers, waiters? The Lord did not choose any of us as the best. He picks "frail vessels." And as we gather together around the Eucharist and look at each other, we recognize in our hearts the truth of Paul's words:

Consider, brethren, the circumstances of your own calling; not many of you are wise, in the world's fashion, not many powerful, not many well born.

(1 Corinthians 1: 26)

We are not the best, otherwise the power of the Gospel would be in us, rather than in the Spirit. But where is this truth better learned than in the presence of the Mystery which seems bread, but is actually Emmanuel; so small that our hands can break it, so full of power that its breaking renews the Passion and Death of Christ? The decreased priest is the increased Christ. When the Eucharist is no more than a remote background to our lives, it is like having the sun low on the horizon behind us. We cast a shadow forward; and the lower the sun, the longer the shadow. If the Lord is far from us, scarcely visible our own ego seems to grow important like our shadow, and with it our opinions and works take on the appearance of great substance. But this is an illusion. If, on the contrary, each day begins with the Eucharist before us as our rising sun, the shadow of the ego no longer hides our true face, and when the Sun of Justice reaches the meridian, no ego survives. Then the souls whom we tend, like the apostles at the Transfiguration, see "no one any more, but Jesus only with them" (Mark 9:7).

The sole requirement is the venture of faith, and the reward is the depths of intimacy for those who cultivate His friendship. To abide with Christ is spiritual fellowship, as He insisted on the solemn and sacred night of the Last Supper, the moment He chose to give us the Eucharist:

You have only to live on in Me, and I will live on in you.

(John 15:4)

He wants us in His dwelling:

That you too, may be where I am.

(John 14:3)

How far we miss the joys of our priesthood, when our only meetings with the Lord are "public audiences" — at Mass, devotions, stations of the Cross, whenever we have to be there. The Lord wants "private audiences." He wants a protracted audience, a full hour. John and Andrew stayed the entire day!

✠ J.M.J. ✠

~ *15* ~

How to Make the Holy Hour

If at all possible, the priest should make his daily Holy Hour before celebrating his Mass. Now that the Church's regulations on the pre-Eucharistic fast have been modified, he will be well advised to take a cup of coffee before he starts. *The average American is physically, biologically, psychologically and neurologically unable to do anything worthwhile before he has a cup of coffee.* And that goes for prayer, too. Even sisters in convents whose rules were written before electric percolators were developed, would do well to update their procedures. Let them have coffee before meditation.

Limit the saying of the Breviary to twenty minutes of the hour. The basic purpose of this hour is to meditate. Some spiritual writers recommend a mechanical division of the hour into four parts: thanksgiving, petition, adoration, and reparation. This is unnecessarily artificial. An hour's conversation with a friend is not divided into four rigid segments or topics. The Holy Hour is not an official prayer; it is personal. Each priest, being a man, has a heart unlike any other in the world. This unique heart must make up the content of his prayer. God no more likes "circular letters" than we do. In addition to liturgical or official prayer, there must be the prayer of the heart. We constantly preach to others; in the Holy Hour we preach to ourselves.

Many books on meditation have a rigid format which is endurable in the seminary, but which the priest soon finds too dry for his purposes. The so-called "methods" of meditation are generally impractical and unsuited to our mentality. What they consist in is an analysis of a meditation *which was already made*, and which proved satisfactory for the one who made it. A child will run after a ball with grace and freedom of movement. But if he is told to narrate what he does every second, how he first lifts the right foot, then the left, all the spontaneity disappears. To base a meditation, first on the intellect, then on the will, and finally on the emotions, is to destroy intimacy. This is not what really happens. The intellect does not work first in meditation, then the will, then the imagination. *The person meditates; all his faculties work together.* To achieve this, the greatest possible freedom should be left to the individual:

> *... where the Lord's Spirit is, there is freedom.*

> (2 Corinthians 3:17)

The best book for meditation is the Scripture. But since many of its depths need to be explained, a good spiritual commentary is valuable. Too often the Lord may have to repeat the complaint He voiced to His disciples:

> *You do not understand the Scriptures or what is the Power of God.*

> (Matthew 22:29)

Read the Scriptures, or a commentary, or any solid spiritual book, until a thought strikes you. Then close the book, and talk to Our Lord about it. But do not do all the talking. Listen also "Speak on, Lord, Thy servant is listening" (1 Kings, 3:10 [1 Samuel 3:10, RSV]) must not be: "Listen, Lord, Thy servant speaketh." we learn to speak through listening, and we grow in love of God through listening. Meditation is at least half listening:

> *It is My turn to ask questions.*
>
> (Job 40:2)

When you are so fatigued and exhausted that you cannot pray, offer up your worthlessness. Does not a dog love to be near the master, even when the master gives him no evident sign of affection?

Allow no difficulty in making the Hour to be an excuse for giving it up. When making it is a pleasure, we can think of ourselves as priests; when it is an effort, we can remember that we are also victims. Then we become like Moses, who asked God to blot his name from the record, if this would win pardon for the people (Exodus 32:31) and like Paul, who was willing to be accursed for his race (Romans 9:1-3). The very effort we put forth each day makes us masters of ourselves, and therefore, better servants of the Sacred Heart.

When tempted to give up the Hour, ask yourself which of these three excuses, which the Lord said would be ours, (Luke 9:57-62) are keeping us back from total service: earthly desires, earthly love, or earthly grief.

Sit or Kneel?

Should one kneel, sit, stand or walk during the Holy Hour? Scripture records examples of each of these various attitudes. The publican who stood in the back of the Temple was accounted justified. St. Simplician, who succeeded St. Ambrose as Bishop of Milan, asked Augustine what was the proper attitude to pray, and why David did not kneel praying before the tabernacle. Augustine replied that one should adopt the bodily position best calculated to move the soul. Aristotle said that the soul by sitting becomes wise. St. Jerome's rule was that in praying and in meditating, the body should always take the position which seemed best for exciting the soul's internal devotion.

Sitting is sometimes associated with despair and weariness in Scripture. When Israel was brought into captivity, and Jerusalem left deserted:

... the prophet Jeremiah sat down there and wept.

(Lamentations 1:1)

242

Elijah, too, in his despair sat down under a juniper tree and "prayed to have done with life" (3 Kings 19:4 [1 KingsI19:4, RSV]). The exiles from Jerusalem are pictured in the Psalm

We sat down by the streams of Babylon and wept there, remembering Sion.

(Psalm 136:1 [137:1, RSV])

And when Moses was praying for victory against Amalek, his "arms grew weary; so they found him a stone to sit on and bade him be seated on it" (Exodus 17: 12).

On the other hand, Our Blessed Lord prayed in the Garden on His knees: "He fell upon his face in prayer" (Matthew 26:39). Stephen prayed in the same position: "Kneeling down, he cried, aloud, Lord, do not count this sin against them" (Acts 7:59). After the miraculous draught of fishes: "Simon Peter fell down and caught Jesus by the knees; Leave me to myself, Lord, I am a sinner" (Luke 5:8). St. Paul evidently prayed kneeling "I fall on my knees to the Father of our Lord Jesus Christ" (Ephesians 3:14). The young man who came to Our Lord inquiring what he must do to receive eternal life "knelt down before him" (Mark 10:17). Even when the soldiers mocked Our Blessed Lord, after beating Him over the head with a rod and spitting upon Him, they "bowed their knees in worship of Him" (Mark 15:19). The gesture of ridicule is an obvious mockery of a gesture of worship.

When Our Lord went into the Garden, He "knelt down to pray" (Luke 22:41). When Peter raised Tabitha from the dead, he "went on his knees to pray" (Acts 9:40). When Paul came to Ephesus, and quoted the only words spoken by Our Lord recorded in Scripture other than in the Gospels ("It is more blessed to give than to receive"), he "knelt down and prayed with them all" (Acts 20:35,36). The Psalmist used a like expression: "Come in, then, fall we down in worship, bowing the knee before God who made us" (Psalm 94:6 [95:6 RSV]). The mother of the sons of Zebedee adopted the same position when seeking preferment for her two boys, "falling on her knees to make a request of Him" (Matthew 20: 20).

The father who had the lunatic son came to Our Lord "and knelt before Him: Lord, he said, have pity on my son, who is a lunatic" (Matthew 17:14). The leper who came up to Our Blessed Lord in the synagogue in Galilee to be healed knelt at His feet and said, "If it be Thy Will, Thou hast power to make me clean" (Mark 1:40). The condition that the devil imposed upon Our Blessed Lord for giving Him all the kingdoms of the world was likewise that of kneeling: "If Thou wilt fall down before me and worship" (Luke 4:7).

Peter, on the contrary, was standing when he warmed himself by the fire (John 18:18,25).

The conclusion is obvious. It is best to kneel during the Holy Hour, for it indicates humility, follows the example of Our Lord in the Garden, makes atonement for our failings, and is a polite gesture before the King of Kings.

How Often?

Should the priest who hears the appeal of the suffering Savior to watch an Hour with Him, make the sacrifice once a week? No! It is too hard. What is done once a week is an interruption of our normal life. The temptation is to put it off until the end of the week, thereby running the risk of not doing it at all.

The weekly Holy Hour can never become a habit. Once a week is not a deep token of love. What mother is content to see her child once a week; what wife, her husband? Love is not intermittent. Medicines taken once a week can give little strength.

If the Holy Hour once a week is too difficult, how often should it be made? The answer is obvious. It should be made every day.

The Holy Hour made once a week is an interruption to the week. But made daily, its absence is an interruption. Furthermore, an act which becomes a habit by daily repetition, loses its difficulty. What at first was imperfectly performed, by habit becomes easier with each progressive stroke. If the Holy Hour is repeated daily at the same hour, we start it without premeditation; it becomes almost automatic. The daily Holy Hour becomes as easy as anything we do daily. It becomes not just a habit, but part of a priest's nature. As Aristotle wrote in his Rhetoric:

> *That which has become habitual becomes, as it were, a part of our nature; habit is something like nature, for the difference between "often" and "always" is not great, and nature belongs to the idea of "always," habit to that of "often."*

In the Old Testament the manna fell each day, not just weekly.

> *But the Lord said to Moses, I mean to rain down bread upon you from heaven. It will be for the people to go out and gather enough for their needs, day by day; and so I shall have a test, whether they are ready to follow My orders or not.*

(Exodus 16:4)

God promised to give them bread every day, but on the day before the Sabbath there fell a double supply, for none would fall on the Sabbath. This daily gathering was a test of love and obedience. The Lord always has a test: in the desert, as well as the Garden. The first parents were tested by the prohibition to eat the fruit of the tree of the knowledge of good and evil. The obedience of the Israelites was tested by the command, not to gather on ordinary days more than enough for that day. All life is probation. The inference suggested is that under the new dispensation, a daily faith in the Eucharist by a Holy Hour is a proof of our faithfulness.

The manna taught a daily lesson of dependence on God, and it played an important part in the spiritual education of Israel. It came not by fits or in starts, but in a regular way. What the Lord gave daily, we can return daily.

The priest should think of the practice of the daily Holy Hour as something to continue for his whole life. The children of Israel ate the manna for forty years (Exodus 16: 35) until they came to the borders of the land of Canaan. The forty years represent the pilgrimage of life. It spiritually implies that every priest should daily gather heavenly manna for his soul.

The daily Holy Hour gives us wisdom. Daily adoration of the Eucharist was not only implied in the type or prefigurement of the manna, but also in the way wisdom is given to those who fulfill the indicated conditions. Our Lord said that those who did His Will would know His doctrine. This means that knowledge is necessary in the beginning in order to love, but that later love deepens knowledge. The Book of Proverbs, speaking of the wisdom that is older than this world, summons the soul to an early and a daily watching:

Love Me, and thou shalt earn My Love; wait early at my doors, and thou shalt gain access to Me.

(Proverbs 8:17)

The mind of the priest who lives close to the tabernacle door gains a special illumination. The priest's mind and heart are best guided when they seek the Eucharistic Lord at dawn. The young priest too is strengthened who begins his watch at the tabernacle door in the first days of his priesthood.

Another passage of the Book of Proverbs describing the daily search for wisdom at the feet of the Lord, is frequently applied to the Blessed Mother:

I was at His side, a master-workman, my delight increasing with each day, as I made play before Him all the while; made play in this world of dust, with the sons of Adam for my playfellows.

(Proverbs 8:30-32)

It is certainly worthy to note that this delight is described not as spasmodic or weekly, but day by day. "Blessed are they who listen to Me, keep vigil, day by day, at My threshold, watching till I open My doors" (Proverbs 8: 34).

Daily exigencies demand a daily Holy Hour. The Lord's Prayer reminds us that yesterday's food does not nourish us today:

Give us this day our daily bread.

(Matthew 6:11)

Vitamins cannot be stored up. Spiritual energy has to be renewed; today's strength must come from the Lord today. Thus the monotony of life is broken, and there comes to the priest new power for each day's apostolate. The Holy Hour each day also destroys in the priest forebodings and worries about the future. Kneeling before the Eucharistic Lord, he receives the rations for each day's march, worrying not at all about the morrow.

The Holy Hour should be a daily event because our crosses are daily, not weekly.

If any man has a mind to come my way, let him renounce self, and take up his cross daily, and follow Me.

(Luke 9:23)

Our children, our missions, our debts, our ulcers, our pet peeves — none of them come in octaves. Their horizontal and vertical weavings form for us a daily cross. These daily crosses will sour us, sear our souls and make us bitter, unless we turn them into crucifixes; and how can that be done except by seeing them as coming from the Lord? That we can do only if we are with Him. The Holy Hour may be a sacrifice, but the Lord does not make the week the unit of sacrifice. He tells us our cross is daily.

One moment in which Our Lord exulted, was when He exclaimed in the midst of His disciples, that "the hour has come" (John 17:1). The word "hour" He used only in relation to His Passion and Death. It was for that time, that hour, that the clock of time had been set in motion; it was for that hour, that the world was created, the Lamb slain, the dust of earth prepared. To it the patriarchs looked forward; to it we look backwards. Without it there would be no Mass, no absolution, no pardon. Will the true priest shrink from such an hour, willing to be a priest but not a victim? To offer, but not to be offered? To be a grain of incense but unready to be consumed in the fire? Rather must he each day take up his cross of watching saying with the Sacred Heart, "the hour has come".

Each day, while it is in his power to do so, because there will be a day and an hour that will not be his over which he will have no control, for

... that day and that hour you speak of, they are known to nobody, not even to the angels in heaven.

(Mark 13:32)

It is not conceivable that a priest who has sanctified each day with its Hour will ever be rejected by the Judge. If Our Lord puts the day and the hour together to make it a symbol of judgment, then shall not we put the day and the hour together unto salvation, unto joy and unto love?

Blessed is that servant who is found doing this when his Lord comes.

(Luke 12:43)

It may be objected, that an hour a day taken out of priestly work, means that much less good can be done. The very same objection was made to Paul's imprisonment. Yet from his prison St. Paul wrote to the Philippians to reassure them that, even if not actively preaching, he was doing good. Each priest in prayer can say as Paul in prison:

I hasten to assure you, brethren, that my circumstances here have only had the effect of spreading the gospel further; so widely has my imprisonment become known, in Christ's honour, throughout the praetorium and to all the world beyond.

(Philippians 1:12)

All the things that were happening to him there, were furthering the Gospel. We all stand committed to Christ under a spiritual obligation to maintain a clear and decisive loyalty, not only for our own sake, but for that of all whom our steadfastness and watchfulness will strengthen. The daily Holy Hour is a limitation on time, but a limitation that is conquered by a superior spiritual good. By human standards nothing could be a greater waste than Paul in prison, just when Christianity was beginning to conquer the world. The same might be said of a pastor beginning a parish. Nothing could seem more wasteful than to sacrifice an hour for the Lord. But God's ways are different. The apparent reverse and discomfiture of man is turned into the triumph of truth. Mercies are garnered and resources found hidden by the priest who knocks on the tabernacle door.

Every pastor may properly ask if he should not give more attention to the tabernacle and the altar in his church, in order to emphasize the Real Presence. An altar which looks like a table and a tabernacle which looks like a box, help little to bring home to the viewer the Divine Presence. Would not the tabernacle perhaps be enriched by restoring the two cherubs prescribed under the law of Moses?

> *Make a throne, too, of pure gold, two and a half cubits long, one and a half cubits broad, and two cherubs of pure beaten gold for the two ends of this throne, one to stand on either side of it; with their wings outspread to cover the throne, guardians of the shrine. They are to face one another across the throne. And this throne is to be the covering of the ark, and the ark's contents, the written law I mean to give thee. Thence will I issue my commands; from that throne of mercy, between the two cherubs that stand over the ark and its records, My Voice shall come to thee, whenever I send word through thee to the sons of Israel.*

(Exodus 25:17-22)

The exact shape of the temple cherubim was kept secret by the Jews. The first-century Jewish historian, Josephus, noted that "no one is able to state or conjecture of what form the cherubim were." The two wings of both cherubs were both so advanced in front of them and elevated, as to overshadow the top of the Ark of the Covenant. Their faces were bent toward one another, so that they both looked downward toward the Ark, as if watching over it. The Cherubs are spoken of as the seraphs of the Temple vision in Isaiah (6:2), and also as the guardians of Paradise (Genesis 3:24). Their wings were also a protecting shade for those who took refuge under them in Divine Mercy (Psalm 90:1-3 [91:1-4 RSV]). St. Peter said later that the angels loved to gaze and meditate upon the mystery of Redemption — an obvious reference to the position of the angels over the Ark of the Covenant.

And now the angels can satisfy their eager gaze.

(1 Peter 1:12)

The top of the Ark, sometimes called the Mercy Seat, was blood-stained, blood being sprinkled on it once a year. As a figure of the New Testament, the faces of the angels are therefore Christ-ward hovering over the cross and the Blood of Redemption.

The angel guarding the Garden of Delight to prevent the return of our first parents (Genesis 3:24), now seems a counterpart of those placed to watch over the prototype of the Eucharist, except that the latter grasp no sword in their hands. Zacharias seems to tell us where the sword will be found, namely, in the Heart of the Shepherd Who offered His life for His sheep.

What wounds be these in Thy Clasped Hands? Thus wounded was I, He shall answer, in the house of my friends. Up, sword, and attack this Shepherd of Mine ... says the Lord of hosts.

(Zachariah 13:6,7)

The pastor's primary concern should be the tabernacle, not the rectory, not the ego, but the Lord, not his comfort, but God's glory. Wall to wall carpeting in a rectory goes poorly with an altar and tabernacle looking like a house on stilts. Should not the King have a better home than his representative? First things first, as David sang:

Never will I come beneath the roof of my house, or climb up into the bed that is strewn for me; never shall these eyes have sleep, these eyelids close, until I have found the Lord a home, the great

God of Jacob a dwelling place.... Let thy priests go clad in the vesture of innocence, thy faithful people cry aloud with rejoicing.

(Psalm 131:3-5,9 [132:3-5,9, RSV])

Some can be forgetful of the Eucharist, as Saul was unmindful of the ark. But David contrasted his own comfortable home with the poverty of the ark: "Here am I dwelling in a house all of cedar, while God's ark has nothing better than curtains of hide about it!" (2 Kings 7:2 [2 Samuel 7:2, RSV]). David could not allow the Eternal God to dwell in an unfitting abode. The Lord rebukes those who build fine houses while neglecting His Temple:

Listen, the Lord said (to them through the prophet Haggai), is it not too early yet for you to have roofs over your heads, and My temple in ruins? ... To your own houses you run helter-skelter, and My temple in ruins! That is why the skies are forbidden to rain on you.

(Haggai 1:4,9,10)

But while we build churches worthy of the Eucharistic Lord, we will give 10 per cent of the cost to build humble homes for the same Lord in Africa and Asia. He who makes the daily Hour will think of this, for he knows that his parish must be a victimhood, as it is also a royal priesthood.

There will come moments when the Hour is difficult — most often on vacation, but sometimes in great distress. What then gives the priest courage? This may be a time of darkness, as when the Greeks had come to Our Lord saying, "We wish to see Jesus," probably because of the majesty and beauty of appearance which they revered so highly as followers of Apollo. But He pointed to His torn and battered Self on a hill, and then added that only through the Cross in their lives will there ever be beauty of soul in the newness of life.

He then paused for a moment as His soul was seized by a frightening apprehension of the Passion and being "made sin," of

251

being betrayed, crucified, and abandoned. Out from the depths of His Sacred Heart welled these words:

And now My soul is distressed. What am I to say? I will say, Father, save Me from undergoing this hour of trial; And yet I have only reached this hour of trial that I might undergo it.

(John 12:27)

These are almost the same words that He used later on in the Garden of Gethsemane — words that are inexplicable except for the fact that He was bearing the burden of the world's sins. It was only natural for Our Blessed Lord to undergo a struggle inasmuch as He was a perfect man. But it was not the physical sufferings alone which troubled Him; He, like Stoics, philosophers, men and women of all ages, could have been calm in the face of great physical trials. But His distress was directed less to the pain, and more to the consciousness of the sins of the world which demanded these sufferings. The more He loved those for whom He was the ransom, the more His anguish would increase, as it is the faults of friends rather than enemies which most disturb hearts!

He certainly was not asking to be saved from the Cross, since He reprimanded His Apostles for trying to dissuade Him. Two opposites were united in Him, separated only in utterance: the desire for release, and *submission* to the Father's will. By laying bare His own soul, He told the Greeks self-sacrifice, was not easy. They were not to be fanatics about wanting to die, for nature does not want to crucify itself; but on the other hand, they were not to turn their eyes from the Cross in cowardly dread. In His own case, now as always, the most sorrowful moods pass into the most blissful; there is never the Cross without the Resurrection; the "Hour" in which evil has mastery passes quickly into the "Day" where God is Victor.

And as at that moment, there came to Him a Voice from heaven, so there will come to the priest-victim a voice from the tabernacle.

~ *16* ~

The Eucharist and the Body of the Priest

One effect of devotion to the Blessed Sacrament is a more lofty concept of the body. Much devotional literature is infected with a Jansenistic emphasis on the vileness of the body. It is represented as a "worm" and "the enemy of the soul," as if the soul could be saved without the body. Such contempt of the body forgets that man is a person, a composite of body and soul. In announcing the Eucharist, Our Blessed Lord spoke of it in relationship not only to the soul but also to the body which will share in the Resurrection.

And He Who sent Me would have Me keep without loss, and raise up at the last day, all He has entrusted to Me.

(John 6:39)

Job, looking forward to the Resurrection while peering at his ulcerous sores, cried out:

This at least I know, that One lives on who will vindicate me, rising up from the dust when the last day comes. Once more my skin shall clothe me, and in my flesh shall I have sight of God.

(Job 19:25)

Similarly, the Lord speaks to Ezekiel:

Will you doubt, then, the Lord's power, when I open your graves and revive you?

(Ezekiel 37:13)

This idea St. Paul developed at length (1 Corinthians 15:35-44), relating it to the Resurrection of Christ. The characteristics the body

253

will assume will reflect those of the soul. If one pours a blue liquid into a glass, the glass looks blue. If one pours red into it, it looks red. If the soul is black within, the body will take on a like corruption. If the soul has a participation of the Divine Nature, the body will take on the radiance of Heaven. As Dante wrote in his *Paradiso*:

Glorious and sanctified flesh shall be put on us again, making our persons more pleasing through being all complete.

What was said of Our Blessed Lord as He came into the world should, therefore, be applicable to every priest.

Thou hast endowed Me instead with a body.

(Hebrews 10:6)

What this means is that God would not be satisfied with the sacrifices of the Old Law (Isaiah 1:11-17; Jeremiah 7:21-23; Hosea 6:6), but that the Body which His Son took was to be the instrument of His divinity. It was thanks to the Body Mary gave Him that He could suffer. It was thanks to the same Body that Divinity walked this earth in the form of man:

In Christ the whole plenitude of Deity is embodied, and dwells in Him.

(Colossians 2:9)

In the wilderness, Satan appealed to the appetite of hunger after Our Lord had been fasting. But Our Lord made reparation for all such sins by offering His Body a Sacrifice on the Cross.

It may be asked why the emphasis in the Epistle to the Hebrews is placed upon the body which Our Lord took, and not upon the soul, as it is in Isaiah (53:10). It was probably to stress the fact that the offering of Christ was to be by death, which required a body; and also to draw attention to the need to confirm the New Covenant by blood as well as the Old. Hence, Our Lord the night of the Last Supper changed the wine into Blood, calling it the Blood of the New Testament or Covenant; but the Blood could not be given without the Body.

Another reason may be to remind us that Christ's Human Nature (Luke 1:35) did not constitute a distinct person, but pertained to the Second Person of the Blessed Trinity. The mystery of the Incarnation is that the Godhead dwelt in the Body; the mystery of Atonement is hidden in One offering of the Body of Christ; the mystery of sanctification is that the Holy Spirit dwells in and sanctifies the Body too.

Since the great High Priest stressed His Body as the source of sanctification for souls, then must not the priest who touches that Body of Christ in the Eucharist, see his own body incorporated in that same Eucharistic Lord?

This respect for the body will manifest itself in two ways: by purity of body, and by a spirit of sacrifice. For all Christians, but particularly for the priest who touches the Body of Christ, the obligation to be pure is clear:

> *But your bodies are not meant for debauchery, they are meant for the Lord, and the Lord claims your bodies.*

> (1 Corinthians 6:13)

> *Have you never been told that your bodies belong to the Body of Christ?*

> (1 Corinthians 6:15)

The body does not belong to the priest; he is only its trustee. He is obligated to use it according to the great High Priest's direction:

> *You are no longer your own masters. A great price was paid to ranson you; glorify God by making your bodies the shrines of His Presence.*

> (1 Corinthians 6:19,20)

It is not only the soul that is the Lord's; it is the body as well. Limb by limb, the body of the priest must be the same as that which the Son of God took, which for us was crucified, and which is now in glory at the right Hand of God. Once the priest actually sees his body as the temple of God, he has to show it a greater respect. The way he dresses, how he presents himself to callers at the door, how he keeps his body disciplined, free from excesses of eating and drinking, these and all his relations to his body, are guided by a sense of what is proper to the temple which is God's. The body of the priest is the temple wall, his senses are its gate, his mind the nave, his heart the altar-priest and his soul the holy of holies.

There will even be a resulting pleasantness about the priest's face. Builders of medieval cathedrals spent much time on the doors to make them as worthy as possible. The face is the doorway of the soul, and it should not be a discredit to the temple. A dreary and sad look, peevishness and discontent, little befit those whose bodies are temples of the Holy Ghost and who touch the Body and Blood of Christ each morning at the altar. In the face will shine forth the Divine Presence.

Purity

The purity of the priest is therefore spiritual before it is physical; it is theological, before it is physiological; it is Eucharistic, before it is hygienic. Purity is a reflection of faith; it is attitude before an act; a reverent inwardness, not a biological intactness.

Purity in the priest is not the result of something he "gives up"; it is reverence for mystery — and the mystery is creativeness. God has allowed creatures to share in His creation. Husband and wife prolong it by begetting fruit to their marriage, an incarnation of their mutual love. The ambassador of Christ is called to another kind of creativeness — he begets souls. He consecrates; he baptizes; he recreates souls in the confessional. In all these acts his body shares. Therefore, he has not surrendered certain functions of the body; he has transformed them, merged them into the Divine plan of redemption.

Consecrated virginity is the highest form of sacral or sacrificial love; it seeks nothing for itself, it seeks only the will of the Beloved. The world makes the mistake of assuming that virginity is opposed to love, as poverty is opposed to wealth. Rather, virginity is related to love, as a university education is related to a grammar-school education. Virginity is the mountain peak of love, as marriage is its hill. Simply because virginity is often associated with asceticism and penance, it is thought to mean only the giving up of something. The true picture is that asceticism is only the fence around the garden of virginity. A guard is always stationed around the crown jewels of England, not because England loves soldiers, but because it needs them to protect the jewels. So, the more precious the love, the greater the precautions to guard it. Since no love is more precious than that of the soul in love with God, the soul must ever be on the watch against lions who would overrun its green pastures. The grating in a Carmelite monastery is not to keep the sisters in, but to keep the world out. As virginity is not the opposite of love, neither is it the opposite of generation. The Christian blessing on virginity did not abrogate the order of Genesis (1:22) to "increase and multiply," for virginity has its own generation. Mary's consecration of virginity was unique in that it resulted in a physical generation — the Word made Flesh. But it also set the pattern for spiritual generation, for she also begot the Christ-like. In like manner, virgin love must not be barren. Rather must it say with Paul:

> *It was I that begot you in Jesus Christ ...*
>
> (1 Corinthians 4:15)

When the woman in the crowd praised the Mother of Our Lord, He turned the praise to spiritual motherhood, and said that she who did the will of His Father in heaven was His mother. Relationship was here lifted from the level of the flesh, to the spirit. To beget a body is blessed; to save a soul, is more blessed, for such is the Father's Will. An idea thus can transform a vital function, not by condemning it to sterility, but by elevating it to a new fecundity of the Spirit. There would, therefore, seem to be implied in all virginity the necessity of apostleship and the begetting of souls for Christ. God, Who hated the man who buried his talent in the ground, will certainly despise those who pledge themselves to be in love with

Him, and yet show no new life — converts or souls saved through contemplation.

Instructing Youths on Purity

In discussing with others the dignity of the body, the true priest will not limit himself to the routine repetition of the traditional prohibitions and the equal routine advice to imitate the Blessed Mother. The "don't" technique is that it makes the young wonder why their instinct of procreation should be so strong, if it has evil associated with it. On the other hand, the young wonder how the Blessed Mother is to be imitated. The ideal is so high and abstract as easily to seem impractical to the young.

As pure water is more than the absence of impurities, as a pure diamond is more than the absence of carbon, and as pure food is more than the absence of poison, so purity is more than the absence of voluptuousness. Because one defends the fortress against the enemy, it does not follow that the fortress itself contains no treasure.

Youth should be told by the priest, that every mystery contains two elements; one visible, the other invisible. For example, in Baptism, water is the visible element and the regenerating grace of the Christ is the invisible element. Sex is a mystery, too, because it has these two characteristics. Sex is something known to everyone, and yet it is something hidden from everyone. The known element is that everyone is either male or female. The invisible, hidden, mysterious element in sex is its capacity for creativeness, a sharing in some way of the creative power by which God made the world and all that is in it. As God's love is the creative principle of the universe, so God willed that the love of man and woman should be the creative principle of the family. This power of human beings to beget one made in their image and likeness partakes of God's creative power.

The young must be made to understand that the torch of life placed by God in their hands, must burn controlled unto the purpose and destiny set by reason and the God of reason. The mystery of creativeness which God put in them is surrounded with awe. A special reverence does envelop the power to be co-creators with God in the making of human life. It is this hidden element which in a special way belongs to God, as does the grace of God in the sacraments. Those who speak of sex alone concentrate on the physical or visible element, forgetting the spiritual or invisible mystery of creativeness. Humans in the sacraments supply the act, the bread, the water, and the words; God supplies the grace, the mystery. In the sacred act of creating life, man and woman supply the unity of the flesh; God supplies the soul and mystery. Such is the mystery of sex as the priest should explain it.

In youth, this awesomeness before the mystery manifests itself in a woman's timidity, which makes her shrink from a precocious or too ready surrender of her secret. In a man, the mystery is revealed in chivalry to women, which is something more than a mere sense of awe in the presence of the unknown. Because, too, of the reverence which envelops this mysterious power which came from God, mankind has always felt that it is to be used only by a special sanction from God and under certain relationships. That is why, traditionally, marriage has been associated with religious rites, to bear witness to the fact that the power of sex which comes from God, should have its use approved by God because it is destined to fulfill His creative designs.

Certain powers may properly be used only in certain relationships. What is lawful in one relationship is not lawful in another. A man can kill another man in a just war, but not in his private capacity as a citizen. A policeman can arrest someone as a duly appointed guardian of the law, but not otherwise. So, too, the "creativeness" of man and woman is lawful under certain relationships sanctioned by God, but not apart from that mysterious relationship called marriage.

Purity is now seen not as something negative, but positive. Purity is such a reverence for the mystery of creativeness, that it will suffer no schism between the use of the power to beget and its Divinely ordained purpose. The pure would no more think of isolating the capacity to share in God's creativeness, than they would think of using a knife for other than its humanly ordained purpose. Those things which God has joined together, the pure would never separate. Never would they use the material sign to dishonor the holy inner mystery, as they would not use the Bread of the altar, consecrated to God, to nourish the body alone.

Purity, then, is not mere physical intactness. The priest will tell the girl it is a firm resolve never to use the power until God sends her a husband. In the boy, it is a steadfast desire to wait upon God's will that he have a wife. In this sense true marriages are made in heaven; for when heaven makes them, body and soul do not pull in opposite directions. The physical aspect, known as sex, is not alienated from the invisible, mysterious aspect which is revealed only to the one willed by God to share in Gods creativeness, in God's own time.

Youth will see that experience bears out the definition of purity as reverence for mystery. No one is scandalized at seeing people eat in public, or read in buses, or listen to music on the street, but they are shocked at dirty shows, foul books, or undue manifestations of affection in public. It is not because youths are prudes, nor because they are educated in Catholic schools, nor because they have not yet come under the "liberating" influence of a Freud, but because these things involve aspects of a mystery so deep, so personal, so incommunicable that they must not be vulgarized.

We like to see the American flag flying over a neighbor's head, but we do not want to see it under his feet. There is a mystery in that flag; it is more than cloth; it stands for the unseen, the spiritual, for love and devotion to country. The pure are shocked at the impure, because of the prostitution of the sacred; it makes the reverent, irreverent. The essence of obscenity is the turning of the inner mystery into a jest. Given a hidden presence of a God-gift in every person, as there is a hidden Divine Presence in the Bread of the altar, each person becomes a host. As one discerns the Bread of Angels under the sign of bread, so one discerns a soul and potential co-partnership with God's creativeness under a body. As the Catholic craves the embrace of Christ in the Sacrament because he first learned to love Him as a Person, so he reveres the body because he first learned to revere the soul. This is adoration in the first instance, and purity in the second.

In dealing with adults, the priest who has given his body to the Lord will explain to them the meaning of "two in one flesh." Not only in marriage, but outside marriage, every such act creates oneness and something that endures through eternity. There is no such thing as drinking the water and forgetting the glass:

> *Am I to take what belongs to Christ and make it one with a harlot? God forbid. Or did you never hear that the man who unites himself to a harlot becomes one body with her? The two, we are told, will become one flesh.*
>
> (1 Corinthians 6:15,16)

Each person possesses a gift which can be given only once, and received only once. In the unity of flesh he makes her a woman; she makes him a man. They may enjoy the gift many times, but once given, it can never be taken back, either in man or in woman. It is not just a physiological experience, but the unraveling of a mystery. As one can pass just once from ignorance to knowledge concerning a given fact or axiom, for example, the principle of contradiction, so one can pass just once from incompleteness to the full knowledge of self which the partner brings. Once that border line is crossed, neither belongs wholly to self. Their reciprocity has created dependence; the riddle has been solved, the mystery has been revealed; the dual have become a unity, either sanctioned by God or in defiance of His Will.

St. Paul also teaches a lesson the priest can communicate about the body.

> *Any other sin a man commits, leaves the body untouched, but the fornicator is committing a crime against his own body.*
>
> (1 Corinthians 6:17,18)

Drunkenness and gluttony are sins done in and by the body, are sins committed through abuse of the body; but they are still outside the body, that is, introduced from without. Fornication is the alienation of a body which is the Lord's and making it the body of someone else; it is the surrendering of the property of the Lord to another. It is a sin against a man's own body in his very nature.

After presenting to others the positive side of purity, then the ideal of the Blessed Mother becomes clear. She is the ideal love we see beyond all creature love, a love to which we instinctively turn when flesh-love fails. She is the ideal that God had in His Heart from all eternity — the Lady Whom He would call our Blessed "Mother." She is the one every man loves when he loves a woman — whether he knows it or not. She is what every woman wants to be, when she looks at herself. She is the woman every man marries in his ideal; she is hidden as an ideal in the discontent of every woman with the carnal aggressiveness of man; she is the secret desire every woman has to be honored and fostered. To know a woman in the hour of possession, a man must first have loved her in the exquisite hour of a dream. To be loved by man in the hour of possession, a woman must first want to be loved, fostered, and honored as an ideal. Beyond all human love is another love; that "other" is the image of the possible. It is that "possible" that each man and each woman loves when they love one another. That "possible" becomes real in the blueprint love of the One beloved of God before the world was made, and in that other love bringing Christ to us and us to Christ: Mary, the Immaculate Virgin, the Mother of God.

The Priest's Body: A Living Sacrifice

The Eucharistic priest lives out Paul's words:

I appeal to you by God's mercy to offer up your bodies as a living sacrifice, consecrated to God and worthy of His acceptance.

(Romans 12:1)

St. Paul may have had in mind some of the sacrifices of the Old Law. The priest, having killed the animal, cut it open and took out all that was unclean. He then washed it, and consumed it on the altar with fire, before the Lord. Our great High Priest would have us wash externally from our guilt in His Blood, and then laying us open, would remove all that was corrupt within us by the washing and regeneration of the Holy Spirit, that we may be laid as holy sacrifices upon the altar and consumed before the Lord.

"Living" may be here understood as opposed to sensual lust which has its source in the body and against which the Apostle later complained (Romans 7:24). "Living" also may mean the continual sacrifice. The Greek word used in this text is the usual one for presenting sacrificial animals at the altar, but here our bodies are specified. The Jew had to present to God the body of an animal, the priest has to present his own body. Under the Law the animal was sacrificed; in the Mass, the priest is "sacrificed" and made a victim.

When the body is offered to God as a "reasonable sacrifice", in the earth is trod not as a golf course, or a market, but as a temple. If our sole sentiment toward our great High Priest was a religious feeling not expressed in an appropriate form of sacrifice, our feelings would eventually die out. Expressing our priestly lives in sacrifice prevents piety from becoming emotional. Nothing gives so much power to the words of the priest in the pulpit, the classroom, or the home, as his self-denials. Nothing in this world is of value until offered or dedicated to a higher end. What is the worth of land, unless we do something with it? What is the worth of our body, unless it is spent for Christ?

The Sacrifice of the Mass which we offer is performed without any satisfaction to the senses. But when does it become sensible, tangible, lived-out, concrete? When the morning sacrifice is made visible in the living sacrifice of the priest's body. Any excesses which dull the spirit and make it unfit to serve Him any absorbing care about outward things which check the growth of Christ in us, such things erect a barrier against the power of the priest to sanctify others *ex opere operantis*. There is no such thing as a "six o'clock Mass." The Mass is continuous — a "living sacrifice." What is mystically presented in the morning Mass must be bodily presented throughout the day.

Having died with Christ on the altar we continue the death in instructing converts, in burying the dead, in consoling the sick, in almsgiving for the Propagation of the Faith. No one will despise the sacrifices which the body ought to make, if the flame sacrifice is kindled at the Consecration.

The continuing sacrifice of the priest is of the heart and mind in thanksgiving (Romans 15: 16; Hebrews 13:15); the sacrifice of good deeds (Hebrews 13:16); the sacrifice of broken hearts and contrite spirits (Psalm 50:17 [51:17 RSV]); the sacrifice of the whole man and the dedication of himself to God (1 Peter 2:15; Romans 12:1; Philippians 2:7).

That the motivation for our living sacrifice is the Eucharist is clear:

So it is the Lord's Death that you are heralding, whenever you eat this Bread and drink this Cup, until He comes.

(1 Corinthians 11:26)

The Eucharist is thus not only an incorporation to the *Life* of Christ, it is also an incorporation to His *Death*. Our Mass not only looks back to the first coming of Christ, but forward to His second coming. The Mass is also a mystical representation of the Death of Christ through the separate consecration of the Bread and Wine, typifying the separation of the Blood from the Body of Christ. This mystical and unbloody representation of the Death of Christ, commits us to the discipline and mortification of the body when we leave the altar. As Christ's Death was not a bare dying, but a death with high and glorious ends, so our re-enactment of it is not a mere historical recalling, but a practical living out of the Cross. Without the prolongation of sacrifice there is only a speculative remembrance, such as one might have of a motion picture, but without a stirring up of mutual love and gratitude.

A decline in reverence in saying the Mass is going to be followed by a decline of sacrifice in the priestly activities of the day. The lazy priest will always work "hardest" to finish his Mass as quickly as possible. He does not want the trumpet call to sacrifice to be loud or too clear. But the saintly priest knows that wheat has to pass through a mill to become fit for the altar and grapes have to be crushed in the wine-press; so too must he be a victim, in order to offer worthily the sacrifice which proclaims and re-enacts the Death of Christ.

Monsignor Ronald Knox bids us reflect on our victimhood. as we say in thanksgiving: "This is His Body which is being given for me; this is His Blood which is being shed for me after all this lapse of time, He still comes to me in the posture of a Victim. And He wants to impress something of Himself on me; I am to be the wax, He the signet ring. Something, then, of the Victim He wants to see in me; does not the *Imitation* say it is up to every Christian to lead a dying life? Not for me, perhaps, to enter very deeply into the dispositions of my Crucified Savior, but to be rather more humble, when I am thwarted; rather more resigned, when things go wrong with me; rather less anxious to make a chart of my own spiritual progress, more ready to let Him do in me what He wants to do, without letting me know about it! If I could only die a little to the world, to my wishes, to myself; be patient and wait for His coming, content to herald His Death by dying with Him!"

Our struggle as priests then is not to become angelic and to live as if we had no body, but to become more Christ-like.

This is my earnest longing and my hope... that this body of mine will do Christ honour....

(Philippians 1:20)

At the end of a busy day when fatigue sets in, because of all we did for Christ's sake, we can read in our body the traces of crucifixion: "We carry about continually in our bodies the dying state of Jesus, so that the living power of Jesus may be manifested in our bodies too" (2 Corinthians 4:10).

In the morning Mass we "announced the death of the Lord"; in parish, home, confessional and everywhere we prolonged it into exhaustion, knowing that such multiple "deaths" for others are the condition of the glorious resurrection of that same body. Some spiritual writers speak of the imitation of Christ as if it were only in the soul. St. Paul insists that the death of Christ is "manifested in our bodies." St. Paul uses two words for body, one is "sarks," which stands for man in his absence from God; the other is "soma," which stands for man in the solidarity of creation and made for God. The first is crucified for Christ's sake, the other is glorified for His sake. The "sarks" cannot inherit the Kingdom of God (1 Corinthians 15:50), but the "soma" can. Since the "body is for the Lord," then our body is not our own. *The priest is not his own.* "You are no longer your own masters. A great price was paid to ransom you; glorify God by making your bodies the shrines of His Presence" (1 Corinthians 6:19,20).

✠ J.M.J. ✠

~ 17 ~

The Priest and His Mother

Every priest has two mothers: one in the flesh, the other in the spirit. Much more is known about the former; much more has been written about the latter. There is no more rivalry between these two mothers than between the priest's earthly father and his heavenly Father. Often, one of the first acts of the mother of the flesh was to lay her son at the feet of the Blessed Mother, as did the author's mother, to symbolize the surrender of filiation. How many were the secret conferences between these two mothers in which the mother in the flesh begged the mother in Christ to have him one day hold a host and a chalice in his hands?

If it is true (as the Fathers say) that Mary conceived in her heart before she conceived in her womb, may not the same be said of the mothers of many priests? Some priests have been called at the eleventh hour, but many mothers may paraphrase the book of Proverbs and say: "The son was not as yet, and I conceived a priest." As God consulted with Mary to ask if she would give Him a human nature, so He often consults with the mother of a priest to ask her consent to the continuation of His priesthood. When the mother's dream is realized, what thoughts pass through the soul of her son, now a priest?

The priest, first, gives up the earthly love of a woman, as Mary gave up the earthly love of a man. His "I have no knowledge of woman" balances her "I have no knowledge of man" (Luke 1:34). The expression in Scripture means carnal union, as in Genesis 4:1 ("Adam had knowledge of his wife, Eve, and she conceived"). From the very beginning, the priest knows that love is simultaneously an affirmation and a negation. Every protestation of love is a limitation on every competing love. True love by its nature imposes restrictions. The married man imposes limitations on himself in respect to all women, but one. The priest admits of no exception, and he does so in the exercise of a perfect freedom. In the Incarnation, God established a beachhead in humanity, through the free choice of a woman; now Our Lord finds an extension of His priesthood in the free act of a priest. He waits upon our consent.

Our earthly mother willed in general to conceive, but when it would be realized was unforeseen and unpredictable. Not so the priest's surrender at ordination. His surrender is like Mary's. She willed her Son and she conceived. So the priest willed to be God's, and he can identify the day and the hour. The more he serves that surrender, the more he knows that only the Christ-fettered are free.

But a priest cannot live without love. The Blessed Mother knew there could be no conception without fire and passion. How could there be a son, since she had "no knowledge of man?" Heaven had the answer. Certainly, there would be fire and passion and love, but that fire and that love would be the Holy Spirit.

Neither can the priest live without love. If there is to be a generation of souls, and if he is to be a "father" begetting other in Christ, there must be love. That love is the same as Mary's; the Fire and Passion of the Holy Spirit overshadowing him. As in her, were united virginity and motherhood, so in the priest, there is to be the unity of virginity and fatherhood. This is not barrenness but fecundity, not the absence of love, but its ecstasy.

The next stage of the priest's love is service.

So it is that the Son of Man did not come to have service done Him; He came to serve others...

(Mark 10:45)

As Mary's spiritual motherhood was not a privilege apart from humanity, so neither is the spiritual fatherhood of the priest. Nothing so provokes the service of others, as a sense of one's unworthiness when visited by the grace of God. Mary hastening over the hills in the Visitation, reveals how she, the handmaid of the Lord, became the handmaid of Elizabeth. She is now the example to the priest that the Christ within him must prompt dedication to "all those who are our friends in the common faith" (Titus 3:15), and to all mankind. As Mary's visit sanctified John the Baptist, so the visit of the priest-victim will always sanctify souls.

Every sick call of the priest will be to him the mystery of the Visitation all over again. Carrying the Blessed Sacrament to his breast, in auto or on foot, makes him another Mary carrying the cloistered Christ within her pure body. No delays on sick calls, no tarrying while the family worries, but like Mary, the priest "hastens" — for nothing demands speed as much as the need of others. The more Christ-possessed the priest is, the more likely he is to hear from those who open the door to him who carries the Blessed Sacrament: "Why, as soon as ever the voice of thy greeting sounded in my ears" (Luke 1:44), my heart leaped with joy. The holy priest inspires Magnificats in every visit to the sick, as the families of the parish say to him: "How have I deserved to be thus visited" (Luke 1:43) by another Christ?

The priest has a deep love of Mary not only in his better moments, but even in his failings. He trusts in her intercession to combat his weakness. Then especially, he looks to her for special attention, knowing that the child who falls most often is apt to get most of the mother's kisses.

If ever the Simon-nature dominates him; if there come moments when, like Demas, he "has fallen in love with this present world" (2 Timothy 4:9); if he becomes known in the parish as a "golfer" or a "swell guy" or "one of the boys" rather than as a good priest, then he knows where he must go to help him find his Lord again. He must go to Mary. She, too, "lost" Christ. That physical loss was a symbol of the spiritual loss which the priest sustains in losing his first ardor. Mary's Heart is pierced with a sword at the loss of every *alter Christus*. But she also is in search of them. To have God and then lose Him is a greater loss than never to have Him. Mary and the weak priest suffer together, but in different ways. She felt the darkness of losing God, when the boy Jesus stayed on in Jerusalem unknown to her (Luke 2:43). It was at this moment that Mary became the Refuge of Sinners. She understood what sin is; for she, a creature, experientially lost the Creator. She lost the Child only in the mystical darkness of soul, while the priest, who falls, feels the moral blackness of an ungrateful heart. But Mary found the Child. To all bishops and priests through the ages, she gave the lesson that we are not to wait for the lost to come back; we must go in search of them. And her intercession will help in the most desperate cases, as we say with Augustine to her: "What all the other saints can do with your help, you alone can do without them."

At the Marriage Feast of Cana, Mary teaches the priest how much he belongs to the Church, and so little to himself. Up to this time and during the feast she is called "Jesus' mother" (John 2:1,3). At its end, however, she becomes "woman" (John 2:4). What happens here is like what happened when Christ was lost for three days. Mary had then said: "Thy father and I" (Luke 2:48), and Our Lord immediately reminded her of His Heavenly Father, recalling the mystery of the Annunciation, and the fact that Joseph was only the putative father.

From that moment, Joseph disappears from Sacred Scripture; he is never seen again. At Cana, "Jesus' mother" asks for a manifestation of His Messianic role and Divinity; Our Lord tells her that the moment He works a miracle and begins His Public Life, He goes to His "Hour," the Cross. Once the "water blushes into wine" at the Divine look, she becomes "woman." As Joseph disappears at the Temple, so Mary as the Mother of Jesus, disappears to become the Mother of all whom He will redeem. She never speaks again in Sacred Scripture. She has spoken her last words, and what a beautiful valedictory they were:

Do whatever He tells you.

(John 2:5)

She now is the "universal Mother," the woman with the seed more numerous than the sands of the sea.

Through Mary's example and influence, there comes a moment in the priest's life when he realizes he does not belong to his family, his parish, his diocese, his country. He belongs to the missions and to the world; he belongs to humanity. The closer the priest gets to the mission of Christ, the more he loves every soul in the world. As Mary "mothered" all men at the Cross, so the priest "fathers" them. No bishop is consecrated for a diocese; he is consecrated for the world. He is assigned to a diocese only for jurisdictional reasons. The priest is not ordained for a diocese; he is ordained for souls. "He does not belong to our parish" is a valid jurisdictional reason for not handling a marriage case, but it is no valid reason for not considering the petitioner as a member of Christ, and therefore, entitled to the milk of human kindness. St. Thomas Aquinas tells us that Mary at the Annunciation spoke in the name of all humanity. At Cana she is given to humanity; at the foot of the Cross, she is confirmed as the mother of mankind.

Devotion to Mary keeps the priest from being the hireling, a hired servant with fixed hours, assigned duties, parish limits, and no lost sheep. There is no "on duty" for a priest. He is "on love" everywhere — on the golf course, in the airplane, in a restaurant, in a hospital. Nothing human is foreign to him. Every soul is either a potential convert, or a potential saint.

In the Passion, Mary teaches compassion to the priest. The saints least indulgent to themselves are the most indulgent to others. But the priest who leads an easy, unmortified life cannot speak the language of the affrighted. Self-raised above need, he cannot bend to console; or if he does, it is with condescension, not compassion. The good priest, on the contrary, sees Mary in the dust of human lives; she lives amidst terror, brain-washings, false accusations, libels, and all the other instruments of terror. The Immaculate is with the maculate, the sinless with the sinner. She bears neither rancor nor bitterness, but only pity, pity that they do not see or know how loving is that Love they are sending to death.

In her purity, Mary is on the mountaintop; in her compassion she is amidst curses, death cells, hangmen, executioners, and blood. A man may become so obsessed with his sinfulness as to refuse to cry to God for forgiveness, but he cannot shrink from invoking the intercession of God's Mother. If the good Holy Mother Mary, who deserved to be spared evil, could nevertheless, in the special Providence of her Son, have a cross, then how shall we, who deserve not to be ranked with her, expect to escape our meeting with a cross? "What have I done to deserve this?" is a cry of pride. What did Jesus do? What did Mary do? Let there be no complaint against God for sending a cross; let there only be wisdom enough to see that Mary is there making it lighter, making it sweeter, making it hers!

Every woe, every wound in the world is ours as a priest. So long as there is an innocent priest in a Siberian jail, I am in prison. So long as a missionary is without a roof over his head, I am homeless. Sharing with these there must be, if there is to be compassion. The priest will never sit and watch the world's enmity against Our Lord, knowing that Mary's co-operation was so real and active that she stood at the foot of the Cross. In every representation of the Crucifixion, the Magdalen is prostrate; she is almost always at the feet of Our Lord. But Mary is standing.

Finally, Mary is present at the death of the priest. Millions of times he has asked Mary to pray for him at the "hour of my death." It is to be hoped that he offered Mass to her once a week during his entire priesthood. Daily, he announced the death of the Lord in the Eucharist (1 Corinthians 11:26), and now he comes not to the end of his priesthood, for that never ends: "A priest forever in the line of Melchizedek" (Psalm 109:4 [110:4 RSV]; Hebrews 5:6). But it is the end of probation. This is the one moment the priest looks most to Mary for her intercession. He sees the Crucifix before him and can hear once again His Lord saying to him, "This is thy mother" (John 19:27). Death to those who are saved is infancy again, a second birth.

That is why it is called *natalitia* or birthday in the liturgy. The world celebrates birthdays when men are born in the flesh; the Church, when souls are born in the Spirit.

But the priest knows that Mary is in labor, for he sees now all his failings in the white light of eternity. At Bethlehem, when she brought forth the High Priest there was no travail, but at the Cross she underwent the pangs of childbirth in becoming the woman or universal mother. The representative of her Divine Son now senses how much extra grief he caused her. But she will not surrender the burden, as she did not refuse John, who was indeed a poor exchange for Jesus.

Two words fall from the priest's lips repeatedly: "Jesus" and "Mary." He had always been a *priest* — now, at last, in death he is also a victim. Twice, the great High Priest had been a *Victim*, on entering the world, and on leaving it. Mary was at both altars, at Bethlehem and at Calvary. Mary was at the priest's altar on the day of ordination, too, and now she is with him at the hour of his death.

Mother of priests! Two loves were always in her life: the love of the Life of her Son, the love of the Death of her Son. The same two loves she bears to every priest. In the Incarnation she was the connecting link between Israel and Christ; at the Cross and Pentecost, she was the connecting link between Christ and His Church. Now she is the link between the priest-victim and the One who is always "making intercession for us in heaven."

Every priest at death wants to be laid in Mary's arms as was the Christ, Whose representative he is. As Mary said after the Crucifixion over her Son Who was laid in her arms: "This is my Body," so she will say at the death of every priest: "This is my body, my victim, my host. As I formed Jesus the Priest in my womb to be a Victim, so I helped Jesus, *Sacerdos Hostia*, to grow in Thee."

Is it any wonder, then, that she is the Woman in every priest's life. No priest is his own. He belongs to the Mother of Jesus, once and always the Priest-Victim.

~ *18* ~

Introduction to Calvary and the Mass

And it came to pass, that as He was in a certain place praying. When He ceased, one of His disciples said to Him Lord, teach us to pray, as John also taught his disciples.

(Luke 11:1)

It was over two thousand years ago that the disciples of Jesus asked Him to teach them to pray. The desire both to know how to pray and to have a prayer life that is satisfying is one that continues to stir in hearts today.

Our Lord lovingly fulfilled the disciples' request when He taught them to pray the Our Father (Luke 11:1–4). By His example, He showed them the necessity of going to a quiet place to pray, to receive guidance and spiritual nourishment (Mark 1:35; Luke 5:16; Matt. 14:23).

While addressing the crowd gathered on the mount, Jesus was likewise reminding the disciples, "When you pray, go into your room and shut the door and pray to your Father who is in secret; and your Father who sees in secret will reward you" (Matt. 6:6).

Archbishop Fulton J. Sheen received this same request that was made of Our Lord: teach us to pray. His students, his parishioners, and his worldwide audience would ask him about ways to pray and about his favorite prayers.

With this in mind, Sheen was keen to encourage people to make prayer a daily, holy habit. To Catholics, he would specifically recommend attending Holy Mass daily whenever possible, to set aside time to pray a Holy Hour, and to pray the Way of the Cross in union with Our Lord's Passion.

Archbishop Fulton J. Sheen was known to have often said: "I do not want my life to be mine. I want it to be Christ's." He had cultivated an intimate prayer life with Christ, and he wanted to share it with everyone.

During the 1930s and '40s, Fulton Sheen was the featured speaker on The Catholic Hour radio broadcast, and millions of listeners heard his radio addresses each week. His topics ranged from politics and the economy to philosophy and man's eternal pursuit of happiness.

Along with his weekly radio program, Sheen wrote dozens of books and pamphlets. One can safely say that through his writings, thousands of people changed their perspectives about God and the Church. Sheen was quoted as saying, "There are not one hundred people in the United States who hate the Catholic Church, but there are millions who hate what they wrongly perceive the Catholic Church to be."

Possessing a burning zeal to dispel the myths about Our Lord and His Church, Sheen gave a series of powerful presentations on Christ's Passion and His seven last words from the Cross. As a Scripture scholar, Archbishop Sheen knew full well the power contained in preaching Christ crucified. With St. Paul, he could say, "For I decided to know nothing among you except Jesus Christ and him crucified" (1 Cor. 2:2).

During his last recorded Good Friday address in 1979, Archbishop Sheen spoke of having given this type of reflection on the subject of Christ's seven last words from the Cross "for the fifty-eighth consecutive time." Whether from the young priest in Peoria, Illinois, the university professor in Washington, D.C., or the bishop in New York, Sheen's messages were sure to make an indelible mark on his listeners.

Given their importance and the impact they had on society, it seemed appropriate to bring back this collection of Sheen's radio addresses that were later compiled into a book titled *Calvary and the Mass* (New York: P.J. Kenedy and Sons, 1936).

In this series of talks, Archbishop Sheen speaks about finding Calvary renewed, re-enacted, and re-presented, in the Mass. Calvary is one with the Mass, and the Mass is one with Calvary, for in both there is the same Priest and Victim. The Seven Last Words are like the seven parts of the Mass. And just as there are seven notes in music admitting an infinite variety of harmonies and combinations, so too on the Cross there are seven divine notes, which the dying Christ rang down the centuries, all of which combine to form the beautiful harmony of the world's redemption.

Each word is a part of the Mass. The First Word, "Forgive," is the Confiteor; the Second Word, "This Day in Paradise," is the Offertory; the Third Word, "Behold Thy Mother," is the Sanctus; the Fourth Word, "Why hast Thou abandoned Me," is the Consecration; the Fifth Word, "I thirst," is the Communion; the Sixth Word, "It is finished," is the Ite, Missa Est; the Seventh Word, "Father, into Thy Hands," is the Last Gospel.

On October 2, 1979, when visiting St. Patrick's Cathedral in New York City, Pope John Paul II embraced Fulton Sheen and spoke into his ear a blessing and an affirmation. He said: "You have written and spoken well of the Lord Jesus Christ. You are a loyal son of the Church." On the day Archbishop Sheen died (December 9, 1979), he was found in his private chapel before the Eucharist in the shadow of the cross. Archbishop Sheen was a man purified in the fires of love and by the wood of the Cross.

It is hoped that upon reading these reflections, the reader will concur with the heartfelt affirmation given by Pope John Paul II about Sheen's giftedness and fidelity. May these writings by Archbishop Fulton J. Sheen evoke a greater love and understanding of the Holy Sacrifice of the Mass. May they reveal to everyone, that the Cross of Jesus Christ, and the Holy Eucharist are the one and true source of all grace, offered for their salvation.

✠ J.M.J. ✠

~ *19* ~

Prologue

There are certain things in life which are too beautiful to be forgotten, such as the love of a mother. Hence we treasure her picture. The love of soldiers who sacrificed themselves for their country is likewise too beautiful to be forgotten; hence, we revere their memory on Memorial Day. But the greatest blessing which ever came to this earth was the visitation of the Son of God in the form and habit of man. His life, above all lives, is too beautiful to be forgotten; hence, we treasure the divinity of His Words in Sacred Scripture and the charity of His Deeds in our daily actions. Unfortunately, this is all some souls remember, namely His Words and His *Deeds*; important as these are, they are not the greatest characteristic of the Divine Saviour.

The most sublime act in the history of Christ was His *Death*. Death is always important for it seals a destiny. Any dying man is a scene. Any dying scene is a sacred place. That is why the great literature of the past, which has touched on the emotions surrounding death, has never passed out of date. But of all deaths in the record of man, none was more important than the Death of Christ. Everyone else, who was ever born into the world, came into it to live; our Lord came into it to die. Death was a stumbling block to the life of Socrates, but it was the crown to the life of Christ. He Himself told us that He came "to give his life redemption for many"; that no one could take away His Life; but He would lay it down of Himself.

If then Death was the supreme moment for which Christ lived, it was, therefore, the one thing He wished to have remembered. He did not ask that men should write down His Words into a Scripture; He did not ask that His kindness to the poor should be recorded in history, but He did ask that men remember His Death. And in order that its memory might not be any haphazard narrative on the part of men, He Himself instituted the precise way it should be recalled.

The memorial was instituted the night before He died, at what has since been called "The Last Supper." Taking bread into His Hands, He said: "This is my body, which shall be delivered for you," i.e., delivered unto death. Then over the chalice of wine, He said, "This is my blood of the new testament, which shall be shed for many unto remission of sins." Thus in an unbloody symbol of the parting of the Blood from the Body, by the separate consecration of Bread and Wine, did Christ pledge Himself to death in the sight of God and men, and represent His death which was to come the next afternoon at three.[1] He was offering Himself as a Victim to be immolated, and that men might never forget that "greater love than this no man hath, that a man lay down his life for his friends." He gave the divine command to the Church: "Do this for a commemoration of me."

The following day, that which He had prefigured and foreshadowed, He realized in its completeness; as He was crucified between two thieves and His Blood drained from His Body for the redemption of the world.

The Church, which Christ founded, has not only preserved the Word He spoke, and the wonders He wrought; it has also taken Him seriously when He said: "Do this for a commemoration of me." And that action whereby we re-enact His Death on the Cross is the Sacrifice of the Mass, in which we do as a memorial what He did at the Last Supper as the prefiguration of His Passion.[2]

Hence the Mass is to us the crowning act of Christian worship. A pulpit in which the words of our Lord are repeated does not unite us to Him; a choir in which sweet sentiments are sung brings us no closer to His Cross than to His garments. A temple without an altar of sacrifice is non-existent among primitive peoples and is meaningless among Christians. And so in the Catholic Church the *altar*, and not the pulpit or the choir or the organ, is the center of worship, for there is re-enacted the memorial of His Passion. Its value does not depend on him who says it, or on him who hears it; it depends on Him who is the One High Priest and Victim, Jesus Christ our Lord. With Him we are united, in spite of our nothingness; in a certain sense, we lose our individuality for the time being; we unite our intellect and our will, our heart and our soul, our body and our blood, so intimately with Christ, that the Heavenly Father sees not so much us with our imperfection, but rather sees us *in Him*, the Beloved Son in whom He is well pleased. The Mass is for that reason the greatest event in the history of mankind; the only Holy Act which keeps the wrath of God from a sinful world, because it holds the Cross between heaven and earth, thus renewing that decisive moment when our sad and tragic humanity journeyed suddenly forth to the fullness of supernatural life.

What is important at this point is that we take the proper mental attitude toward the Mass, and remember this important fact, that the Sacrifice of the Cross is not something which happened two thousand years ago. It is still happening. It is not something past like the signing of the Declaration of Independence; it is an abiding drama on which the curtain has not yet rung down. Let it not be believed that it happened a long time ago, and therefore no more concerns us than anything else in the past. *Calvary belongs to all times and to all places.* That is why, when our Blessed Lord ascended the heights of Calvary, He was fittingly stripped of His garments: He would save the world without the trappings of a passing world. His garments belonged to time, for they localized

Him, and fixed Him as a dweller in Galilee. Now that He was shorn of them and utterly dispossessed of earthly things, He belonged not to Galilee, not to a Roman province, but to the world. He became the universal poor man of the world, belonging to no one people, but to all men.

To express further the universality of the Redemption, the cross was erected at the crossroads of civilization, at a central point between the three great cultures of Jerusalem, Rome, and Athens, in whose names He was crucified. The cross was thus placarded before the eyes of men, to arrest the careless, to appeal to the thoughtless, to arouse the worldly. It was the one inescapable fact that the cultures and civilizations of His day could not resist. It is also the one inescapable fact of our day, which we cannot resist.

The figures at the Cross were symbols of all who crucify. We were there in our representatives. What we are doing now to the Mystical Christ, they were doing in our names to the historical Christ. If we are envious of the good, we were there in the Scribes and Pharisees. If we are fearful of losing some temporal advantage by embracing Divine Truth and Love, we were there in Pilate. If we trust in material forces and seek to conquer through the world instead of through the spirit, we were there in Herod. And so the story goes on for the typical sins of the world. They all blind us to the fact that He is God. There was, therefore, a kind of inevitability about the Crucifixion. Men who were free to sin were also free to crucify.

As long as there is sin in the world, the Crucifixion is a reality. As the poet Rachel Annand Taylor has put it:

"I saw the son of man go by,
Crowned with a crown of thorns.
'Was it not finished Lord,' said I,
'And all the anguish borne?'

He turned on me His awful eyes;
'Hast Thou not understood?
So every soul is a Calvary
And every sin a rood.'"

We were there then during that Crucifixion. The drama was already completed as far as the vision of Christ was concerned, but it had not yet been unfolded to all men and all places and all times. If a motion picture reel, for example, were conscious of itself, it would know the drama from beginning to end, but the spectators in the theater would not know it until they had seen it unrolled upon the screen. In like manner, our Lord on the Cross saw His eternal mind, the whole drama of history, the story of each individual soul and how later on it would react to His Crucifixion; but though He saw all, we could not know how we would react to the Cross until we were unrolled upon the screen of time. We were not conscious of being present there on Calvary that day, but He was conscious of our presence. Today we know the role we played in the theater of Calvary, by the way, we live and act now in the theater of the twentieth century.

That is why Calvary is actual; why the Cross is the Crisis; why in a certain sense the scars are still open; why Pain still stands deified, and why blood like falling stars is still dropping upon our souls. There is no escaping the Cross, not even by denying it as the Pharisees did; not even by selling Christ as Judas did; not even by crucifying Him as the executioners did. We all see it, either to embrace it in salvation or to fly from it into misery.

But how is it made visible? Where shall we find Calvary perpetuated? We shall find Calvary renewed, re-enacted, re-presented, as we have seen, in the Mass. Calvary is one with the Mass, and the Mass is one with Calvary, for in both there is the same Priest and Victim. The Seven Last Words are like the seven parts of the Mass. And just as there are seven notes in music admitting an infinite variety of harmonies and combinations, so too on the Cross there are seven divine notes, which the dying Christ rang down the centuries, all of which combine to form the beautiful harmony of the world's redemption.

Each word is a part of the Mass. The First Word, "Forgive," is the Confiteor; the Second Word, "This Day in Paradise," is the Offertory; the Third Word, "Behold Thy Mother," is the Sanctus; the Fourth Word, "Why hast Thou abandoned Me," is the Consecration; the Fifth Word, "I thirst," is the Communion; the Sixth Word, "It is finished," is the Ite, Missa Est; the Seventh Word, "Father, into Thy Hands," is the Last Gospel.

Picture then the High Priest Christ leaving the sacristy of heaven for the altar of Calvary. He has already put on the vestment of our human nature, the maniple of our suffering, the stole of priesthood, the chasuble of the Cross. Calvary is his cathedral; the rock of Calvary is the altar stone; the sun turning to red is the sanctuary lamp; Mary and John are the living side altars; the Host is His Body; the wine is His Blood. He is upright as Priest, yet He is prostrate as Victim. His Mass is about to begin.

(1) "Death is put before us in a symbol, by means of that sacramental parting of the Blood from the Body; but death at the same time already pledged to God for all its worth, as well as all its awful reality, by the expressive language of the Sacred Symbol. The price of our sins shall be paid down on Calvary, but here the liability is incurred by our Redeemer and subscribed in His very Blood"-Maurice de la Taille, S.J.-Catholic Faith in the Holy Eucharist, p. 115. "There were not two distinct and complete sacrifices offered by Christ, one in the Cenacle, the other on Calvary. There was a sacrifice at the Last Supper, but it was the sacrifice of Redemption, and there was a sacrifice on the Cross, but it was the

selfsame sacrifice continued and completed. The Supper and the Cross made up one complete sacrifice."- Maurice de la Taille, S.J., The Mystery of Faith and Human Opinion, p. 232.

(2) "He offered the Victim to be immolated; we offer it as immolated of old. We offer the eternal Victim of the Cross, once made and forever enduring... The Mass is a sacrifice because it is our oblation of the Victim once immolated, even as the Supper was the oblation of the Victim to be immolated." ibid. p. 239-240. The Mass is not only a commemoration; it is a living representation of the sacrifice of the cross. "In this Divine Sacrifice, which takes place at the Mass is contained and immolated, in an unbloody manner, the same Christ that was offered once for all in the blood upon the Cross ... It is one and the same Victim, one and the same High Priest, who made the offering through the ministry of His priests today, after having offered Himself upon the cross yesterday; only the manner of the oblation is different" (Council of Trent, Session 22).

✠ J.M.J. ✠

~ *20* ~

The Confiteor

"Father, forgive them,

for they know not what they do."

The Mass begins with the Confiteor. The Confiteor is a prayer in which we confess our sins and ask the Blessed Mother and the saints to intercede to God for our forgiveness, for only the clean of heart can see God. Our Blessed Lord also begins His Mass with the Confiteor. But His Confiteor differs from ours in this: He has no sins to confess. He is God and therefore, is sinless. "Which of you shall convince me of sin?" His Confiteor then cannot be a prayer for the forgiveness of *His* sins, but it can be a prayer for the forgiveness of our sins.

Others would have screamed, cursed, wrestled, as the nails pierced their hands and feet. But no vindictiveness finds place in the Saviour's breast; no appeal comes from His lips for vengeance on His murderers; He breathes no prayer for strength to bear His pain. Incarnate Love forgets injury, forgets pain, and in that moment of concentrated agony reveals something of the height, the depth, and the breadth of the wonderful love of God, as He says His Confiteor: "Father, forgive them, for they know not what they do."

He did not say, "Forgive Me," but "Forgive them." The moment of death was certainly the one most likely to produce confession of sin, for conscience in the last solemn hours does assert its authority;

and yet not a single sigh of penitence escaped His lips. He was associated with sinners but never associated with sin. In death as well as life, He was unconscious of a single unfulfilled duty to His heavenly Father. And why? Because a sinless Man is not just a man; He is more than mere man. He is sinless because He is God – and there is the difference. We draw our prayers from the depths of our consciousness of sin: He drew His silence from His own intrinsic sinlessness. That one word, "Forgive" proves Him to be the Son of God.

Notice the grounds on which He asked His heavenly Father to forgive us – "Because they know not what they do." When anyone injures us or blames us wrongly, we say: "They should have known better." But when we sin against God, He finds an excuse for forgiveness – our ignorance.

There is no redemption for the fallen angels. The blood drops that fell from the cross on Good Friday in that Mass of Christ did not touch the spirits of the fallen angels. Why? Because they knew what they were doing? They saw all the consequences of their acts, just as clearly as we see that two and two make four, or that a thing cannot exist and not exist at the same time. Truths of this kind when understood cannot be taken back; they are irrevocable and eternal. Hence when they decided to rebel against Almighty God, there was no taking back the decision. They knew what they were doing!

But with us it is different. We do not see the consequences of our acts as clearly as the angels; we are weaker; we are ignorant. But if we did know that every sin of pride wove a crown of thorns for the head of Christ; if we knew that every contradiction of His divine command made for Him the sign of contradiction, the Cross; if we knew that every grasping avaricious act nailed His hands, and every journey into the byways of sin dug His feet; if we knew how good God is and still went on sinning, we would never be saved. It is only our ignorance of the infinite love of the Sacred Heart that brings us within the hearing of His Confiteor from the Cross: "Father, forgive them, for they know not what they do."

These words, let it be deeply graven on our souls, do not constitute an excuse for continued sin, but a motive for contrition and penance. Forgiveness is not a denial of sin. Our Lord does not deny the horrible fact of sin, and that is where the modern world is wrong. It explains sin away: it ascribes it to a fall in the evolutionary process, to a survival of ancient taboos; it identifies it with psychological verbiage.

In a word, the modern world denies sin. Our Lord reminds us that it is the most terrible of all realities. Otherwise, why does it give Sinlessness a cross? Why does it shed innocent blood? Why does it have such awful associations: blindness, compromise, cowardice, hatred, and cruelty? Why does it now lift itself out of the realm of the impersonal and assert itself as personal by nailing Innocence to a gibbet? An abstraction cannot do that. But sinful man can.

Hence He, who loved men unto death, allowed sin to wreak its vengeance upon Him, in order that they might forever understand its horror as the crucifixion of Him who loved them most.

There is no denial of sin here – and yet, with all its horror, the Victim forgives. In that one and the same event, there is the sign of sin's utter depravity and the seal of divine forgiveness. From that point on, no man can look upon a crucifix and say that sin is not serious, nor can he ever say that it cannot be forgiven. By the way He suffered, He revealed the reality of sin; by the way, He bore it, He shows His mercy toward the sinner.

It is the Victim who has suffered that forgives: and in that combination of a Victim so humanly beautiful, so divinely loving, so wholly innocent, does one find a Great Crime and a Greater Forgiveness. Under the shelter of the Blood of Christ, the worst sinners may take their stand; for there is a power in that Blood to turn back the tides of vengeance which threaten to drown the world.

The world will give you sin explained away, but only on Calvary do you experience the divine contradiction of sin forgiven. On the Cross, supreme self-giving and divine love transforms sin's worst act in the noblest deed and sweetest prayer the world has ever seen or heard, the Confiteor of Christ: "Father, forgive them, for they know not what they do."

That word "Forgive," which rang out from the Cross that day when sin rose to its full strength and then fell defeated by Love, did not die with its echo. Not long before, that same merciful Saviour had taken means to prolong forgiveness through space and time, even to the consummation of the world. Gathering the nucleus of His Church round about Him, He said to His Apostles: "Whose sins you shall forgive, they are forgiven."

Somewhere in the world today then, the successors of the Apostles have the power to forgive. It is not for us to ask: But how can man forgive sins? – For man cannot forgive sins. But God can forgive sins *through* man, for is not that the way God forgave His executioners on the cross, namely through the instrumentality of His human nature?

Why then is it not reasonable to expect Him still to forgive sins through other human natures to whom He gave that power? And where find those human natures?

You know the story of the box, which was long ignored and even ridiculed as worthless; and one day it was opened and found to contain the great heart of a giant. In every Catholic Church, that box exists. We call it the confessional box. It is ignored and ridiculed by many, but in it is to be found the Sacred Heart of the forgiving Christ, forgiving sinners through the uplifted hand of His priest, as He once forgave through His own uplifted hands on the Cross. There is only one forgiveness – the Forgiveness of God. There is only one 'Forgive' – the 'Forgive' of an eternal Divine Act in which we come in contact at various moments of time.

As the air is always filled with symphony and speech, but we do not hear it unless we tune it in on our radios, so neither do souls feel the joy of that eternal and divine 'Forgive' unless they are attuned to it in time; and the confessional box is the place where we tune in to that cry from the Cross.

Would to God that our modern mind instead of denying the guilt, would look to the Cross, admit its guilt, and seek forgiveness; would that those who have uneasy consciences that worry them in the light and haunt them in the darkness, would seek relief, not on the plane of medicine but on the plane of Divine Justice; would that they who tell the dark secrets of their minds, would do so not for the sake of sublimation, but for the sake of purgation; would that those poor mortals who shed tears in silence would find an absolving hand to wipe them away. Must it be forever true that the greatest tragedy of life is not what happens to souls, but rather what souls miss? And what greater tragedy is there than to miss the peace of sin forgiven? The Confiteor is at the foot of the altar our cry of unworthiness: the Confiteor from the Cross is our hope of pardon and absolution. The wounds of the Saviour were terrible, but the worst wound of all would be to be unmindful that we caused it all. The Confiteor can save us from that, for it is an admission that there is something to be forgiven – and more than we shall ever know.

There is a story told of a nun who was one day dusting a small image of Our Blessed Lord in the chapel. In the course of her duty, she let it slip to the floor. She picked it up undamaged, she kissed it, and put it back again in its place, saying, "If you had never fallen, you never would have received that." I wonder if our Blessed Lord does not feel the same way about us, for if we had never sinned, we never could call Him "Saviour."

~ *21* ~

The Offertory

"Amen I say to thee, this day thou

shalt be with me in paradise."

This is now the offertory of the Mass, for our Lord is offering Himself to His heavenly Father. But in order to remind us that He is not offered alone, but in union with us, He unites with His offertory the soul of the thief at the right. To make His ignominy more complete, in a masterstroke of malice, they crucified Him between two thieves. He walked among sinners during His life, so now they let Him hang between them at death. But He changed the picture and made the two thieves the symbols of the sheep and the goats, which will stand at His right and left hand when He comes in the clouds of heaven, with His then triumphant cross, to judge both the living and the dead.

Both thieves at first reviled and blasphemed, but one of them, whom tradition calls Dismas, turned his head to read the meekness and dignity on the face of the crucified Saviour. As a piece of coal thrown into the fire is transformed into a bright and glowing thing, so the black soul of this thief thrown into the fires of the Crucifixion glowed with love for the Sacred Heart.

While the thief on the left was saying: "If thou be Christ, save thyself and us," the repentant thief rebuked him saying: "Neither dost thou fear God, seeing thou art under the same condemnation. And we indeed justly, for we receive the due reward of our deeds; but this man hath done no evil." That same thief then emitted a plea, not for a place in the seats of the mighty, but only not to be forgotten: "Remember me, when thou shalt come into thy kingdom."

Such sorrow and faith must not go unrewarded. At a moment when the power of Rome could not make Him speak when His friends thought all was lost, and His enemies believed all was won, our Lord broke the silence. He, who was the accused, became the Judge: He, who was the crucified, became the Divine Assessor of souls. As to the penitent thief, He trumpeted the words: "This day thou shalt be with me in paradise." This day – when you said your first prayer and your last; this day – thou shalt be with me – and where I am, there is paradise.

With these words our Lord who was offering Himself to His heavenly Father as the great Host, now unites with Him on the paten of the cross the first small host ever offered in the Mass, the host of the repentant thief, a brand plucked from the burning, a sheaf torn from the earthly reapers; the wheat ground in the mill of the crucifixion and made bread for the Eucharist.

Our Lord does not suffer alone on the Cross: He suffers with us. That is why He united the sacrifice of the thief with His own. It is this St. Paul means when he says that we should fill up those things that are wanting to the sufferings of Christ. This does not mean our Lord on the cross did not suffer all He could. It means rather that the physical, historical Christ suffered all He could in His own human nature, but that the Mystical Christ, which is Christ and us, has not suffered to *our* fullness. All the other good thieves in the history of the world have not yet admitted their wrong and pleaded for remembrances. Our Lord is now in heaven. He, therefore, can suffer no more in His human nature, but He can suffer more in our human natures.

So He reaches out to other human natures, to yours and mine, and asks us to do as the thief did, namely, to incorporate ourselves to Him on the Cross, that sharing in His Crucifixion we might also share in His Resurrection, and that made partakers of His Cross we might also be made partakers of His glory in heaven.

As our Blessed Lord on that day chose the thief as the small host of sacrifice, He chooses us today as the other small hosts united with Him on the paten of the altar. Go back in your mind's eye to a Mass, to any Mass which was celebrated in the first centuries of the Church, before civilization became completely financial and economic. If we went to the Holy Sacrifice in the early Church, we would have brought to the altar each morning some bread and some wine. The priest would have used one piece of that unleavened bread and some of that wine for the sacrifice of the Mass. The rest would have been put aside, blessed, and distributed to the poor. Today we do not bring bread and wine. We bring its equivalent: we bring that which buys bread and wine. Hence the offertory collection.

Why do we bring bread and wine or its equivalent to the Mass? We bring bread and wine because these two things, of all things in nature, most represent the substance of life. Wheat is as the very marrow of the ground, and the grapes its very blood, both of which give us the body and blood of life. In bringing those two things, which give us life, nourish us, *we are equivalently bringing ourselves to* the Sacrifice of the Mass.

We are therefore present at each and every Mass under the appearance of bread and wine, which stand as symbols of our body and blood. We are not passive spectators as we might be watching a spectacle in a theater, but we are co-offering our Mass with Christ. If any picture adequately describes our role in this drama, it is this: There is a great cross before us on which is stretched the great Host, Christ. Round about the hill of Calvary are our small crosses on which we, the small hosts, are to be offered. When our Lord goes to

His Cross, we go to our little crosses, and offer ourselves in union with Him, as a clean oblation to the heavenly Father.

At that moment we literally fulfill to the smallest detail the Saviour's command: Take up your cross daily and follow Me. In doing so, He is not asking us to do anything He has not already done Himself. Nor is it any excuse to say: "I am a poor unworthy host." So was the thief.

Note that there were two attitudes in the soul of that thief, both of which made him acceptable to our Lord. The first was the recognition of the fact that He deserved what He was suffering, but that the sinless Christ did not deserve His Cross; in other words, he was *penitent*. The second was *faith* in Him whom men rejected, but whom the thief recognized as the very King of Kings.

Upon what conditions do we become small hosts in the Mass? How does our sacrifice become one with Christ's and as acceptable as the thief's? Only by reproducing in our souls the two attitudes in the soul of the thief: *penitence* and *faith*.

First of all, we must be penitent with the thief and say: "I deserve punishment for my sins. I stand in need of sacrifice." Some of us do not know how wicked or how ungrateful to God we are. If we did, we would not so complain about the shocks and pains of life. Our consciences are like darkened rooms from which light has been long excluded. We draw the curtain and lo! Everywhere what we thought was cleanliness, we now find dust.

Some consciences have been so filmed over with excuses that they pray with the Pharisee: "I thank Thee, O God, that I am not as the rest of men." Others blaspheme the God of heaven for their pain and sins but repent not. The World War, for example, was meant to be a purgation of evil; it was meant to teach us that we cannot get along without God, but the world refused to learn the lesson. Like the thief on the left, it refuses to be penitent: it refuses to see any relation of justice between sin and sacrifice, between rebellion and a cross.

But the more penitent we are, the less anxious we are to escape our cross. The more we see ourselves as we are, the more we say with the good thief: "I deserved this cross." He did not want to be excused; he did not want to have his sin explained away; he did not want to be let off; he did not ask to be taken down. He wanted only to be forgiven. He was willing even to be a small host on his own little cross – but that was because he was penitent. Nor is there given to us any other way to become little hosts with Christ in the Mass than by breaking our hearts with sorrow; for unless we admit we are wounded how can we feel the need of healing? Unless we are sorry for our part in the Crucifixion, how could we ever ask to be forgiven its sin?

The second condition of becoming a host in the offertory of the Mass is faith. The thief looked above the head of our Blessed Lord and saw a sign which read: "KING." Strange king that! For a crown: thorns. For royal purple: His own blood. For a throne: a cross. For courtiers: executioners. For a coronation: a crucifixion. And yet beneath all that dross, the thief saw the gold; amidst all those blasphemies he prayed.

His faith was so strong he was content to remain on his cross. The thief on the left asked to be taken down, but not the thief on the right. Why? Because he knew there were greater evils than crucifixions and another life beyond the cross. He had faith in the Man on the central cross who could have turned thorns into garlands and nails into rosebuds if He willed; but he had faith in a Kingdom beyond the cross, knowing that the sufferings of this world are not worthy to be compared with the joys that are to come. With the Psalmist, his soul cried: "Though I should walk in the midst of the shadow of death, I will fear no evils, for thou art with me."

The Offertory

Such faith was like that of the three youths in the fiery furnace who were commanded by the king, Nebuchadnezzar, to adore the golden statue. Their answer was: "For behold, our God, whom we worship, is able to save us from the furnace of burning fire, and to deliver us out of thy hands, O king. But if He will not, be it known to thee, O king, that we will not worship thy gods, nor adore the golden statue which thou hast set up." Note that they did not ask God to deliver them from the fiery furnace, though they knew God could do it, "for He is able to save us from the furnace of burning fire." They left themselves wholly in God's hands, and like Job, they trusted Him.

So likewise, with the good thief: He knew our Lord could deliver Him. But *he did not ask to be taken down from the cross*, for our Lord did not come down Himself even though the mob challenged Him. The thief would be a small host, if need be, unto the very end of the Mass. This did not mean the thief did not love life: He loved life as much as we love it. He wanted life and a long life, and he found it, for what life is longer than Life Eternal. To each and every one of us in like manner, it is given to discover that Eternal Life. But there is no other way to enter it than by penance and by faith, which unite us to that Great Host – the Priest and Victim Christ. Thus do we become spiritual thieves and steal heaven once again.

✠ J.M.J. ✠

~ 22 ~

The Sanctus

"Woman, behold thy son . . .

behold thy mother."

Five days ago Our Blessed Lord made a triumphal entry into the city of Jerusalem: Triumphant cries rang about His ears; palms dropped beneath His feet, as the air resounded with hosannas to the Son of David and praises to the Holy One of Israel. To those who would have silenced the demonstration in His honour, our Lord reminds them that if their voices were silent, even the very stones would have cried out. That was the birthday of Gothic cathedrals.

They did not know the real reason why they were calling Him *holy*; they did not even understand why He accepted the tribute of their praise. They thought that they were proclaiming Him a kind of earthly king. But He accepted their demonstration because He was going to be the King of a spiritual empire. He accepted their tributes, their hosannas, and their pæans of praise because He was going to His cross as a Victim. And every victim must be holy – *Sanctus, Sanctus, Sanctus*. Five days later came the *Sanctus* of the Mass of Calvary. But at that *Sanctus* of His Mass, He does not say "holy" – He speaks to the holy ones; He does not whisper "Sanctus" – He addresses Himself *to* saints, to His sweet Mother Mary, and His beloved disciple, John.

Striking words they are: "Woman, behold thy son . . . behold thy mother." He was speaking now to saints. He had no need of saintly intercession, for He was the Holy One of God. But we have need of holiness, for every victim of the Mass must be holy, undefiled, and unpolluted. But how can we be holy participants in the Sacrifice of the Mass? He gave the answer: namely, by putting ourselves under the protection of His Blessed Mother. He addresses the Church and all its members in the person of John, and says to each of us: "Behold thy mother." That is why He addressed her not as "Mother" but as "Woman." She had a universal mission, to be not only His Mother but to be the Mother of all Christians. She had been His Mother; now, she was to be the Mother of His Mystical Body, the Church. And we were to be her children.

There is a tremendous mystery hidden in that one word, "Woman." It was really the last lesson in detachment which Jesus had been teaching her these many years and the first lesson of the new attachment. Our Lord had been gradually 'alienating,' as it were, His affections from His Mother, not in the sense that she was to love Him less, or that He was to love her less but only in the sense that she was to love us more. She was to be detached from motherhood in the flesh, only to be more attached to that greater motherhood in the spirit. Hence the word: "Woman." She was to make us *other Christs*, for as Mary had raised the Holy One of God, so only she could raise us as holy ones for God, worthy to say *Sanctus, Sanctus, Sanctus*, in the Mass of that prolonged Calvary.

The story of the preparation for her role as Mother of the Mystical Body of Christ is unfolded in three scenes in the life of her divine Son, each one suggesting the lesson which Calvary itself was to reveal: namely, that she was called to be not only the Mother of God but also the Mother of men; not only the Mother of holiness but the Mother of those who ask to be holy.

The first scene took place in the Temple, where Mary and Joseph found Jesus after a three-day search. The Blessed Mother reminds Him that their hearts were broken with sorrow during the long search, and He answers: "Did you not know that I must be about my Father's business?" Here He was equivalently saying: "I have another business, Mother, than the business of the carpenter shop. My Father has sent Me into this world on the supreme business of Redemption, to make all men adopted sons of My heavenly Father in the greater kingdom of the brotherhood of Christ, Thy Son." How far the full vision of those words dawned upon Mary, we know not; whether she then understood that the Fatherhood of God meant that she was to be the Mother of men, we know not. But certainly, eighteen years later, in the second scene, the marriage feast of Cana, she came to a fuller understanding of that mission.

What a consoling thought it is to think that our Blessed Lord, who talked penance, who preached mortification, who insisted upon taking up the cross daily and following Him, should have begun His public life by assisting at a wedding festival! What a beautiful understanding of our hearts!

When in the course of the banquet, the wine was exhausted, Mary, always interested in others, was the first to notice, and the first to seek relief from the embarrassment. She simply said to our Blessed Lord, "They have no wine." And our Blessed Lord said to her, "Woman, what is that to me and to thee? my hour is not yet come." "Woman, what is that to me?" He did not call her "Mother," but "Woman" – the same title she was to receive three years later.

He was equivalently saying to her: "You are asking Me to do something which belongs to Me as the Son of God. You are asking Me to work a miracle which only God can work; you are asking Me to exercise My divinity, which has relationship to all mankind, namely as its Redeemer. But once that divinity operates for the salvation of the world, you become not only My Mother but the

Mother of redeemed humanity. Your physical motherhood passes into the wider world of spiritual motherhood, and for that reason, I call you: 'Woman.'" And in order to prove that her intercession is powerful in that role of universal motherhood, He ordered the pots filled with water, and in the language of Crashaw the first miracle was worked: "the conscious waters saw their God and blushed."

The third scene happens within two years. One day as our Lord was preaching someone interrupted His discourse to say, "Thy mother . . . stands without, seeking thee." Our Blessed Lord said, "Who is my mother?" and stretching forth His hands toward His disciples He said: "Behold my mother and my brethren. For whosoever shall do the will of my Father, that is in heaven, he is my brother, and my sister, and mother." The meaning was unmistakable. There is such a thing as spiritual maternity; there are bonds other than those of the flesh; there are ties other than the ties of blood, namely spiritual ties which band together those of the Kingdom where reign the Fatherhood of God and the Brotherhood of Christ.

These three scenes have their climax at the Cross, where Mary is called "Woman." It was the second Annunciation. The angel said to her in the first: "Hail, Mary." Her Son speaks to her in the second: "Woman." This did not mean she ceased to be His Mother; she is always the Mother of God; but her Motherhood enlarged and expanded; it became spiritual, it became universal, for at that moment she became our mother. Our Lord created the bond where it did not exist by nature as only He could do.

And how did she become the Mother of men? By becoming not only the mother but also the spouse of Christ. He was the new Adam; she is the new Eve. And as Adam and Eve brought forth their natural progeny, which we are, so Christ and His Mother brought forth at the Cross their spiritual progeny, which we are: children of Mary or members of the Mystical Body of Christ. She brought forth her First-born at Bethlehem. Note that St. Luke calls our Lord the *First-born*

– not that our Blessed Mother was to have other children *according to the flesh*, but only because she was to have other children *according to the spirit*. That moment when our Blessed Lord said to her, "Woman," she became in a certain sense the spouse of Christ, and she brought forth in sorrow her first-born in the spirit, and his name was John. Who the second-born was we know not. It might have been Peter. It might have been Andrew. But we, at any rate, are the millionth-and-millionth-born of that woman at the foot of the Cross. It was a poor exchange indeed, receiving the son of Zebedee in place of the Son of God. But surely our gain was greater, for while she acquired but undutiful and often rebellious children, we obtained the most loving Mother in the world – the Mother of Jesus.

We are children of Mary – literally, *children*. She is our Mother, not by title of fiction, not by title of courtesy; she is our Mother because she endured at that particular moment the pains of childbirth for all of us. And why did our Lord give her to us as Mother? Because He knew *we could never be holy without her*. He came to us through her purity, and only through her purity can we go back to her. There is no Sanctus apart from Mary. Every victim that mounts that altar under the species of bread and wine must have said the Confiteor, and become a holy victim – but there is no holiness without Mary.

Note that when that word was spoken to our Blessed Mother, there was another woman there who was prostrate. Have you ever remarked that practically every traditional representation of the Crucifixion always pictures Magdalene on her knees at the foot of the crucifix? But you have never yet seen an image of the Blessed Mother prostrate. John was there, and he tells in his Gospel that she stood. He saw her stand. But why did she stand? She stood to be of service to us. She stood to be our minister, our Mother.

If Mary could have prostrated herself at that moment as Magdalene did, if she could have only wept, her sorrow would have had an outlet. The sorrow that cries is never the sorrow that breaks the heart. It is the heart that can find no outlet in the fountain of tears which cracks; it is the heart that cannot have an emotional breakdown that breaks. And all that sorrow was part of our purchase price paid by our Co-Redemptrix, Mary the Mother of God!

Because our Lord willed her to us as our Mother, He left her on this earth after He ascended into heaven, in order that she might mother the infant Church. The infant Church had need of a mother, just as the infant Christ. She had to remain on earth until her family had grown. That is why we find her on Pentecost abiding in prayer with the Apostles, awaiting the descent of the Holy Spirit. She was mothering the Mystical Body of Christ.

Now she is crowned in heaven as Queen of Angels and Saints, turning heaven into another marriage feast of Cana when she intercedes with her divine Saviour on behalf of us, her other children, brothers of Christ and sons of the heavenly Father.

Virgin Mother! What a beautiful conjunction of virginity and motherhood, one supplying the defect of the other. Virginity alone lacks something: there is an incompleteness about it; something unfulfilled; a faculty unused. Motherhood alone loses something: there is a surrender, an unflowering, a plucking of a blossom. Oh! For a *rapprochement* in which there would be a virginity that never lacked anything and a motherhood that never lost anything! We have both in Mary, the Virgin Mother: Virgin by the overshadowing of the Holy Spirit in Bethlehem and Pentecost; Mother by the millions of her progeny from Jesus unto you and me.

There is no question here of confusing our Lady and our Lord; we venerate our Mother, we worship our Lord. We ask of Jesus those things which only God can give: mercy, grace, and forgiveness. We ask that Mary should intercede for us with Him, and especially at the hour of our death. Because of her nearness to Jesus, which her vocation involves, we know our Lord listens especially to her appeal. To no other saint can we speak as a child to its mother: no other virgin, or martyr, or mother, or confessor has ever suffered as much for us as she has; no one has ever established better claim to our love and patronage than she.

As the Mediatrix of all graces, all favors come to us from Jesus through her, as Jesus himself came to us through her. We wish to be holy, but we know there is no holiness without her, for she was the gift of Jesus to us at the *Sanctus* of His Cross. No woman can ever forget the child of her womb; then certainly Mary can never forget us. That is why we feel way down deep in our hearts that every time she sees another innocent child at the First Communion rail, or another penitent sinner making his way to the Cross, or another broken heart pleading that the water of a wasted life be changed into the wine of God's love, that she hears once again that word: "Woman, behold thy son."

✠ J.M.J. ✠

~ 23 ~

The Consecration

"My God, My God, why hast thou forsaken me?"

The Fourth Word is the Consecration of the Mass of Calvary. The first three Words were spoken to men, but the last four Words were spoken to God. We are now in the final stage of the Passion. In the fourth Word, in all the universe, there is but God and Himself. This is the hour of darkness. Suddenly out of its blackness, the silence is broken by a cry – so terrible, so unforgettable, that even those who did not understand the dialect remembered the strange tones: "*Eli, Eli, lamma sabacthani.*" They recorded it so, a rough rendering of the Hebrew because they could never get the sound of those tones out of their ears all the days of their life.

The darkness, which was covering the earth at that moment, was only the external symbol of the dark night of the soul within. Well indeed might the sun hide its face, at the terrible crime of Deicide. A real reason why the earth was made was to have a Cross erected upon it. And now that the Cross was erected, creation felt the pain and went into darkness.

But why the cry of darkness? Why the cry of abandonment: "My God, my God, why hast thou forsaken me?" It was the cry of atonement for sin. Sin is the abandonment of God by man; it is the creature forsaking the Creator, as a flower might abandon the sunlight, which gave its strength and beauty. Sin is a separation, a

307

divorce – the original divorce from unity with God, whence all other divorces are derived.

Since He came on earth to redeem men from sin, it was therefore fitting that He *feels* that abandonment, that separation, that divorce. He felt it first internally, in His soul, as the base of a mountain, if conscious, might feel abandoned by the sun when a cloud drifted about it, even though its great heights were radiant with light. There was no sin in His soul, but since He willed to feel the effect of sin, an awful sense of isolation and loneliness crept over Him – the loneliness of being without God.

Surrendering the divine consolation which might have been His, He sank into an awful human aloneness, to atone for the solitariness of a soul that has lost God by sin; for the loneliness of the atheist who says there is no God, for the isolation of the man who gives up his faith for things, and for the broken-heartedness of all sinners who are homesick without God. He even went so far as to redeem all those who will not trust, who in sorrow and misery curse and abandon God, crying out: "Why this death? Why should I lose my property? Why should I suffer?" He atoned for all these things by asking a "Why" of God.

But in order better to reveal the intensity of that feeling of abandonment, He revealed it by an external sign. Because man had separated himself from God, He, in atonement, permitted His Blood to be separated from His Body. Sin had entered into the blood of man; and as if the sins of the world were upon Him, He drained the chalice of His Body of His sacred Blood. We can almost hear Him say: "Father, this is My Body; this is My Blood. They are being separated from one another as humanity has been separated from Thee. This is the consecration of My Cross."

What happened there on the Cross that day is happening now in the Mass, with this difference: On the Cross the Saviour was alone;

in the Mass, He is with us. Our Lord is now in heaven at the right hand of the Father, making intercession for us. He, therefore, can never suffer again *in His own human nature*. How then can the Mass be the re-enactment of Calvary? How can Christ renew the Cross? He cannot suffer again in His own human nature, which is in heaven enjoying beatitude, but He can suffer again in our human natures. He cannot renew Calvary in His *physical body*, but He can renew it in *His Mystical Body* – the Church. The Sacrifice of the Cross can be re-enacted provided we give Him our body and our blood, and give it to Him so completely that as His own, He can offer Himself anew to His heavenly Father for the redemption of His Mystical Body, the Church.

So the Christ goes out into the world gathering up other human natures who are willing to be Christs. In order that our sacrifices, our sorrows, our Golgothas, our crucifixions, may not be isolated, disjointed, and unconnected, the Church collects them, harvests them, unifies them, coalesces them, masses them, and this massing of all our sacrifices of our individual human natures is united with the Great Sacrifice of Christ on the Cross in the Mass.

When we assist at the Mass we are not just individuals of the earth or solitary units, but living parts of a great spiritual order in which the Infinite penetrates and enfolds the finite, the Eternal breaks into the temporal, and the Spiritual clothes itself in the garments of materiality. Nothing more solemn exists on the face of God's earth than the awe-inspiring moment of Consecration; for the Mass is not a prayer, nor a hymn, nor something said – it is a Divine Act with which we come in contact at a given moment of time.

An imperfect illustration may be drawn from the radio. The air is filled with symphonies and speech. We do not put the words or music there; but, if we choose, we may establish contact with them by tuning in our radio. And so with the Mass. It is a singular, unique

Divine Act with which we come in contact each time it is re-presented and re-enacted in the Mass.

When the die of a medal or coin is struck, the medal is the material, visible representation of a spiritual idea existing in the mind of the artist. Countless reproductions may be made from that original as each new piece of metal is brought in contact with it, and impressed by it. Despite the multiplicity of coins made, the pattern is always the same. In like manner in the Mass, the Pattern – Christ's sacrifice on Calvary – is renewed on our altars as each human being is brought in contact with it at the moment of consecration; but the sacrifice is one and the same despite the multiplicity of Masses. The Mass then is the communication of the Sacrifice of Calvary to us under the species of bread and wine.

We are on the altar under the appearance of bread and wine, for both are the sustenance of life; therefore, in giving that which gives us life we are symbolically giving ourselves. Furthermore, wheat must suffer to become bread; grapes must pass through the winepress to become wine. Hence both are representative of Christians who are called to suffer with Christ, that they may also reign with Him.

As the consecration of the Mass draws near our Lord is equivalently saying to us: "You, Mary; you, John; you, Peter; and you, Andrew – you, all of you – give Me your body; give Me your blood. Give Me your whole self! I can suffer no more. I have passed through My cross, I have filled up the sufferings of My physical body, but I have not filled up the sufferings wanting to My Mystical Body, in which you are. The Mass is the moment when each one of you may literally fulfill My injunction: 'Take up your cross and follow Me.'"

On the cross, our Blessed Lord was looking forward to you, hoping that one day you would be giving yourself to Him at the moment of consecration. Today, in the Mass, that hope our Blessed

Lord entertained for you is fulfilled. When you assist at the Mass, He expects you now actually to give Him yourself.

Then as the moment of consecration arrives, the priest in obedience to the words of our Lord, "Do this for a commemoration of me," takes bread in his hands and says, "This is my body"; and then over the chalice of wine says, "This is the chalice of my blood of the new and eternal testament." He does not consecrate the bread and wine together, but separately. The separate consecration of the bread and wine is a symbolic representation of the separation of body and blood, and since the Crucifixion entailed that very mystery, Calvary is thus renewed on our altar. But Christ, as has been said, is not alone on our altar; we are with Him. Hence the words of consecration have a double sense; the primary signification of the words is: "This is the Body of Christ; this is the Blood of Christ;" but the secondary signification is "This is my body; this is my blood."

Such is the purpose of life! To redeem ourselves in union with Christ; to apply His merits to our souls by being like Him in all things, even to His death on the Cross. He passed through His consecration on the Cross that we might now pass through ours in the Mass. There is nothing more tragic in all the world than wasted pain.

Think of how much suffering there is in hospitals, among the poor, and the bereaved. Think also of how much of that suffering goes to waste! How many of those lonesome, suffering, abandoned, crucified souls are saying with our Lord at the moment of consecration, "This is my body. Take it," And yet that is what we all should be saying at that second:

I GIVE MYSELF TO GOD. HERE IS MY BODY. TAKE IT. HERE IS MY BLOOD. TAKE IT. HERE IS MY SOUL, MY WILL, MY ENERGY, MY STRENGTH, MY PROPERTY, MY

WEALTH – ALL THAT I HAVE. IT IS YOURS. TAKE IT! CONSECRATE IT! OFFER IT! OFFER IT WITH THYSELF TO THE HEAVENLY FATHER IN ORDER THAT HE, LOOKING DOWN ON THIS GREAT SACRIFICE, MAY SEE ONLY THEE, HIS BELOVED SON, IN WHOM HE IS WELL PLEASED. TRANSMUTE THE POOR BREAD OF MY LIFE INTO THY DIVINE LIFE; THRILL THE WINE OF MY WASTED LIFE INTO THY DIVINE SPIRIT; UNITE MY BROKEN HEART WITH THY HEART; CHANGE MY CROSS INTO A CRUCIFIX. LET NOT MY ABANDONMENT, AND MY SORROW AND MY BEREAVEMENT GO TO WASTE. GATHER UP THE FRAGMENTS, AND AS THE DROP OF WATER IS ABSORBED BY THE WINE AT THE OFFERTORY OF THE MASS, LET MY LIFE BE ABSORBED IN THINE; LET MY LITTLE CROSS BE ENTWINED WITH THY GREAT CROSS SO THAT I MAY PURCHASE THE JOYS OF EVERLASTING HAPPINESS IN UNION WITH THEE.

"CONSECRATE THESE TRIALS OF MY LIFE WHICH WOULD GO UNREWARDED UNLESS UNITED WITH THEE; TRANSUBSTANTIATE ME SO THAT LIKE BREAD WHICH IS NOW THY BODY, AND WINE WHICH IS NOW THY BLOOD, I TOO MAY BE WHOLLY THINE. I CARE NOT IF THE SPECIES REMAIN, OR THAT, LIKE THE BREAD AND THE WINE I SEEM TO ALL EARTHLY EYES THE SAME AS BEFORE. MY STATION IN LIFE, MY ROUTINE DUTIES, MY WORK, MY FAMILY – ALL THESE ARE BUT THE SPECIES OF MY LIFE WHICH MAY REMAIN UNCHANGED; BUT THE *substance* OF MY LIFE, MY SOUL, MY MIND, MY WILL, MY HEART – TRANSUBSTANTIATE THEM, TRANSFORM THEM WHOLLY INTO THY SERVICE, SO THAT THROUGH ME ALL MAY KNOW HOW SWEET IS THE LOVE OF CHRIST." AMEN.

~ 24 ~

The Communion

"I thirst."

Our Blessed Lord reaches the communion of His Mass when out from the depths of the Sacred Heart, there wells the cry: "I thirst." This was certainly not a thirst for water, for the earth is His and the fullness thereof; it was not a thirst for any of the refreshing draughts of earth, for He calmed the seas with doors when they burst forth in their fury. When they offered Him a drink, He took it not. It was another kind of thirst which tortured Him. He was thirsty for the souls and hearts of men.

The cry was a cry for communion – the last in a long series of shepherding calls in the quest of God for men. The very fact that it was expressed in the most poignant of all human sufferings, namely, thirst, was the measure of its depth and intensity. Men may *hunger* for God, but God *thirsts* for men. He thirsted for man in Creation as He called him to fellowship with divinity in the garden of Paradise; He thirsted for man in Revelation, as He tried to win back man's erring heart by telling the secrets of His love; He thirsted for man in the Incarnation when He became like the one He loved and was found in the form and habit of man.

Now He was thirsting for man in Redemption, for greater love than this no man hath, that he lay down his life for his friends. It was the final appeal for communion before the curtain rang down on the Great Drama of His earthly life. All the myriad loves of parents for children, of spouse for spouse, if compacted into one great love, would have been the smallest fraction of God's love for man in that cry of thirst. It signified at once, not only how much He thirsted for the little ones, for hungry hearts and empty souls, but also how intense was His desire to satisfy our deepest longing.

Really, there should be nothing mysterious in our thirst for God, for does not the heart pant after the fountain, and the sunflower turn to the sun and the rivers run into the sea? But that He should love us, considering our own unworthiness, and how little our love is worth – *that is the mystery!* And yet such is the meaning of God's thirst for communion with us.

He had already expressed it in the parable of the Lost Sheep when He said He was not satisfied with the ninety-nine; only the lost sheep could give Him perfect joy. Now the truth was expressed again from the Cross: Nothing could adequately satisfy His thirst, but the heart of every man, woman, and child, who were made for Him, and therefore could never be happy until they found their rest in Him.

The basis of this plea for communion is Love, for Love by its very nature tends to unity. Love of citizens one for another begets the unity of the state. Love of man and woman begets the unity of two in one flesh. The love of God for man, therefore, calls for a unity based upon the Incarnation, namely, the unity of all men in the Body and Blood of Christ.

In order, therefore, that God might seal His love for us, He gave us to Himself in Holy Communion, so that as He and His human nature taken from the womb of the Blessed Mother were one in the unity of His Person, so He and we taken from the womb of humanity might be one in the unity of the Mystical Body of Christ. Hence, we use the word "receive" when speaking of communion with our Lord in the Eucharist, for literally we do "receive" Divine Life, just as really and truly as a babe receives the life of its mother.

All life is sustained by communion with a higher life. If the plants could speak, they would say to the moisture and sunlight, "Unless you enter into communion with me, become possessed of my higher laws and powers, you shall not have life in you."

If the animals could speak, they would say to the plants: "Unless you enter into communion with me, you shall not have my higher life in you." We say to all lower creation: "Unless you enter into communion with me, you shall not share in my human life."

Why then should not our Lord say to us: "Unless you enter into communion with Me, you shall not have life in you"? The lower is transformed into, the higher, plants into animals, animals into man, and man, in a more exalted way, becomes "divinized," (if I may use that expression) through and through by the life of Christ.

Communion then is first of all the receiving of Divine Life, a life to which we are no more entitled than marble is entitled to blooming. It is a pure gift of an all-merciful God who so loved us that He willed to be united with us, not in the bonds of flesh, but in the ineffable bonds of the Spirit where love knows no satiety, but only rapture and joy.

And oh, how quickly we should have forgotten Him could we not, like Bethlehem and Nazareth, receive Him into our souls! Neither gifts nor portraits take the place of the beloved one. And our Lord knew it well. We needed Him, and so He gave us Himself.

But there is another aspect of Communion of which we but rarely think. Communion implies not only *receiving* Divine Life; it means also God *giving* human life. All love is reciprocal. There is no one-sided love, for love by its nature demands mutuality. God thirsts for us, but that means that man must also thirst for God. But do we ever think of Christ receiving Communion from us? Every time we go to the Communion rail, we say we 'receive' Communion, and that is all many of us do, just 'receive Communion.'

There is another aspect of Communion than receiving Divine Life, of which St. John speaks. St. Paul gives us the complementary truth in his Epistle to the Corinthians. Communion is not only an incorporation to the *life* of Christ; it is also an incorporation to His *death*. "As often as you shall eat this bread, and drink the chalice, you shall show the death of the Lord, until He come." (1 Cor. 11:26)

Natural life has two sides: the anabolic and the katabolic. The supernatural also has two sides: the building up of the Christ-pattern and the tearing down of the old Adam. Communion, therefore, implies not only a "receiving" but also a "giving." There can be no ascent to a higher life without death to a lower one. Does not an Easter Sunday presuppose a Good

Friday? Does not all love imply mutual self-giving which ends in self-recovery? This being so, should not the Communion rail be a place of exchange, instead of a place of exclusive receiving? Is all the *Life* to pass from Christ to us and nothing to go back in return? Are we to drain the chalice and contribute nothing to its filling? Are we to receive the bread without giving wheat to be ground, to receive the wine and give no grapes to be crushed? If all we did during our lives was to go to Communion to receive Divine Life, to take it away, and leave nothing behind, we would be parasites on the Mystical Body of Christ.

The Pauline injunction bids us fill up in our body the sufferings wanting to the Passion of Christ. We must, therefore, bring a spirit of sacrifice to the Eucharistic table; we must bring the mortification of our lower self, the crosses patiently borne, the crucifixion of our egotism, the death of our concupiscence, and even the very difficulty of our coming to Communion. Then does Communion become what it was always intended to be, namely, a commerce between Christ and the soul, in which we give His Death shown forth in our lives, and He gives His Life shown forth in our adopted sonship? We give Him our time; He gives us His eternity. We give Him our humanity; He gives us His divinity. We give Him our nothingness; He gives us His all.

Do we really understand the nature of love? Have we not sometimes, in great moments of affection for a little child, said in language which might vary from this, but which expresses the idea, "I love that child so much, I should just like to possess it within myself?" Why? Because all love craves for unity. In the natural order, God has given great pleasures to the unity of the flesh. But those are nothing compared to the pleasure of the unity of the spirit when divinity passes out to humanity, and humanity to divinity – when our will goes to Him, and He comes to us so that we cease to be men and begin to be children of God.

If there has ever been a moment in your life when a fine, noble affection made you feel as if you had been lifted into the third or the seventh heaven; if there has ever been a time in your life when a noble love of a fine human heart cast you into an ecstasy; if there has ever been a time when you have really loved a human heart – then, I ask you, think of what it must be to be united with the great Heart of Love! If the human heart in all of its fine, noble, Christian riches can so thrill, can so exalt, can make us so ecstatic, then what must be the great heart of Christ? Oh, if the spark is so bright, what must be the flame!

Do we fully realize how much Communion is bound up with Sacrifice, both on the part of our Lord and on the part of us, His poor weak creatures? The Mass makes the two inseparable: there is no Communion without a Consecration. There is no receiving the bread and wine we offer until they have been transubstantiated into the Body and Blood of Christ. Communion is the consequence of the Calvary: namely, we live by what we slay. All nature witnesses this truth; our bodies live by the slaying of the beasts of the fields and the plants of the gardens. We draw life from their crucifixion. We slay them not to destroy, but to fulfill; we immolate them for the sake of communion.

And now by a beautiful paradox of Divine Love, God makes His Cross the very means of our salvation. We have slain

Him; we nailed Him there; we crucified Him, but Love in His eternal Heart willed not to be defeated. He willed to give us the very life we slew; to give us the very Food we destroyed; to nourish us with the very Bread we buried, and the very Blood we poured forth. He made our very crime a *happy fault*; He turned a Crucifixion into a Redemption; a Consecration into a Communion; a death into life everlasting.

And it is just that which makes man all the more mysterious! Why man should be loved is no mystery, but why he does not love in return is the great mystery. Why should our Lord be the Great Unloved; why should Love not be loved? Why then, whenever He says: "I thirst," do we give Him vinegar and gall?

✠ J.M.J. ✠

~ 25 ~

The Ite, Missa Est

"It is finished."

Our Blessed Saviour now comes to the *Ite, missa est* of His Mass, as He utters the cry of triumph: "It is finished."

The work of salvation is finished, but when did it begin? It began back in the agelessness of eternity when God willed to make man. Ever since the beginning of the world, there was a Divine "Impatience" to restore man to the arms of God.

The Word was impatient in heaven to be the 'Lamb slain from the beginning of the world.' He was impatient in prophetic types and symbols, as His dying face was reflected in a hundred mirrors stretching through all Old Testament history. He was impatient to be the real Isaac carrying the wood of His sacrifice in obedience to the commands of His heavenly Abraham. He was impatient to fulfill the mystic symbol of the Lamb of the Jewish Pasch, who was slain without a single bone of its body being broken. He was impatient to be the new Abel, slain by his jealous brethren of the race of Cain that His Blood might cry to Heaven for forgiveness. He was impatient in His mother's womb, as He saluted His precursor John. He was impatient in the Circumcision, as He anticipated His blood-shedding and received the name of "Saviour." He was impatient at the age of twelve, as He reminded His Mother that He had to be about His Father's business. He was impatient in His public life, as He said He had a baptism wherewith He was to be baptized, and He was "straightened until it be accomplished." He was impatient in the Garden, as He turned His back to the consoling twelve legions of angels, to crimson olive roots with His redemptive Blood. He was impatient at His Last Supper, as He anticipated the separation of His Body and Blood under the appearance of bread and wine. And then, impatience closed as the hour of darkness drew near at the end of that Last Supper – He sang. It was the only time He ever sang, the moment He went to His death.

It was a trivial matter for the world if the stars burned brightly, or the mountains stood as symbols of perplexity, or the hills made their tribute to valleys, which gave them birth. What was important was that every single word predicted of Him should be true. Heaven and earth would not pass away until every jot and tittle had been fulfilled. There was only a little iota remaining, one tiny little jot; it was a word of David's about every prediction being fulfilled. Now that all else was fulfilled, He fulfilled that iota; He, the true David, quoted the prophetic David: "It is finished."

What is finished? The Redemption of man is finished. Love had completed its mission, for Love had done all that it could. There are two things Love can do. Love by its very nature tends to an Incarnation, and every Incarnation tends to a Crucifixion. Does not all true love tend toward an Incarnation? In the order of human love, does not the affection of husband for wife create from their mutual loves, the incarnation of their confluent love in the form of a child? Once they have begotten their child, do not they make sacrifices for it, even to the point of death? And thus their love tends to a crucifixion.

But this is just a reflection of the divine order, where the love of God for man was so deep and intense that it ended in an Incarnation, which found God in the form and habit of man, whom He loved. But our Lord's love for man did not stop with the Incarnation. Unlike everyone else who was ever born, our Lord came into this world to redeem it. Death was the supreme goal He was seeking. Death interrupted the careers of great men, but it was no interruption to our Lord; it was His crowning glory; it was the unique goal He was seeking.

His Incarnation thus tended to the Crucifixion, for "greater love than this no man has, that he lay down his life for his friends" (John 15:13). Now that Love had run its course in the Redemption of man, Divine Love could say: "I have done all for my vineyard that I can do." Love can do no more than die. It is finished: "Ite, missa est."

His work is finished. But is ours? When He said, "it is finished," He did not mean that the opportunities of His life had ended; He meant that His work was done so perfectly that nothing could be added to it to make it more perfect – but with us, how seldom that is true. Too many of us end our lives, but few of us see them *finished.* A sinful life may end, but a sinful life is never a finished life.

If our lives just "end," our friends will ask: "How much did he leave?" But if our life is "finished" our friends will ask: "How much did he take with him?" A finished life is not measured by years but by deeds; not by the time spent in the vineyard, but by the work done. In a short time, a man may fulfill many years; even those who come at the eleventh hour may finish their lives; even those who come to God like the thief at the last breath may finish their lives in the Kingdom of God. Not for them the sad word of regret: "Too late, O ancient Beauty, have I loved Thee."

Our Lord finished His work, but we have not finished ours. He pointed the way we must follow. He laid down the Cross at the finish, but we must take it up. He finished Redemption in His physical Body, but we have not finished it in His Mystical Body. He has finished salvation; we have not yet applied it to our souls. He has finished the Temple, but we must live in it. He has finished the model Cross; we must fashion ours to its pattern. He has finished sowing the seed; we must reap the harvest. He has finished filling the chalice, but we have not finished drinking its refreshing draughts. He has planted the wheat field; we must gather it into our barns. He has finished the Sacrifice of Calvary; we must finish the Mass.

The Crucifixion was not meant to be an inspirational drama, but a pattern act on which to model our lives. We are not meant to sit and watch the Cross as something done and ended like the life of Socrates. *What was done on Calvary avails for us only in the degree that we repeat it in our own lives.*

The Mass makes this possible, for at the renewal of Calvary on our altars we are not on-lookers but sharers in Redemption, and there it is that we "finish" our work. He has told us: "And I if I be lifted up from the earth, will draw all things to myself" (John 12:32). He finished His work when He was lifted up on the Cross; we finish ours when we permit Him to draw us unto Himself in the Mass.

The Mass is that which makes the cross visible to every eye; it placards the Cross at all the crossroads of civilization; it brings Calvary so close that even tired feet can make the journey to its sweet embrace; every hand may now reach out to touch its Sacred Burden, and every ear may hear its sweet appeal, for the Mass and the Cross, are the same. In both there is the same offering of a perfectly surrendered will of the beloved Son, the same Body broken, the same Blood flowed forth, the same Divine Forgiveness. All that has been said and done and acted during Holy Mass is to be taken away with us, lived, practiced, and woven into all the circumstances and conditions of our daily lives. His sacrifice is made our sacrifice by making it the oblation of ourselves in union with Him; His life given for us becomes our life given for Him. Thus do we return from Mass as those who have made their choice, turned their backs upon the world, and become other Christs for the generation in which we live – living potent witnesses to the Love that died that we might live with Love.

This world of ours is full of half-completed Gothic cathedrals, of half-finished lives and half-crucified souls. Some carry the Cross to Calvary and then abandon it; others are nailed to it and detach themselves before the elevation; others are crucified, but in answer to the challenge of the world "Come down," they come down after one hour . . . two hours . . . after two hours and fifty-nine minutes. Real Christians are they who persevere unto the end. Our Lord stayed until He had finished.

The priest must likewise stay at the altar until the Mass is finished. He may not come down. So we must stay with the Cross until our lives are finished. Christ on the Cross is the pattern and model of a finished life. Our human nature is the raw material; our will is the chisel; God's grace is the energy and the inspiration.

Touching the chisel to our unfinished nature, we first cut off huge chunks of selfishness. Then by more delicate chiselings, we dig away smaller bits of egotism until finally only a brush of the hand is needed to bring out the completed masterpiece – a finished man made to the image and likeness of the pattern on the Cross. We are at the altar under the symbol of bread and wine; we have offered ourselves to our Lord; He has consecrated us.

We must therefore not take ourselves back, but remain there unto the end, praying unceasingly, that when the lease of our life has ended, and we look back upon a life lived in intimacy with the Cross, the echo of the Sixth Word may ring out on our lips: "It is finished."

And as the sweet accents of that Ite, missa est reach beyond the corridors of Time and pierce the "hid battlements of eternity," the angel choirs and the white-robed army of the Church Triumphant will answer back: "*Deo Gratias.*"

✠ J.M.J. ✠

~ 26 ~

The Last Gospel

"Father, into thy hands, I commend my spirit."

It is a beautiful paradox that the Last Gospel of the Mass takes us back to the beginning, for it opens with the words "In the beginning." And such is life: the last of this life is the beginning of the next. Fittingly indeed, then, that the Last Word of our Lord was His Last Gospel: "Father, into thy hands, I commend my spirit." Like the Last Gospel of the Mass, it too takes Him back to the beginning, for He now goes back to the Father whence He came. He has completed His work. He began His Mass with the word: "Father." And He ends it with the same word.

"Everything perfect," the Greeks would say, "travels in circles." Just as the great planets only after a long period of time complete their orbits, and then go back again to their starting point, as if to salute Him who sent them on their way, so the Word Incarnate, who came down to say His Mass, now completes His earthly career and goes back again to His heavenly Father who sent Him on the journey of the world's redemption. The Prodigal Son is about to return to His Father's House, for is He not the Prodigal Son? Thirty-three years ago He left the Father's House and the blessedness of heaven and came down to this earth of ours, which is a foreign country – for every country is foreign which is away from the Father's House.

For thirty-three years, He had been spending His substance. He spent the substance of His Truth in the infallibility of His Church;

He spent the substance of His Power in the authority He gave to His apostles and their successors. He spent the substance of His Life in the Redemption and the Sacraments. Now every drop of it is gone, He looks longingly back again to the Father's House, and with a loud cry throws His Spirit into His Father's arms, not in the attitude of one who is taking a plunge into the darkness, but as one who knows where He is going – to a homecoming with His Father.

In that Last Word and Last Gospel, which took Him back to the Beginning of all beginnings, namely, His Father is revealed the history and rhythm of life. The end of all things must, in some way, get back to their beginning. As the Son goes back to the Father; as Nicodemus must be born again; as the body returns to the dust – so the soul of man, which came from God, must one day go back to God.

Death is not the end of all. The cold clod falling upon the grave does not mark finis to the history of a man. The way he has lived in this life determines how he shall live in the next. If he has sought God during life, death will be like the opening of a cage, enabling him to use his wings to fly to the arms of the divine Beloved. If he has fled from God during life, death will be the beginning of an eternal flight away from Life and Truth and Love – and that is hell.

Before the throne of God, whence we came on our earthly novitiate, we must one day go back to render an account of our stewardship. There will not be a human creature who, when the last sheaf is garnered, will not be found either to have accepted or rejected the divine gift of Redemption and in accepting or rejecting it to have signed the warrant of his eternal destiny.

As the sales on a cash register are recorded for the end of our business day, so our thoughts, words, and deeds are recorded for the final Judgment. If we but live in the shadow of the Cross, death will not be an ending but a beginning of eternal life. Instead of a parting, it will be a meeting; instead of a going away, it will be an arriving; instead of being an end, it will be a Last Gospel – a return to the beginning. As a voice whispers, "You must leave the earth," the Father's voice will say, "My child, come unto Me."

We have been sent into this world as children of God, to assist at the Holy Sacrifice of the Mass. We are to take our stand at the foot of the Cross and, like those who stood under it the first day, we will be asked to declare our loyalties. God has given us the wheat and the grapes of life, and as the men who, in the Gospel, were given talents; we will have to show return on that divine gift.

God has given us our lives as wheat and grapes. It is our duty to consecrate them and bring them back to God as bread and wine – transubstantiated, divinized, and spiritualized. There must be harvest in our hands after the springtime of the earthly pilgrimage.

That is why Calvary is erected in the midst of us, and we are on its sacred hill. We were not made to be mere on-lookers, shaking our dice like the executioners of old, but rather to be participants in the mystery of the Cross.

If there is any way to picture Judgment in terms of the Mass, it is to picture it in the way the Father greeted His Son, namely, by looking at His hands. They bore the marks of labour, the callouses of redemption, and the scars of salvation. So too, when our earthly pilgrimage is over, and we go back to the beginning, God will look at both of our hands. If our hands in life touched the hands of His divine Son they will bear the same livid marks of nails; if our feet in life have trod over the same road that leads to eternal glory through the detour of a rocky and thorny Calvary, they too shall bear the same bruises; if our hearts beat in unison with His, then they too shall show the riven side which the wicked lance of jealous earth did pierce.

Blessed indeed are they who carry in their Cross-marked hands the bread and wine of consecrated lives signed with the sign and sealed with the seal of redemptive Love. But woe unto them who come from Calvary with hands unscarred and white.

God grant that when life is over, and the earth is vanishing like a dream of one awakening when eternity is flooding our souls with its splendours, we may with humble and triumphant faith re-echo the Last Word of Christ: "Father, into thy hands I commend my spirit."

And so the Mass of Christ ends. The *Confiteor* was His prayer to the Father for the forgiveness of our sins; the *Offertory* was the presentation on the paten of the Cross of small hosts of the thief and ourselves; the *Sanctus* was His commending ourselves to Mary, the Queen of Saints; the *Consecration* was the separation of His Blood from His Body, and the seeming separation of divinity and humanity; the *Communion* was His thirst for the souls of men; the *Ite, missa est* was the finishing of the work of salvation; the *Last Gospel* was the return to the Father whence He came.

And now that the Mass is over, and He has commended His Spirit to the Father, He prepares to give back His Body to His Blessed Mother at the foot of the Cross. Thus once again will the end be the beginning, for at the beginning of His earthly life He was nestled on her lap in Bethlehem, and now, on Calvary, He will take His place there once again.

Earth had been cruel to Him; His feet wandered after lost sheep, and we dug them with steel; His hands stretched out the Bread of everlasting life, and we fastened them with nails; His lips spoke the Truth, and we sealed them with dust. He came to give us Life, and we took away His. But that was our fatal mistake. We really did not take it away. We only tried to take it away. He laid it down of Himself. Nowhere do the Evangelists say that He died. They say, "He gave up the spirit." It was a willing, self-determined relinquishment of life.

It was not death which approached Him; it was He who approached death. That is why, as the end draws near, the Saviour commands the portal of death to open unto Him in the presence of the Father. The chalice is gradually being drained of its rich red wine of salvation. The rocks of earth open their hungry mouths to drink as if more thirsty for the draughts of salvation than the parched hearts of man; the earth itself shook in horror because men had erected God's Cross upon its breast. Magdalene, the penitent, as usual, clings to His feet, and there she will be again Easter morn; John, the priest, with a face like a cast moulded out of love, listens to the beating of the Heart whose secrets He learned and loved and mastered; Mary thinks how different Calvary is from Bethlehem.

Thirty-three years ago, Mary looked down at His sacred face; now He looks down at her. In Bethlehem, heaven looked up into the face of earth; now, the roles are reversed. Earth looks up into the face of heaven – but a heaven marred by the scars of earth. He loved her above all the creatures of earth, for she was His Mother and the Mother of us all. He saw her first on coming to earth; He shall see her last on leaving it. Their eyes meet, all aglow with life, speaking a language all their own. There is a rupture of a heart through a rapture of love, then a bowed head, a broken heart. Back to the hands of God, He gives, pure and sinless, His spirit, in loud and ringing voice that trumpets eternal victory. And Mary stands alone a Childless Mother. Jesus is dead!

Mary looks up into His eyes which are so clear even in the face of death: "High Priest of Heaven and earth, Thy Mass is finished! Leave the altar of the Cross and repair into Thy Sacristy. As High Priest Thou didst come forth from the sacristy of Heaven, panoplied in the vestments of humanity and bearing Thy Body as Bread and Thy Blood as Wine.

Now the Sacrifice has been consummated. The Consecration bell has rung. Thou didst offer Thy Spirit to Thy Father; Thy Body and Thy Blood to man. There remains now nothing but the drained chalice. Enter into Thy Sacristy. Take off the garments of mortality and put on the white robes of immortality. Show Thy hands, and feet, and side to Thy heavenly Father and say: "With these was I wounded in the house of those that love me."

"Enter, High Priest, into Thy heavenly Sacristy, and as Thy earthly ambassadors hold aloft the Bread and Wine, do Thou show Thyself to the Father in loving intercession for us even unto the consummation of the world. Earth has been cruel to Thee, but Thou wilt be kind to earth. Earth lifted Thee on the Cross, but now Thou shalt lift earth unto the Cross. Open the door of the heavenly Sacristy, O High Priest! Behold, it is now we who stand at the door and knock!

"And Mary, what shall we say to Thee? Mary, Thou art the Sacristan of the High Priest! Thou wert a Sacristan in Bethlehem when He did come to Thee as wheat and grapes in the crib of Bethlehem. Thou wert His Sacristan at the Cross, where He became the Living Bread and Wine through the Crucifixion. Thou art His Sacristan now, as He comes from the altar of the Cross wearing only the drained chalice of His sacred Body.

"As that chalice is laid in your lap it may seem that Bethlehem has come back again, for He is once more yours. But it only seems – for in Bethlehem He was the chalice whose gold was to be tried by fire, but now at Calvary, He is the chalice whose gold has passed through the fires of Golgotha and Calvary. In Bethlehem He was white as He came from the Father: now He is red as He came from us. But thou art still His Sacristan! And as the Immaculate Mother of all hosts who go to the altar, do thou, O Virgin Mary, send us there pure, and keep us pure, even unto the day when we enter into the heavenly Sacristy of the Kingdom of Heaven, where thou wilt be our eternal Sacristan and He our eternal Priest."

And you, friends of the Crucified, your High Priest has left the Cross, but He has left us the Altar. On the Cross He was alone; in the Mass, He is with us. On the Cross He suffered in His physical Body; on the altar, He suffers in the Mystical Body which we are. On the Cross He was the unique Host; in the Mass, we are the small hosts, and He the large host receiving His Calvary through us. On the Cross He was the wine; in the Mass, we are the drop of water united with the wine and consecrated with Him. In that sense He is still on the Cross, still saying the Confiteor with us, still forgiving us, still commending us to Mary, still thirsting for us, still drawing us unto the Father, for as long as sin remains on earth, still will the Cross remain.

"Whenever there is silence around me
By day or by night –
I am startled by a cry.

It came down from the Cross.
The first time I heard it
I went out and searched –
And found a man in the throes of Crucifixion.

And I said: 'I will take you down,'
and I tried to take the nails out of His Feet,
But He said: 'Let them be for I cannot be taken down until every man, every woman, and every child come together to take me down.'

And I said: 'But I cannot bear your cry. What can I do?'
And He said: 'Go about the world –
Tell everyone that you meet –
There is a Man on the Cross.'"

Elizabeth Cheney

Books by Fulton J. Sheen

Calvary and the Mass

The Cross and the Beatitudes

The Cross and the Crisis

Liberty, Equality and Fraternity

The Rainbow of Sorrow

Victory Over Vice

The Seven Virtues

For God and Country

The Holy Hour Prayer Book

God and War

Missions and the World Crisis

Love One Another

The Divine Verdict

God Love You

The Priest Is Not His Own

Philosophies at War

Seven Words to the Cross

Seven Pillars of Peace

Love One Another

Seven Words of Jesus & Mary

The Seven Last Words

Distributed by Bishop Sheen Today

www.bishopsheentoday.com

www.ingramcontent.com/pod-product-compliance
Lightning Source LLC
Chambersburg PA
CBHW070904120626
46546CB00001B/128